Where's the Money?

Sure-Fire Financing Solutions
For Your Small Business

By Art Beroff
and Dwayne Moyers

Current titles from Entrepreneur Media Inc.:

Business Plans Made Easy:
It's Not as Hard as You Think

Start Your Own Business:
The Only Start-up Book You'll Ever Need

303 Marketing Tips
Guaranteed to Boost Your Business

Young Millionaires:
Inspiring Stories to Ignite Your
Entrepreneurial Dreams

Forthcoming titles from Entrepreneur Media Inc.:

Knockout Marketing:
Powerful Strategies to Punch Up Your Sales

Success for Less:
100 Low-Cost Businesses You Can Start Today

Gen E: Generation Entrepreneur is Rewriting
the Rules of Business—and You Can, Too

Get Smart: 365 Tips to
Boost Your Entrepreneurial IQ

Entrepreneur MAGAZINE'S

Where's the Money?

Sure-Fire Financing Solutions
For Your
Small Business

By Art Beroff
and Dwayne Moyers

ENTREPRENEUR MEDIA INC.
2392 Morse Ave., Irvine, CA 92614

Managing Editor: Marla Markman
Copy Editor: Karre Lynn
Interior Book Design: Sylvia H. Lee
Proofreader: Guen Sublette
Production Design: Creative Graphics Group
Cover Design: Olson Kotowski & Co.
Indexer: Alta Indexing

Library of Congress Cataloging-in-Publication Data
Where's the money?: sure-fire financing solutions for your small business/by Art Beroff and Dwayne Moyers.
    p.   cm.
Includes bibliographical references and index.
ISBN 1-891984-03-9
    1. Small business—Finance. 2. Small business—Management.
I. Moyers, Dwayne. II. Entrepreneur Media, Inc. III. Title.
    HG4027.7.B484 1999
    658.15'92—dc21
                                       98-51284
                                         CIP

Printed in the United States of America

09 08 07 06 05 04 03 02 01 00   10 9 8 7 6 5 4 3 2 1

This book is for Carole, David and Ilana,
who remind me what I am working for.

— *Art Beroff*

This book is dedicated to Lindy Moyers.
The world is a better place because she is in it.

— *Dwayne Moyers*

Acknowledgments

We owe a debt of gratitude to many people for the completion of this book.

First, we would like to thank the editors at Entrepreneur, who took an interest in our ideas and gave us the forum and resources to express them.

We would also like to thank our investors and clients. There are too many to mention here, but you must know that we hold all of you in high esteem. Furthermore, we recognize that without your enthusiasm for the entrepreneurial process, we would not be able to participate in the financing of so many exciting companies. Thank you.

Finally, we owe a debt of extreme gratitude to this great country. We firmly believe that the many freedoms it offers is the driving force behind our capital markets. These markets do more than simply make fortunes. As the following pages will testify, they make dreams come true.

TABLE OF CONTENTS

Table Of Contents

Table Of Contents

Introduction

This book has something for everyone, regardless of their stage of development. It was also written with a singular premise in mind. Specifically, that most businesses fail to raise the money they need, not because they are not viable, but because they approach the wrong sources of capital. For example, untold numbers of entrepreneurs approach institutional venture capital firms for capital, when in fact, these investors rarely finance start-up companies. And the kinds of companies they do finance are so narrowly defined, that few need apply.

To address this problem, each chapter in this book begins with a section called "The Scoop" that details a particular source of capital. Read these "resumes" carefully because they tell you whether you should be pursuing the source of capital they describe. Sometimes it's difficult to accept a truth so easily offered in black and white, but these resumes offer this truth as it relates to the kinds of capital you should try to pursue as you grow your business.

As a general guide, however, if you are just starting, you might want to read the chapters on start-up financing, angel investors, venture capital and business incubators. The chapter on venture capital offers you a test to take to see whether you should pursue this channel.

If your business is up and running, make sure you review all of the book's earlier chapters about the sources of loan financing. Some of these forms of financing are expensive, but they'll not cost you any equity. In particular, it's worth looking at the chapters titled "Royalty Financing," "Federal Government Venture Capital," "Private Loan Guarantees" and "Asset-based Loans."

If your business is up, running, profitable and has the opportunity to grab for the brass ring, look at the chapters on various kinds of equity financing. In particular, you'll want to look at the chapter on initial public offerings (IPOs), alternatives to an IPO and institutional venture capital.

Regardless of the kind of financing you need, it's worth reading the chapters titled "Preparing A Business Plan," and "How Investors Use Your Financial Statements." These two chapters will help you understand how lenders and investors view you and your company.

It's also worth noting that some thought went into the sequence of the chapters in this book. Take a brief look at the table of contents. The sources of capital are listed by what we call the degree of imposition. That is, the earlier chapters cover sources of financing, which if successfully acquired, do not change the degree of control outsiders exert on your business. The later chapters discuss sources of financing that have a significant impact on the control you as the entrepreneur will have after you have been financed by these sources of capital.

You might also note that the organization of the chapters runs from debt sources of financing and quasi-debt to equity. This organization will lead you to one of the central truths of early-stage finance. Equity financing is expensive and dramatically changes the destiny of your business.

The only exceptions to this organization are the chapters titled "Angel Investors," "Electronic Matching Services" and "Business Incubators." These are not specific kinds of investment capital, but more accurately, are good conduits to capital. However, their placement in the latter half of the sources section indicates that more often than not these conduits will lead to equity sources of capital.

Throughout this book you will find tip boxes, which are designed to call your attention to basic or fundamental concepts. These tip boxes and their purpose are as follows:

Shop Talk

Finance is often intimidating because it comes with a language all its own. These tip boxes highlight terms or phrases that might confuse financial neophytes.

A Good Deal

Every financing technique has its hidden costs and opportunities for savings. These tip boxes help you by highlighting the not-so-obvious costs, as well as the benefits.

Don't Forget

These tip boxes are designed to give you a reality check. Sometimes in finance it's easy to get caught up in the minutiae or in the larger picture without being able to see the obvious and to understand how it might influence what you are trying to accomplish.

Taking Action

If you want to run with the dogs, you cannot sit on the porch. These tip boxes offer you a concrete action step to set you in motion, which is a key to raising capital.

Also keep in mind that finance has a language of its own. So, in addition to the "Shop Talk" tip boxes throughout the book, we have added a glossary at the end, covering some frequently used technical terms.

You will also notice that this book is divided into two parts, which can be described as sources and techniques. The sources are just that, sources. But the technique section owes its existence to this book's other central idea: Specifically, not only do entrepreneurs tend to look in all the wrong places for capital, but they are also often ill-prepared from the start. The techniques section of the book therefore is designed to give you the tools you need to approach investors, with a likelihood of achieving success.

Perhaps the final "large idea" that lines the subtext of this book is that raising money is a discipline of networking. Except in rare instances, capital will not come to you; you must go out and get it. And nobody will write you a check just because you can make a good case that you need it. Raising money is a personal affair that hinges largely on personal relationships.

So go forth, multiply your contacts, and you will be fruitful.

> Most of the business owners' names in this book have been changed at the entrepreneurs' request.

PART 1

SOURCES

Chapter 1

Start-up Financing

The Scoop

Definition Or Explanation: Start-up financing is the initial infusion of money that advances an idea or an intention into something tangible.

Appropriate For: Any business that wants to be a business.

Supply: Even though it's everywhere, it's sometimes difficult to find.

Best Use: Commencing initial operation to the point where outside investors can see and feel the venture, as well as understand that you took some risk getting it to that point.

Cost: Start-up financing will possess two of the following three qualities: good, cheap and fast. It will never possess all three qualities.

Ease Of Acquisition: If you have nothing, it's difficult. If you have personal assets, the hard part is putting them at risk. But doing so is the rite of passage to both success and failure.

The Way It Is

If you are starting a business, it's your baby. This idea may leave you feeling simultaneously liberated and inspired. But it also has an edge. Specifically, if it's your baby, it's also your obligation to finance it beyond the "I've got an idea" stage.

How about the entrepreneur who wants to raise $25,000 from outside investors to start a restaurant? It's unlikely he will succeed in getting people to reach for their checkbooks.

Why not? First, if the would-be restaurateur can't scratch together $25,000 out of his own resources or credit, it's highly unlikely that an investor would view him or her as having the kind of chutzpah needed to make a go of it in the restaurant business.

Second, and more to the point, if this entrepreneur can raise these funds from his own resources but did not want to for fear of losing them, then any investor is sure to ask, "If you won't take a chance on this, why should I?"

The fact is, if you're not willing to take the maximum amount of risk your circumstances will allow, then no one else will be willing to, either.

According to entrepreneur Jim Young of Long Beach, California, who has started more than 10 businesses, it's sort of like a plate of ham and eggs. "The chicken makes a contribution," he says. "But the pig makes a commitment." When starting a new business, the investor is the chicken. The entrepreneur must take the other role.

So the question is, How do you get that first dollop of funds that will either advance your idea to the point where it can attract outside capital, or perhaps jump-start you into profitable operations?

Sell Assets

If you own things, you can sell them. It's that simple. Jewelry, rugs, pool tables, boats, time-shares, second proper-

A Piece Of The Pie

The Small Business Administration's (SBA) 8(a) Program is a small-business set-aside that gives certified MBEs (Minority Business Enterprises) access to government contracts as well as management and technical assistance to help develop their businesses. The 8(a) Program is envisioned as a starter program for minority businesses, which must leave the nest after nine years.

Entrepreneurs who participate in the 8(a) Program are eligible for the 7(a) Loan Guaranty and Minority Pre-qualification programs. The 8(a) Program has faced challenges in recent years because federal courts are increasingly questioning the legality of affirmative action and set-aside programs. This may mean new avenues for the program.

ties. For most people their largest assets are their homes and cars. Homes are covered later. Here's what you can do with automobiles.

If you drive a nice, late-model car, you can sell it and lease a cheap one without a down payment. If your car is nice, this might net you $15,000 to $20,000 and leave you with a small monthly lease payment.

Even if you lease your car, a variation on this theme applies. Suppose you lease a brand-new sport utility vehicle for $449 per month. Get rid of it and lease an economy car for $99 per month. Granted, the savings of $350 each month isn't much to start a business on. However, this new monthly cash flow should allow you to secure a personal loan. With that much, you would be able to borrow as much as $12,000.

Borrow Against Your Home

This is the oldest trick in the book. It's also one of the best because you can exert almost total control over the process. Here's how it works: Say you need $50,000, your home is worth $250,000 and you owe the bank $100,000 on your mortgage. You can borrow against the equity, in this case $150,000.

Most banks and mortgage companies will lend up to 70 percent of the equity in your home. So in our hypothetical example, the $150,000 of equity would allow the homeowner/entrepreneur to borrow up to $105,000.

Of course, once the loan kicks in, you'll have monthly payments. If you're starting a new business, it's a wise idea to set aside some of the proceeds from the home equity loan to help make these payments until the business can pay you a steady salary.

Another way to get money out of your home but maintain a lower monthly payment is to refinance the mortgage with a new one.

Using the above hypothetical example, rather than

Don't Forget

If you trade down on your auto, you can save even more money by passing on the collision insurance. It may not be much, but the extra monthly cash flow translates into even more cash you can borrow.

borrowing against the equity, our homeowner/entrepreneur would get a new 30-year mortgage for $150,000 and with the proceeds pay off the $100,000 mortgage. The difference, $50,000, can be used for any purpose the borrower wants, including investing in a new business.

The refinancing option is less expensive because payments on the $50,000 are spread across 30 years instead of perhaps 10 years for a home equity loan. In the long run, the lower payments prove to be more expensive, since the borrower is paying interest on the outstanding balance for perhaps as long as 30 years.

> **Shop Talk**
> The equity in your home is the difference between what you owe on it and what it's worth. This means even if your loan payments pay off very little principal, you can still build up equity through increases in the value of your home.

Borrow Against Insurance Policies

If you want to know where all your money is, look at your insurance payments. Each month you probably pay for health insurance, life insurance, disability insurance, auto insurance and perhaps homeowner's insurance.

Unfortunately, you can only borrow against whole life policies, but most have some cash value after three years. Simply write your agent or insurance company, saying you want a policy loan. Most companies will lend up to 90 percent of the cash value, and your policy stays intact, as long as you keep paying the premiums as they come due. Unfortunately, if you die with a policy loan outstanding, the benefits might be diminished, although that varies by policy. But the good news is that loans against your insurance policy are fairly reasonable, since the rates charged are tied to the key money-market rate.

Friends And Family

They believe in you the most. Therefore, they should be one of the first outside sources of capital you try to tap.

Friends and family present a formidable source of capital.

Your typical friend or family investor is male, has been successful in his own business and wants to invest because he wishes someone had done it for him, according to Kirk Neiswander, director of entrepreneurial programs at Case Western Reserve University's Weatherhead School of Management. "They are not reckless investors, and they have shallow pockets," he says. "They will invest once but not a second or a third time and generally in an industry they know that is close to home. Typically, friends and family will invest up to $100,000."

However, investments with friends and family can turn out bad when things don't go as planned. The situation can be even worse than with professional investors because friends and family react to bad news as much with emotion as with logic. Take the following steps to protect everyone from each other:

- Get an agreement in writing, which will eliminate all conversations that start with, "You never said that."
- Emphasize debt (loans) rather than equity (ownership). You don't want friends and family in your company for-

Meet Me In The Middle

The Small Business Administration has two unique programs, called the Minority and Women's Pre-qualification Loan programs, which help women and minority entrepreneurs. Working with the aid of private intermediary organizations chosen by the SBA, eligible entrepreneurs prepare a business plan and complete a loan application. The intermediary submits the application to the SBA. If it is approved, the SBA issues the borrower a prequalification letter, which is taken, along with a loan package, to a commercial lender. The idea being that with the SBA's guarantee already in place, the bank is more likely to approve the loan.

Under the women's program, entrepreneurs can apply for loans of up to $250,000; under the minority program, you can get up to $250,000 or more on a case-by-case basis.

ever. Before you know it, they start telling you how to run the place, and long-buried emotions emerge. Make it a loan, and pay it back as fast as you can.

- Put some cash flow on their investment. If Dad says, "Here's $50,000—try not to lose it, and pay it back as soon as you can," that's great. But consider paying some nominal interest at regular intervals so that you and he have a reality check. And it's better to pay this quarterly rather than monthly. This way, when things are teetering, your lender won't immediately know it.

Taking Action

Fill out an application with your broker for margin privileges. The process will take 10 days to a month. This way, if you need cash in a hurry, you can get it with just one call to your stockbroker.

Borrow Against Your Investments

So-called margin loans are cheap and easy. They can also be dangerous.

Margin loans are easy because any brokerage firm with which you have an account will lend you money against the value of your holdings. For instance, you can borrow up to 90 percent of the value of federal government bills, bonds and notes. For municipal bonds the advance rate is 75 percent, for government agencies it's 65 percent, and for stocks and mutual funds the advance rate is 50 percent. Margin loans are cheap because the underlying collateral is accessible (it's in your account) and it's liquid (it can be sold and quickly turned into cash).

Assuming you have $50,000 worth of blue-chip stocks in your portfolio and you have applied for margin privileges, one phone call to your broker will get you $25,000. It's that easy.

Margin loans are great when stock prices are steady or rising, but they aren't the best choice when they are falling. Suppose your marginable common stocks are worth $50,000 and you borrow the maximum amount, $25,000. If the value of those stocks falls to $40,000 it can cause a problem. Specifically, to keep the loan amount ($25,000) in the proper proportion (50 percent) to the value of the collateral, it must be $50,000 or more at all times. When it dips to $40,000 your broker will ask you to deposit $10,000 into your account to set everything straight again.

If you don't deposit the cash into the account, the broker simply liquidates stocks in your portfolio to pay back the loan. This unplanned sale of securities can provoke serious tax consequences in the form of capital gains taxes.

Margin loans are not for everyone. In fact, they might even be a last resort. But if they are, then you've got to do what you've got to do.

If you're starting your business part time while keeping your full-time job, another more potentially stable investment is borrowing against your employer's 401(k) retirement plan. It's common for such plans to let you borrow a percentage of your money that doesn't exceed $50,000. The interest rate is usually about 6 percent, with a specified repayment schedule. The downside of borrowing from your 401(k) is that if you lose your job, the loan must be repaid quickly, often within 30 days. To see if this is an option, consult your plan's documentation.

You may also want to consider using the funds in your IRA. Within the laws governing IRAs, you can actually withdraw money from an IRA as long as you replace it within 60 days. This is not a loan, so you don't pay interest; rather, this is a withdrawal that you're allowed to keep for 60 days. A highly organized person could possibly juggle funds among several IRAs. But if you're one day late—for any reason—you'll be hit with a 10 percent premature withdrawal fee, and the money you haven't returned will become taxable.

Credit Cards

They're not terribly creative. But credit cards are quick and easy. In a perverse way, they are also cheap. That is, a minimum payment of $50 per month can hold down a whole lot of debt. Of course, if you only make the minimum payment, your balance continues to grow, and if the business fails, you have to pay the piper. But if things go well and the business pays off the balances without missing a beat, then you look back at your early credit card financing with a nostalgic fondness, and perhaps a twinge of longing for simpler days.

Chapter 2

Equipment Leasing

The Scoop

Definition Or Explanation: Equipment leasing is basically a loan in which the lender buys and owns equipment and then "rents" it to a business at a flat monthly rate for a specified number of months. At the end of the lease the business may purchase the equipment for its fair market value (or a fixed or predetermined amount), continue leasing, lease new equipment or return it.

Appropriate For: Any business at any stage of development. For start-up businesses with no revenues, "small ticket" leases, those of $150,000 or less, are feasible on the personal credit of the founders or owners—if they are willing to make the monthly payments.

Supply: Abundant. Of the billions of dollars individual and institutional investors pour into the capital markets each month, a good hunk finds its way to leasing companies that use these funds to purchase equipment on behalf of small businesses. With more and more money flowing into the markets, leasing companies are flush with capital, eager to do business and respond to competition with lower monthly rates.

Best Use: Financing equipment purchases. Leasing can also finance the soft costs often associated with equipment purchases, such as installation and training services.

Cost: Lease financing is generally more expensive than bank financing, but in most instances it is more easily obtained.

Ease Of Acquisition: Easy for leases of less than $150,000. An application for a small-ticket lease is generally no more complex than a credit card application. Leases for more than $150,000 require detailed financial information from the business, and the leasing company conducts the same credit analysis a conventional bank would.

Range Of Funds Available: Unlimited

A Case In Point

When Bill and Peggy Brown took over Royal Laundry, which provides laundry services to institutions, the company was breaking even on sales of approximately $500,000. With some focused marketing efforts, the potential the couple saw in the business quickly materialized, with customers such as Electronic Data Systems, American Airlines and a large hospital group. "Our customers," Bill recalls, "were offering us lots of opportunities to grow with new services and a higher level of volume."

To take advantage of this demand, the Browns needed new equipment—and lots of it. The dry-cleaning machines, automated folders and high-speed irons they needed totaled about $500,000.

Bill says he tried to get a bank loan but was summarily rejected by national, regional and local lending institutions. "Even though the business was almost 10 years old when we sought the loans, in the eyes of the bankers it was technically a start-up since we recently purchased it." No one was willing to finance a company that was less than 2 years old." And even if they found a bank, the Browns' personal guarantee, which would be required, wasn't worth much. "We put everything we had into buying the business," says Bill. "We were cash poor."

Enter Jim Lahti, president of Affiliated Corporate Services Inc., a Lewisville, Texas, equipment-leasing company. Lahti took a real interest in what the Browns were trying to accomplish, and over the course of two years, structured approximately seven leases that got Royal Laundry the equipment it needed. With the added capacity and new services, annual sales at Royal Laundry mushroomed to $2.8 million.

Advantages Of Leasing

Equipment leasing is big business. In fact, it is the single largest source of financing for U.S. businesses, totaling more than $180 billion annually. The dollar volume of equipment leases exceeds the annual dollar volume of commercial loans. It even exceeds the dollars raised through the issuance of bonds or the sale of stock. Leasing is bigger than commercial mortgages. And perhaps best of all, because of the high volume of available lease capital, equipment lease financing is readily obtainable for small businesses.

Here are some of the most important competitive advantages of lease financing:

- **One hundred percent financing:** With leasing, the lessor (i.e., the company that purchases, then rents, the equipment) finances 100 percent of the cost of the equipment being purchased. In fact, lessors often finance some of the soft costs — such as training and installation — associated with the purchase of new equipment.

- **Easy application and rapid approval times:** Most applications for leases of less than $150,000 are a single page in length, and approvals can occur within 24 hours.

- **Tax treatment:** In general, the tax implications of leasing can be quite complex; they could be the subject of a book itself. However, for small-ticket leases, which in most instances are so-called capital leases, the tax treatment is straightfor-

L easing By The Numbers

Companies of every size use leasing. Commercial airlines lease jets. Caterers lease tables, chairs and chafing dishes. So how do the professionals who serve these diverse businesses segment the market? Basically, the leasing business is divided into three distinct markets:

- **Small-ticket leases:** less than $100,000
- **Middle-market leases:** $100,000 to $1 million
- **Large-ticket leases:** greater than $1 million

A Good Deal

Leasing companies also frequently finance the soft costs that come with equipment purchases, such as training, installation fees, service contracts and even consulting fees you may have paid to get help figuring out which piece of equipment was right for you.

ward and favorable. The business leasing the equipment writes off the entire monthly payment as an expense. Conversely, when a business takes out a loan to buy equipment—i.e., places it on its books as an asset—the company can only deduct the interest portion of the payment plus a depreciation expense.

• **Flexible terms:** Most leasing companies can structure the term of the lease to fit a certain monthly payment that the business owner is willing or able to make.

Not A Bank

The distinction between an equipment-leasing company and a bank runs deep, according to Lahti, who is also the president of Oakland, California–based trade group United Association of Equipment Leasing. "When the bank makes a loan, you have some discretion over the proceeds," Lahti says. "And if you buy equipment with the loan, you own the equipment, depreciate it and pay the bank back. But with a leasing company, we buy and own the equipment and rent it to you. So one of the primary differences is ownership."

Another difference is orientation. "The leasing company is more adventurous than a conventional lender," Lahti says, "because we do not labor under the same federal regulations as a bank and we do not have the same audit trails as a bank." Underscoring this difference, Lahti says his firm will lend up to $75,000 on a so-called "app only" basis. That is, the loan underlying the lease can be approved on the basis of information provided in the lease

A Good Deal

When you take out a lease for equipment, the entire lease payment is deductible as an expense. When you take out a loan to purchase equipment, only the interest portion of your payment to the lender is deductible as an expense.

application, which is generally no more complex than an ordinary credit card application. Lahti says there are leasing companies that will make deals of up to $250,000 on an app-only basis.

Finally, whereas most banks are geared for credit analysis — a detailed study of a business's financial position and assessment of its ability to repay a loan — leasing companies are not. Says Lahti, "We all take the path of least resistance and try to figure out ways to make loans even faster."

Adding It Up

Credit-scoring streamlines the credit process because it looks at relatively few variables out of many that constitute a company's full financial picture. Each variable is scored, and the credit decision-making is done either by computers or clerks. Often, the credit-scoring models are adjusted over time to reflect a lender's experience. As these models evolve, many lenders regard their credit-scoring system to be proprietary and a trade secret. Below are the main criteria that are evaluated in a credit-scoring system:

- time in business
- lessee's industry
- type of equipment
- bank's rating of lessee
- trade creditor's rating of lessee
- personal credit bureau reports on the principals
- landlord rating
- quality of the vendor supplying equipment to be leased
- structure of the lease
- new or used equipment
- credit reports of outside reporting agencies

Source: The Leasing Professional's Handbook

Improving Your Chances
Of Getting A Lease

A small-ticket lease is comparatively easier to land than a traditional loan because of the widespread use of credit-scoring systems by leasing companies. Banks are starting to use credit-scoring systems for business, though most still use credit analysis. Under the credit-analysis model, a business's ability to meet a monthly payment and to pay off a debt is examined. This analysis is time-consuming and expensive. In fact, the same credit analysis that goes into a $2 million loan is also applied to a $200,000 loan—a fact that makes applying for a small-business loan difficult and time-intensive.

But under the credit-scoring model, businesses are analyzed not so much on their ability to repay a loan as on the probability that they will repay a loan. In fact, Lahti says, for leases of less than $100,000, a leasing company may simply credit-score the business owner's personal credit and check trade and bank references to reach a decision.

And as a general rule, for leases of more than $100,000 but less than $150,000, the leasing company credit-scores the business and its owners and asks for a full set of financial statements. However, the overall application process is streamlined, with the actual application still only being a page long in most cases. When leases are for more than $150,000, Lahti says, would-be lessors face the same kind of scrutiny and analysis they would with almost any commercial lender.

So what red flags appear in a credit score that might cause your would-be lease to be denied?

- **Personal credit problems:** Past delinquencies, slow payments or nonpayments reduce your overall credit score.

- **A high number of credit inquiries:** If several lending

> **Don't Forget**
> A lease can be a superior alternative to a term loan because the leasing company finances 100 percent of the equipment, whereas a bank generally requires a sizable down payment for any major asset purchases it is financing.

institutions are scoring your credit, it could be a sign that you have made too many credit applications and are carrying too much debt.

- **Lengthy payments on trade credit:** If you stretch out the payments to your vendors to 90 days, it comes home to roost when you fill out an equipment lease application.

- **A high number of NSFs:** Continually writing checks that are returned for nonsufficient funds seriously undermines your credit score.

- **Lawsuits and judgments:** These are never a good sign to a lender.

- **Frequent change in banking institutions:** "If you change banks often," Lahti says, "you're not doing yourself any favors." Most lenders, he says, like to see at least two years of history with the same institution.

- **Being a bad tenant:** If your landlord thinks you're a lousy tenant, it causes a lessor to think you will be a lousy lessee.

- **Exotic equipment:** The harder it is to resell whatever equipment you are leasing (which is what you will have to do if the whole deal goes south), the lower your score.

Shop Talk
The "residual" is the value of the equipment at the end of the lease period. The lessee often has the option to purchase the equipment for its residual value.

P.S. The lessee is the entity taking out the lease, and the lessor is the entity granting the lease.

If your credit score comes up poor, Lahti says, most leasing companies will take steps to make the deal doable. "In the trade, we all do this structuring," he says.

Popular "structuring" techniques include making down payments on equipment, finding additional guarantors (i.e., other people or institutions that will pay off the lease if the original lessee runs into financial difficulty), and anteing up additional collateral in the form of real estate, publicly traded stock, letters of credit and, of course, equipment a company already has on hand. "If you already have equipment on your floor, I can use it as additional collateral," Lahti says. "In fact, if you need working capital, we can buy your equipment [for a lump sum] and lease it back to you."

Scoring The Lease

There are ways to gauge how expensive or economical lease financing is. But you must know the residual value of the equipment you are leasing. For instance, suppose you lease a $12,000 warehouse forklift for $300 per month for three years, and at the end of the lease, the value of the forklift, or the residual, is $4,000. If you buy the forklift for $4,000, your total cash outlay is $10,800 (36 payments x $300), plus $4,000, for a total of $14,800. Since the forklift cost $12,000 new, the difference between the original price and the total cash outlay is the implied financing cost, in this case $2,800.

If the residual were higher, say, $5,000, and the payments remained the same, $300, the resulting financing costs, $3,800, are much higher than in the previous scenario.

Such an analysis represents a good starting point for analyzing a lease, but other factors must come into play as well, Lahti maintains. "The flexibility to extend or modify a lease, search and documentation fees, speed of approval, and the ease with which you can upgrade to new equipment are all [elements] that must be taken into account when weighing one lease against another."

Taking Action
For a leasing company referral, call or write the United Association of Equipment Leasing at 520 Third St., #201, Oakland, CA 94607, (510) 444-9235, www.uael. org.

Let's Make A Deal

Finding an equipment-leasing company is easy. Almost any equipment a business could conceivably need offers a lease option. Though it's not apparent at first glance, the company offering the lease financing is not the same one that is selling the equipment. The company selling the equipment simply makes a direct referral to a leasing company with which it does business.

It's a good idea to get a quote from the leasing firm referred by the company that wants to sell you the equipment. The quote should be competitive. After all, the company selling products wants to sell as many as possible, and it surely doesn't win any points by referring a leasing company that gouges its customers. But it also pays to get another quote. Usually, the company selling the equipment has more than one leasing company on hand. Or, ask a friend or business associate.

As a final point, when looking for a leasing company you should understand whether you are talking to a broker—the person who simply structures deals, then gets them financed through any of the leasing companies he or she works with—or a leasing company that is actually putting its own funds on the line.

There's nothing wrong with brokers. The situation is analogous to working with an independent insurance agent. He or she might have intimate knowledge of the marketplace and know where to go to get the kind of insurance, or lease, you need. In theory, at least, this generates savings in excess of his or her fees. But with brokers, the same advice applies: Buyer beware.

Chapter 3

Community Development Financial Institutions

The Scoop

Definition Or Explanation: Community Development Financial Institutions (CDFIs) provide primarily loan financing to businesses in areas that need economic development. CDFIs make loans that are generally "unbankable" by traditional industry standards.

Appropriate For: Start-up to established companies that can demonstrate the ability to repay a loan but whose loan proposal is unbankable because of past credit problems, the size of the loan request, limited equity from founders or limited collateral.

Supply: Good. There are hundreds of CDFIs in urban, rural and reservation-based communities with billions of dollars to lend. Unfortunately, despite their numbers, CDFIs can be difficult to track down.

Best Use: To start a new business or to expand an established one. Also, when the application of the proceeds can create a second bottom line in the form of community job creation — the introduction or preservation of a service that is vital to a community or stabilizing a community in decline.

Cost: Relatively inexpensive. Most CDFI loans are priced according to risk as opposed to the cost of funds. Since CDFI loans tend to be riskier than bank loans, they cost more as well. Typical pricing may be from 0.5 to 3 percentage points higher than conventional loan rates.

Ease Of Acquisition: Easier than commercial lenders, but challenging, since for loans, a company must still undergo the scrutiny of traditional credit analysis. The difficulty of securing CDFI financing is sometimes compounded by the relatively narrow focus and agenda these institutions may maintain.

Range Of Funds Typically Available: $25,000 to $500,000.

The Power Of The People

The idea behind a CDFI is simple and powerful. In a nutshell, a community makes viable loans to businesses that can help the area grow and prosper.

That was certainly the case with two unlikely entrepreneurs from the Northwest. Sawmill managers Mike Brine and Dave Miles had always wanted their own company. As a result, when the opportunity arose to take control of a closed mill and call it their own, the two didn't waste any time looking into it. The only problem is, when opportunity knocks, it usually wants money. In the case of the two rough-hewn entrepreneurs, the opportunity required a capital commitment of $100,000.

There were plenty of risks. First, the business, despite its heritage, would be a pure start-up. Second, operating a sawmill is a risky business. Mills had closed by the score throughout the Pacific Northwest. By almost any yardstick, the deal Brine and Miles had in mind was not bankable. But the Cascadia Revolving Loan Fund, a community development financial institution in Seattle, had a different perspective.

According to loan officer Josh Drake, Cascadia, true to the credo of a CDFI, saw its way through the risks and anted up the $100,000 financing package. The deal consisted of a $25,000 five-year term loan and a $75,000 equity investment. Drake says that the equity investment, though by his-

A Good Deal

Although CDFI financing is generally more expensive than conventional loan financing, it is often still the way to go because the alternative may be no financing at all.

torical standards is unusual for a community loan development fund, is a growing and positive trend, since equity investments do not carry the regular interest payments that can so cripple a new enterprise.

Cascadia and the surrounding community reaped significant rewards on its investment: The lumber company the two entrepreneurs started about 150 miles southwest of Seattle turned in a profitable performance during its first full year in business and generated $5 million in revenue. In addition, the company's payroll grew from the initial two entrepreneurs with a dream to more than 50 hard-working saw men in the Northwest.

Where It Comes And Goes

These charts show where CDFIs get their capital and, more important, how and where it's disbursed.

Sources:

A. Foundations, 20%
B. Individuals, 19%
C. Financial institutions, 16%
D. Religious institutions, 15%
E. Government, 12%
F. Other, 13%

Uses By Stage Of Development:

A. Expansions, 27%
B. Facilities, 27%
C. Start-ups, 20%
D. Other, 20%

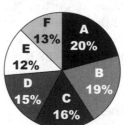

Uses By Geography:

A. Rural areas, 45%
B. Major urban centers, 33%
C. Smaller urban centers, 20%
D. Mixed, 2%

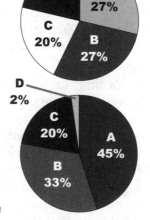

Source: National Community Capital Association

Real Businesses, Please

Don't be fooled into thinking that helping a community develop economically means the CDFIs will back any local entrepreneur with a gleam in his eye for a new business.

Quite the contrary. The way most loan officers at CDFIs see it, their capital is the dearest of all. Because without it, the surrounding communities would have access to hardly any (and in some cases no) capital. As a result, they can't pick losers. They need their capital back so they can recycle it into the community and jump-start the process of economic development.

> **Don't Forget**
> Community Development Financial Institutions offer loans, not grants. As such, they are looking to finance companies that demonstrate an ability to pay them back.

Testimony to the loan standards of CDFIs are their national loan loss rates. These rates measure the percentage of loans lost to failure and non-performance. According to the National Community Capital Association, a trade group of CDFIs, the national loan loss rate is about 1.4 percent, a figure that rivals, and, in some instances, actually beats the performance of traditional commercial lenders.

However, according to Mark Pinsky, executive director of the National Community Capital Association, lenders at CDFIs tend to take greater risk because they look more at present facts and circumstances than historical patterns. "More and more banks that make small-business loans are using credit-scoring systems," he says. "These systems work great, but since they are numerically driven, a lot of companies that might otherwise be viable credits are weeded out."

> **Shop Talk**
> Commercial lenders tend to think of loans in terms of being "bankable" or "unbankable." Your loan proposal is not bankable if you cannot demonstrate a viable source of repayment.

CDFIs, Pinsky says, are different: "We deal with the entrepreneur and the specific opportunity at hand, not necessarily the fact that there is a blemish on his or her personal credit report."

5 Steps To CDFI Financing

1. **Contact the CDFI and schedule an appointment.** Not only are they willing to discuss your loan proposal, but many CDFIs also assist companies in getting loan financing from other institutions.

2. **Be ready to demonstrate your "second bottom line."** Specifically, how will the loan result in job creation or the introduction of an important service in the community, or how will it help stabilize the local economy or community? For instance, Pinsky recalls an urban neighborhood that did not have a Laundromat. It was a Latino community and many of the families did laundry every day. With the closest Laundromat 20 blocks away, it took all day.

Evolution In The Air

There is a growing trend among CDFIs to provide equity financing as well as loan financing, according to the National Community Capital Association's Mark Pinsky. In fact, the National Community Capital Association recently changed its name from the National Association of Community Development Loan Funds because the membership and the kinds of financing they were becoming involved with were changing. "Our mission is more than to create CDFIs," says Pinsky. "We are striving to create institutions that can use capital to create stronger communities," he says.

As part of this mission, Pinsky adds, often members readily recognize that debt financings do not address the needs of many small businesses because their cash flow is not stable enough to support regular interest payments. In short, debt financing, even when small companies can get it, can prove debilitating. "As a result, many of our members are now putting equity into companies that generally do not attract the interest of traditional equity investors and venture capitalists."

But then a couple of the residents got together to open a new neighborhood Laundromat, which was funded by a CDFI. The new facility, Pinsky says, spawned a small grocery, an eating establishment and a newsstand. "In essence," he says, "this one small business helped stabilize the economy of the entire neighborhood."

Taking Action

To find out if there is a CDFI in your area, request a list from the National Community Capital Association. Send a self-addressed stamped envelope to the National Community Capital Association, 924 Cherry St., Philadelphia, PA 19107, or call (215) 923-4754.

3. **Show that you are committed to the community,** and that your long-range plans are to stay there, not grow up and move on.

4. **Set aside ample time.** CDFI loan officers tend to spend more time with you than a traditional commercial lender. Give them their due because it might result in the creative solution that delivers your financing.

5. **Be ready to commit some of your own funds.** If possible, set aside some of your personal capital to put into the business as an incentive for the CDFI to make a commitment. Nothing gives a lender more comfort than a founder who puts in everything he can.

Chapter 4

Microloans

The Scoop

Definition Or Explanation: The Microloan Program was developed by the Small Business Administration (SBA) in 1992 to increase the availability of very small loans to small-business borrowers. It achieved permanent status in 1997. The program uses nonprofit intermediaries to make loans to new and existing borrowers, and from 1993 through January 1998, accounted for 6,380 loans totaling more than $65 million.

Appropriate For: These funds may be used for working capital, inventory, supplies, furniture, fixtures, machinery and equipment.

Supply: Microloans are available from private, nonprofit intermediaries. Currently, the program is administered by 105 nonprofit organizations serving their communities in 49 states, plus Washington, DC, and Puerto Rico. According to the SBA, there is a sufficient supply of funds due in part to a self-sustaining revolving fund.

Best Use: For start-up companies with lower capital requirements and limited operating history. Microloan borrowers may benefit from the intermediary's expertise in business.

Cost: Negotiable with intermediary, but rates tend to be higher than for standard business loans. Most loans are collateralized by equipment, contracts, inventory or other property, and require personal guarantees.

Ease Of Acquisition: This is an especially good source of funds for businesses that have never borrowed from a bank. And it provides a source of smaller loans that many banks are reluctant to service, especially as a business loan. One of the difficulties in obtaining microloan funding, however, lies in the nonprofit intermediary distribution system. These intermediaries distribute funds in their own communities and/or regions, so if one does not exist in your area, SBA microloan financing may be difficult to get. If this is the case, however, there are other microloan programs—often backed by state and local governments—that can offer an alternative.

Range Of Funds Typically Available: Less than $100 to a maximum of $25,000. Average loan size is $10,400, with an average loan maturity of 37 months. Maximum term for a loan is six years.

Small Is Beautiful

Often, it's the small loan that can be hardest to get; most commercial banks are reluctant to make business loans of less than $10,000. Business owners who need less, or do not qualify for more, are out of luck unless they want to borrow the money personally. This latter option is often more expensive, typically ignores any business collateral and, perhaps most important, does nothing to advance the credit of the business.

"Microloans enable businesspeople to get small loans that are treated as business loans," says Millard Owens, director of microlending for Self-Help, a nonprofit commercial development financial institution. "This is not to say that personal issues are not factored in, but the strength of the business can help offset some personal inadequacies."

For a new business, new borrower, or a borrower with some blemishes in his or her credit history, the microloan program can provide an answer to the Catch-22 of lending—being unable to get money unless you have it. These loans have a range starting at just $100, with a maximum of $25,000. Different lenders may have their own minimums, so it's wise to clarify this upfront when shopping for a loan. Starting small allows small businesses an excellent means of establishing business credit and improving their credit profile.

Some microloan lenders focus extensive resources on offering management training and other critical business skills to their small-business borrowers, while others focus primarily on lending. Many microloan borrowers can benefit from these services, and availability may be a consideration when choosing a microloan lender.

A Good Deal

If your choice is to obtain a personal loan and use the proceeds for your business or get a microloan with the business as the borrower, take the microloan. Even though you must personally guarantee the loan, it helps your business establish a sound credit rating. And as bankers like to say, "A good credit rating is your best asset!"

Microloan lenders can often be more flexible than traditional lenders in their underwriting criteria, especially for smaller loans. They do look at credit history, collateral and debt history, but they also tend to spend more time and attention on individual applicants. In addition, because of the nature of their lending practices, many microloan lenders have already had experience with businesses that are considered to be risky by traditional lenders. With this experience they are often more open to these types of ventures and better able to offer managerial assistance.

Owens also suggests that potential borrowers—and other small businesses as well—check other sources of technical and managerial assistance. Try local colleges and universities, chambers of commerce and the SBA (see "Help Is On The Way" on page 38). You will not only gain useful information, but this effort will also help demonstrate your seriousness and commitment to a prospective lender.

When Small Isn't Beautiful

Microloan lenders are not trying to compete with other lenders, so you may find that the loan rates are higher than for other loans. On the other hand, the rates are lower than on credit cards and other avenues often used to finance small amounts.

Convenient access to a microloan lender may be an issue for some borrowers due to the limited number of SBA microloan lenders and their mandate to serve local and regional economic development. To find an SBA microloan lender in your region, call your district SBA office, or go to www.sba.gov and check under "Local SBA Resources." There are other types of non-SBA microloan lending programs, generally backed by state or local governments. Ask your banker, or contact state or local chambers of commerce or your state department of commerce for more information about these programs. Some universities also offer assistance to small businesses through the SBA; it may be worth a call to the business department of a nearby university.

Don't Forget
Lenders speak the language of finance. You cannot converse with them without financial documentation. Even if you are a tiny business seeking a small loan, you must still have personal and business tax returns if you are to take the process beyond the "nice to meet you" stage.

Another drawback of the microloan program is the limited product line. Self-Help, for example, does not offer a credit line under the SBA program. Not all microloan lenders offer a full range of loan products, or even the full range of microloan amounts. So if you anticipate needing larger amounts of funds in the future, you should establish a relationship with a traditional lender.

Shop Talk
Every lender has so-called underwriting criteria, but what are they? These criteria spell out the standards and guidelines the lender lives by. "Companies that have been in business at least two years with positive cash flow" gives examples of two very simple underwriting criteria. When meeting with a lender, ask about its criteria to gain some idea of how your company matches or mismatches the lender's profile.

The Microloan Application Process

Self-Help is one of the nation's most active SBA microloan lenders, and Owens has been involved in many of these loans. He says that the process of applying for the

Help Is On The Way

The SBA provides a variety of business counseling and training services to current and prospective small-business owners. You can find out where these services are offered by calling the nearest Small Business Administration district office or by visiting the SBA's Web site at www.sba.gov.

- **The Service Corps of Retired Executives:** The collective experience of SCORE counselors spans the full range of American enterprise. SCORE volunteers provide free management and technical assistance in all aspects of running a business — from writing a business plan to accounting and marketing. Counseling is available at SBA district offices, business information centers and some Small Business Development Centers.

- **Small Business Development Centers:** SBDCs offer a broad spectrum of free to low-cost business information and guidance, from assisting with market research to help in preparing business plans. In addition, SBDCs offer assistance in preparing loan applications. The program is a cooperative effort of the private sector, the educational community, and federal, state and local governments.

- **Business Information Centers:** BICs provide the latest in access to high-tech hardware, software and telecommunications to help small businesses get started and grow strong. Supported by local SBA offices, BICs also offer expert counseling by SCORE volunteers. Assistance is free to low-cost.

- **One-Stop Capital Shops:** OSCSs are the SBA's contribution to the Empowerment Zones/Enterprise Communities Program, an interagency initiative that provides resources to economically distressed communities. The shops provide a full range of free to low-cost SBA lending and technical-assistance programs, such as credit counseling or help with preparing financial statements or loan applications.

loan can be made easier by understanding what is involved, and describes what happens when a potential microloan borrower initiates the loan process at his organization.

During the first call, a Self-Help staff member takes the time to gather preliminary information. In this initial conversation, the borrower is asked a number of basic questions, including:

- Is this a start-up or existing business?
- How much money is needed, and for what purpose are the funds intended?
- Who is included in the management team, and what is their experience?
- What collateral is available?
- How much have you already invested or are you willing to invest?

A Good Deal

Check out the SBA's Women's Business Center, a Web site for women who want to start or expand their businesses. Free online counseling and a world of information about business practices, management techniques, technology training, market research and SBA services are available. Go to www.on-linewbc.org.

Taking Action

Raising money is about making connections with other people. After all, it's somebody else who has what you need. And often it's a random path that leads you to the gold at the end of the rainbow. Pick any of the resources we've mentioned, make an appointment, see a counselor or consultant and ask him or her to point you in a direction—any direction.

Following this preliminary information-gathering call, applications are sent via mail, along with a form from which applicants are asked to develop a personal financial statement.

Business plans are not required at all levels, according to Owens, but borrowers must have a complete understanding of their market, capacity and competition. Previous financial statements are required for existing businesses, but in the case of start-ups, personal tax returns are often substituted.

Once this data is reviewed,

Self-Help contacts the applicant by phone, usually within a few days. During this period, Self-Help adds a credit report to the information supplied by the applicant. Often, Owens notes, the application is incomplete and requires additional information. It is generally the tax returns that are among the missing pieces. The best advice, especially if you're in a hurry, is to supply all requested information and, almost as important, make it as clear as possible in terms of its presentation. In other words, if the lender can't read it, it may as well not be included.

From there, if the loan request is small—that is, $5,000 and less—the process can be completed in a few days. Larger amounts take longer—generally, three to four weeks—because additional information is required.

In summary, the Microloan Program can offer a cash and credit jump-start to small or start-up businesses. Unlike many of their counterparts, these lenders are comfortable with the needs, collateral and experience level of small borrowers and are flexible in their dealings with this important segment of the economy.

Chapter 5

Asset-based Loans

The Scoop

Definition Or Explanation: Asset-based loans are usually from commercial finance companies (as opposed to banks) that are offered on a revolving basis and collateralized by a company's assets, specifically accounts receivable and inventory.

Appropriate For: Companies that may be rapidly growing, highly leveraged, in the midst of a turn-around or undercapitalized. In addition, asset-based financing works only for companies with proven accounts receivable, and a demonstrated track record of turning over their inventory several times each year.

Supply: Overall, the supply of asset-based financing is vast. A large number of commercial finance companies, as well as many banks, have massive pools of capital to lend to businesses. However, for smaller asset-based loans, those of $500,000 or less, the market is considerably smaller. Most asset-based lenders would prefer to make larger loans because the cost to monitor an asset-based loan is generally the same whether it is large or small.

Best Use: Financing rapid growth in the absence of sufficient equity capital to fund receivables and inventory. Asset-based loans can also be used to finance acquisitions.

Cost: More expensive than bank financing since asset-based lenders generally have higher expenses than bankers. Still, pricing is competitive among asset-based lenders. Small asset-based loans can be pricey, though, running 12 percent to 28 percent.

Ease Of Acquisition: Comparatively easy if your company has good financial statements, good reporting systems, inventory that is not exotic and, finally, customers who have a track record of paying their bills. If you don't have any of these, your path to an asset-based loan will be challenging.

Funds Typically Available: $100,000 and greater.

Asset-based Lending—What Is It?

Conceptually, asset-based loans are easy to understand, according to William Barnett, a partner with law firm Herrick, Feinstein in New York City, who specializes in asset-based lending. "Asset-based lending is formula lending based on the liquidation value of accounts receivable and inventory," he says.

While term lenders certainly consider the value of these assets when making a loan, they are secondary. For the most part, when a banker makes a term loan, he or she looks at the enterprise's cash flow and tries to determine whether it is sufficient to service the debt and whether it can be sustained for the term of the loan.

Asset-based lenders, on the other hand, do not focus on cash flow. They look at two asset classes: accounts receivable and inventory. With a knowledge of these assets, the asset-based lender makes a short-term loan. Although this short-term loan is paid off as accounts receivable and inventory liquidate, for growing businesses, more accounts receivable and more inventory are being created all the time. As a result, an asset-based loan has a revolving quality, and may remain on a company's books for a while. This can be beneficial because it gives a company time to catch its breath. But is can also work against a company because an asset-based

Shop Talk

When a lender takes a "security interest" in an asset it means he or she is granted possession of and ownership in the assets in the event of a default. The security interest that lenders are able to take on inventory and accounts receivable is the basis of their collateral and, as a result, is the loan's underpinning.

loan may not be renewed and must then be paid back before a company may be prepared to do so.

An asset-based lender's emphasis on assets rather than cash flow significantly affects the relationship between lender and borrower, according to Barnett. First, the asset-based lender is taking a security position in the underlying assets and views liquidation of them as a viable means of recovering the loan principal. Second, because the asset-based lender is lending against assets that can fluctuate rapidly in value, he or she monitors these assets more intensively. "It's not uncommon," Barnett says, "for asset-based lenders to look at the inventory or accounts receivable once a month, sometimes even more frequently." Conventional lenders making term loans, on the other hand, might review financial data once a quarter, and never look at inventory once the initial loan is made.

Estimating Your Borrowing Capacity

Your borrowing capacity for an asset-based loan rests on what your assets will support, as well as the maximum line a lender is willing to grant you.

The Factor Factor

A close relative of asset-based financing is factoring. The primary difference between the two is that the former is a loan against an asset, while the latter is the outright sale of an asset. That's right—when you factor your accounts receivable, you sell to a third party your right to receive payment. Of course, if you sell the asset, you receive payment—just not as much as you would have received if you had waited until your customer made his payment. A factor makes money by purchasing your $100 receivable for $87.50 and then receiving from your customer the full $100 payment.

One of the drawbacks of factoring is that once you sell your accounts receivable, you lose control over how they are collected. A factor that collects aggressively might turn off your customers and damage the relationship you have built with them.

Barnett says that most asset-based lenders lend 90 percent of "eligible" receivables, and 50 percent of "eligible" inventory. So what is meant by "eligible"?

Basically, just because you have an asset on the books does not necessarily mean that a lender will advance you funds against it. "Asset-based lenders deduct ineligible receivables, such as those from mom-and-pop shops, or ones that are more than 45 days old, or ones from customers who have had a bad debt on prior receivables, or perhaps receivables due from customers overseas," Barnett explains.

So on the receivables side, the equation looks like this:

total receivables – ineligible receivables = net eligible receivables

and

net eligible receivables x 0.9 = total borrowing capacity from receivables

The same concepts apply to inventory. That is, the inventory on hand must be adjusted by the lender. Specifically, ineligible components must be removed to estimate what constitutes the eligible portion. Ineligible inventory might include items that are more than 180 days old, certain exotic goods that would be difficult to liquidate and material that may have spoiled or been damaged.

total inventory – ineligible inventory = net eligible inventory

and

net eligible inventory x 0.5 = total borrowing capacity from inventory.

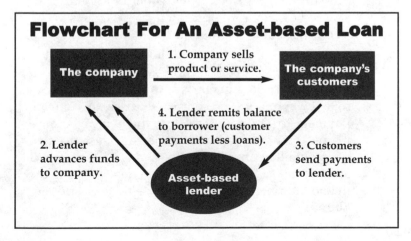

Flowchart For An Asset-based Loan

The company

1. Company sells product or service.

The company's customers

4. Lender remits balance to borrower (customer payments less loans).

2. Lender advances funds to company.

3. Customers send payments to lender.

Asset-based lender

Supply And Demand

Slightly farther up—or farther down the food chain, depending on your perspective—is another source of asset-based financing: suppliers. In fact, suppliers already offer financing by giving most of their customers 30 days to pay their invoices. Many businesses need asset-based financing because their sales cycle is longer than their accounts payable cycle. After all, if you could purchase goods on 30-day terms, sell them and be paid within 15, who would need financing? Unfortunately, most sales cycles take more time.

So before talking to a commercial finance company, start with your suppliers. There are two ways to do this. The first is simply not to pay invoices until they are 90 days old. This gives you three months of financing—in some cases free. You will know this strategy is working if your supplier does not freeze shipments to you after your first invoice is more than 60 days old. The second way is to simply ask your supplier to extend your payment terms. If this is offered in conjunction with a lien on the materials it sells you, the vendor might just bite. After all, even if it doesn't have the cash from you, it has still booked the sale. If your supplier is under pressure to show sales growth quarter to quarter, or year to year, your sale, even if it takes 90 days to collect, is helpful to its cause.

Another way to get a couple of extra days out of your supplier is to test its limits. For instance, if you pay your invoices in 30 days, pay them at 35 days for a few months. If no complaint arises, then stretch payment to 44 days. Why does this work? Because many accounts receivable collection systems flag payments that are older than 45 days. Therefore, if 35 days isn't a problem, chances are 45 days is the magic number to avoid to keep your supplier happy.

Adding the two sums together and subtracting any outstanding debt represents the total availability of what can be borrowed, Barnett explains, as long as it does not exceed the total line available to the company, which is spelled out in the agreement between the company and the borrower.

Why does inventory get such a low advance rate, just 50 percent of eligible inventory, while accounts receivable get 90 percent of the eligible amount? "The accounts receivable are self-liquidating, while the inventory is not," says Timothy Gannon of Sterling Bank in New York City, which specializes in small-business loans. "If a lender must liquidate to recover the loan, it must take possession of the inventory and sell it, which can be difficult, time-consuming and expensive." By contrast, he says, most accounts receivable will, over time—ideally within 30 days—turn themselves into cash through payments from customers.

Asset-based Loans—How They Work

The diagram below shows the cash flow of a typical asset-based loan:

Step 1: The process starts with the company selling its product or service to customers. Unless it's a cash business or a business in which customers pay for all of their purchases by credit card, a receivable is created. The receivable, a debt to the company, is, in most cases, repaid to the company in 10, 15, 30 or 45 days. This asset, in combination with inventory, which is not shown in the diagram on page 47, starts the process.

Step 2: The lender makes a loan to the company based on the value of the receivables. As discussed, the lender won't advance 100 percent of the receivables but will advance 90 percent of the eligible receivables. The moment funds are advanced, the company starts paying interest, and the lender starts earning interest.

Step 3: Pay close attention here. Note that with an asset-based loan, in most cases, the customers do

Don't Forget
Lenders want accounts receivable and inventory that can be turned into cash quickly. If you deal in exotic products, which cannot be easily sold, and exotic customers, asset-based lending may not be for you.

A Good Deal

You cannot look at the cost of asset-based loans—which can carry annual interest rates of 24 percent, or more—in absolute terms. It appears too expensive. Most experts counsel that smart borrowers treat the cost of an asset-based loan like another cost of doing business. If the loan's expensive but you can stay in business and make a profit, then that's what you must do.

not send their payments to the company that sold them the product or service but instead directly to the finance company. Asset-based lending can be uncomfortable for some businesses because a third party gains control of the company's cash flow.

This discomfort is warranted. Under such a scenario, certain events may turn out bad for the borrower. For instance, suppose a borrower has a large outstanding balance that is continuously revolving, and an entire group of the borrower's customers experienced some sort of financial peril. Say they all sold products to a region of the world that experienced financial meltdown. The lender, who closely monitors the assets, and begins to see the length of these customers' receivables expanding, may take a "reserve" to protect itself against possible loan losses. This reserve might come from the company's customer payments. Instead of remitting customer payments to the company, the lender hangs on to some of them to create this reserve against future loan losses. Suddenly, the company does not have the funds it was counting on.

Step 4: The lender remits to the company invoices paid, less the principal on loans it has already advanced, less interest.

Requirements And Scenarios

Sterling Bank's Gannon says that to successfully negotiate an asset-based deal, borrowers must come to the table with financial information that not only paints a positive picture but also is detailed and accurate. They must also be willing to make the lender comfortable. Among the requirements he cites:

- The business must have a reasonable net worth and long-term viability.
- Financial statements must be reviewed by a certified pub-

lic accountant whom the lender deems acceptable.

- Borrowers must submit a year's worth of monthly projections.
- The business's principals must guarantee the loan, and the guarantee must be supported by personal financial statements.
- Keyman (or keywoman) life insurance may be required.

Even if you qualify for an asset-based loan, it might not be the way to go, Gannon warns. "Asset-based loans are more expensive than bank lines of credit and are often much more intrusive on the borrower."

For instance, he says, if you have a good guarantee, are profitable and need to borrow, say, $500,000 twice a year for 60 days, go to a commercial bank. "That's the cheapest, easiest route."

Similarly, if you have a good guarantee and need a line of credit to support inventory and receivables that can be "cleaned up" (i.e., paid back) within one year, there's a good chance a bank will take a security interest in your inventory and receivables and offer a line of credit or a revolving line of credit. "This also will be cheaper than traditional asset-based loans," Gannon says.

"But if your guarantee is not that strong, you are not profitable, your business is undercapitalized, you need working capital and there is no way you can pay off a line for perhaps two or three years," Gannon says, "you present a problem for most banks even if, in spite of these circumstances, your business is a good one." He says that the bank may take a flier, but in most instances such as these, a bank would refer you to a commercial finance company that offers asset-based financing. A commercial finance company is sometimes your only salvation.

Taking Action

Looking for an asset-based lender? One of the fastest and easiest ways to start your search is to visit the Web site for the Commercial Finance Association. Enter the amount and type of capital you are looking for, and the site will give you the name, telephone number and a contact person at all the commercial finance companies that match your initial criteria. Visit www.cfa.com.

Chapter 6

Bank Term Loans

The Scoop

Definition Or Explanation: Bank term loans are the basic vanilla commercial loan. They typically carry fixed interest rates, monthly or quarterly repayment schedules and a set maturity date. Bankers tend to classify term loans into two categories:

- **Intermediate-term loans:** Usually running less than three years, these loans are generally repaid in monthly installments (sometimes with balloon payments) from a business's cash flow. Repayment is often tied directly to the useful life of the asset being financed, according to the American Bankers Association (ABA).

- **Long-term loans:** These loans are commonly set for more than three years. Most are between three and 10 years, and some run for as long as 20 years. Long-term loans are collateralized by a business's assets and typically require quarterly or monthly payments derived from profits or cash flow. These loans usually carry wording that limits the amount of additional financial commitments the business may take on (including other debts but also dividends or principals' salaries), and they sometimes require a profit set-aside earmarked to repay the loan, according to the ABA.

Appropriate For: Established small businesses that can leverage sound financial statements and substantial down payments to minimize monthly payments and total loan costs. Repayment is typically linked in some way to the item financed. Term loans require collateral and a relatively rigorous approval process but can help reduce risk by minimizing costs. Before deciding to finance equipment, borrowers should be sure they can they make full use of ownership-related benefits, such as depreciation, and should compare the cost with that leasing.

Supply: Large but highly differentiated. The degree of financial strength required to receive loan approval can vary tremendously from bank to bank, depending on the level of risk the bank takes on.

Best Use: Construction; major capital improvements; large capital investments, such as machinery; working capital; purchases of existing businesses.

Cost: Inexpensive if the borrower can pass the financial litmus tests. Rates vary, making it worthwhile to shop, but generally run around 2.5 points over prime for loans of less than seven years and 2.75 points over prime for longer loans. Fees totaling up to 1 percent are common (though this varies greatly, too), with higher fees on construction loans.

Ease Of Acquisition: Challenging but sometimes a moderate challenge when smaller amounts are involved. However, for loans more than $100,000 (sometimes up to $200,000), you need a complete set of financial statements and must undergo a complete financial analysis by the lending institution.

Funds Typically Available: $25,000 and greater.

Term Loans Are Still
The Cheapest Vehicle

The bank term loan was the old standby for decades before some of today's popular and innovative financial methods offered so many alternatives. But despite myriad new instruments, the term loan is far from dead, and for good reason: It is often still the cheapest way to go, if you can meet sometimes hefty qualification requirements.

"When you look at venture capital, they want a piece of your business," says Rob Fazzini, president of commercial lending at Busey Bank in Illinois. "Leasing puts someone in the middle, and they have to make a profit, so the rate will be higher; national prime plus 5 percent is common. As for asset-based loans, there is greater risk and more monitoring effort for the bank, so the rate has to be higher. That is why the traditional way of lending is still often the best choice—if you qualify."

How Do You Qualify?

You will most likely have to cough up a good bit of your own cash. Expect banks to ask you to put down 20 percent to 25 percent of the total cost of what is being financed because they want the borrower to carry some risk.

But there's more to it. "You want a customer who has thought enough ahead to save some of the money to reduce the risk," says Fazzini, who is also one of seven of ABA's national banking advisors. "Otherwise, they have to finance the full amount, and that increases the chances of failure because they face higher payments."

Sure, if you don't have the seed money, you can still rent or lease, Fazzini notes. "But the payments will be higher than the principle and interest payments on a loan, and you are not building equity." In other words, a term loan has much in common with a home mortgage. You get ownership (assuming you want it), lower overall costs and the ability to lower payments by spreading them out.

As you might guess, people applying for term loans are most often turned down because they lack that down payment. But, Fazzini says,

Shop Talk

Almost every loan has covenants. These are promises that borrowers make to lenders about their actions and responsibilities. A typical covenant specifies the amount of debt the borrower is allowed to take on in the future. If you want to see just how restrictive your loan will be, look at the covenants section of the loan agreement.

"Most banks will not say, 'term loans are the traditional and best way to go, and if you don't have the down payment, go away.'" In fact, he says, there's nothing to feel bad about if you're turned down for a loan. Banks often counsel applicants against buying, say, a building, suggesting instead a rent-with-an-option-to-buy clause until it is clear that the new asset is producing as projected.

Be Prepared

What do banks look for when making decisions about term loans? Well, the "five C's" continue to be of utmost importance.

- **Character:** How have you managed other loans (business and personal)? What is your business experience? "If a corporate executive wants to open a restaurant, then he'd better have restaurant experience," Busey Bank's Fazzini says.

- **Credit capacity:** The bank will conduct a full credit analy-

Line Of The Times

You may need a line of credit rather than a term loan. One of the key differences between the two, from a financial management perspective, is that a term loan can provide working capital that is always on hand, while a line of credit offers working capital only when it's needed. One of the costs of always having funds on hand is that you pay for them each and every month.

Financing the seasonality of a product or service—such as making bathing suits or distributing road salts—is one of the primary reasons to seek a line of credit. If you can draw down funds and pay them back in 60 to 90 days, that is often less intrusive than the demands of a full-blown term loan. If, on the other hand, your business is not seasonal but undercapitalized, and the advance of funds may stay on your books for more than a year, then a term loan, or asset-based financing (discussed in the previous chapter) may be more appropriate.

sis, including a detailed review of financial statements and personal finances to asses your ability to repay.

- **Collateral:** The primary source of repayment. Expect the bank to want this source to be larger than the amount you're borrowing.
- **Capital:** What assets do you own that can be quickly turned into cash if necessary? The bank wants to know what you own outside of the business—bonds, stocks, apartment buildings—that might be an alternate repayment source. If there is a loss, your assets are tapped first, not the bank's. Or, as one astute businessman puts it, "Banks like to lend to people who already have money." You will most likely have to add a personal guarantee to all of that, too.
- **Comfort/confidence with the business plan:** How accurate are the revenue and expense projections? Expect the bank to make a detailed judgment. What is the condition of the economy and the industry: "Are you selling buggy whips or computers?" Fazzini asks.

Financial Statements

Expect to supply the bank with a complete range of financial statements. A surprising number of businesses approach banks with poor or insufficient documentation, which does not create a great impression. The following are the documents a bank is likely to request:

- Balance sheet
- Income statements for five years
- Cash flow reports for two years
- Accounts receivable and payables (in some cases)
- Tax returns for at least two years. Don't bother arguing that your revenues are really more than your tax returns indicate. Many small-business owners try this sideways claim (especially those in cash businesses), but trust

Don't Forget

It's not all numbers. Bankers look at the person as much as the business. Make a good impression. Show them you understand your business and industry. Don't hide your entrepreneurial spirit and enthusiasm; they like to see it. And give them a taste of your sales skills; this can only increase their confidence in you.

us, it cuts no ice with the banker. And, they do not want to hear this even if it is true.

Other statements are also often required, such as aging of accounts receivable. What's more, expect to be asked to supply financial statements regularly during the life of the loan.

You should also expect that the banks will use these documents to do some financial ratio analysis, including the following:

- Total debt-to-net worth: a measure of total debt against net worth (or equity)
- Long-term debt to net worth
- Current ratio: This liquidity measurement compares current assets to current liabilities

(See Chapter 21 for more insight on how a lender looks at your financial statements.)

Other ratios, such as the inventory turnover, may be used in the financial analysis, depending on the industry. Acceptable ratio numbers will also vary by industry and by bank. And there are other measurements the banks will probably make. The point is, there may be key financial-analysis hurdles to clear, so a consultation with your accountant is a good way to start.

Other documents that may be required include organizational charts and insurance information.

> **Don't Forget**
> You don't have to do business in town. Lots of banks are now scouring the country looking for small-business customers. In fact, many of the top names in banking now show up in your mailbox in the form of loan offers. These loans, which are often unsecured lines of credit, can be a ready source of capital. So don't toss all that junk mail. Some of it may be the debt financing you're looking for.

Red Flags

Pay special attention to the following items—your bank certainly will, according to Fazzini:

- **Poor credit reports:** If your credit bureau report is blemished, the bank will naturally wonder why you would pay it on time when you have failed to do so for others. If you have problems, you better have good explanations.

- **Absence of a down payment:** If you don't have one, expect the bank to think that you have not thought ahead.
- **A bad rap:** Your reputation in town should be good. "We will ask, believe me," Fazzini says.
- **Poor collateral:** Quality of the collateral. Uncle Joe's sealing wax collection won't cut it. Banks want to see liquid assets, which will be assessed on their market value, not what you paid for them or what you think they are worth.
- **A poor business plan, or none at all:** Make sure you have one, and be sure it is realistic. (See Chapter 23 on strategies for preparing a business plan.)

The Great Divide

More and more banks are willing to forgo a full-scale credit analysis for smaller loans in lieu of working up a credit scoring similar to that used by leasing companies and others. In some cases, the information required is not much different from a credit card application.

A Good Deal

Beware of "compensating balances," which is the level of funds the bank stipulates you must leave in the bank if it grants you a loan. If the bank lends you $500,000 but says to keep a balance of $50,000 at all times, then your loan proceeds are really $450,000. The compensating balance has the effect of ratcheting up the effective interest you are paying.

The cutoff point varies from bank to bank: $50,000 for some, and up to $100,000 for others. BankAmerica, for example, requires financial statements only for loan requests of more than $100,000. Fazzini's Busey Bank, on the other hand, doesn't offer a credit-scoring option for term loans. It does full-scale analyses for every loan (and has a default rate that is just a fraction of the industry's as a result). As with most things, it pays to shop; however, the real point is that if you are looking for a smaller loan, of $100,000 or less, you might obtain it more quickly by working with banks that use a credit-scoring rather than a credit-analysis model.

You Know You Should Look Elsewhere When . . .

Loans are like any other product or service you buy. There are good deals and not-so-good deals. Following are some of the elements of the latter:

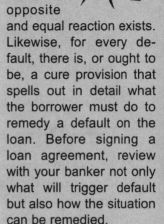

Shop Talk
For every action an opposite and equal reaction exists. Likewise, for every default, there is, or ought to be, a cure provision that spells out in detail what the borrower must do to remedy a default on the loan. Before signing a loan agreement, review with your banker not only what will trigger default but also how the situation can be remedied.

- **High fees:** Bank fees of up to about 1 percent on these loans are common. "Fees above this point," Fazzini says, "are generally higher than you should pay for a regular term loan." Exceptions involve construction loans because the banks have to do a lot more work to analyze and monitor the loan.

- **Difficult personalities:** Be certain that the banker working with you understands your business. Perverse though it may seem, you should leave a meeting with your banker feeling as if you have been challenged. A good one will be a sounding board and help you skirt the avoidable mistakes. After all, your banker has probably been through the process hundreds of times. This may be your first time. A good banker has clear ideas of which businesses fail and which succeed, and why. He should know your industry and be able to offer insights. And his views should not be limited to finances. A good banker also pumps you for answers to detailed marketing questions.

- **The bank you are working with is going to be acquired:** The consolidation of the banking industry has two potentially unpleasant side effects for small-business borrowers. First, your once friendly bank may, as a result of changing policy dictated by the new parent company, decide that entire industries or sectors are no longer desirable. If you're in that sector or industry, your bank may be itching for a reason to revoke your credit. The other possible side effect is that your lender may be replaced by a new one at increasingly frequent intervals. Now here is an institution that holds the destiny of your company in its hand, has a lien on all your personal and corporate assets, and every six months there's someone new on your account, who wants to play by a different set of rules. No thanks!

What Else You Need To Know

Here are some typical concepts that may be built into a loan, depending on the variables of the specific deal:

- **Commitment fees:** When a bank makes a commitment to lend you money, it could end up costing you 3 percent to 25 percent of the loan value. The bank often finances the commitment fee or takes it out of the loan proceeds. Perhaps more than any other aspect of a loan, commitment fees are variable—and negotiable. If you are not getting the rate or term you want, work on the commitment fee.

- **Balance fees:** Banks typically charge fees on unused portions of a line of credit. That is, if you have a $250,000 line of credit, but are not using it, the bank may charge you a fee for any portion of the line that is not drawn down. The bank's reasoning? There is a cost and a value associated with making money available to you at all times, even if you are not using it. In addition, many banks require borrowers

Taking Action

If you want to find a small-business–friendly bank, check out the Small Business Administration's banking studies, which identify the nation's top small-business commercial bank lenders. The study rates banks in each state on their performance in small-business lending. You can find this information in Appendix C or at www.sba.gov/advo/stats. Under "Finance," look for "Banking Studies."

to maintain a certain balance in the bank. A borrower with a $500,000 loan may be required to have a balance of at least $25,000 at all times. In theory, this is expensive, since in the example given on page 60, the borrower has access to only $450,000 of his or her funds but is paying interest on $500,000. Balance fees are common. But the good news for entrepreneurs is that they are often negotiable.

- **Prepayment penalties:** Banks figure they go to a lot of trouble and expense to commit funds over a long period. When a business decides to pay off early, there can be costs to the bank. A prepayment penalty helps to defer that cost.

- **Covenants:** Here the borrower may agree to secure certain actions, such as the owner maintaining full-time employment with the company during the assigned period of the loan, or not taking on additional debt. (By the way, this is one reason companies already saddled with debt might turn to leasing.)

- **Default treatment:** Some action, or inaction, on the part of the borrower grants the lender the right to demand immediate full payment, to sell collateral or some similar move. Obviously, missing payments can kick in such clauses. But so can piling on additional debt in violation of your covenants. The bank may try to stick a business with onerous terms. These terms must be vigorously negotiated.

Choosing A Bank

Use the following guidelines when selecting a business bank:

- Ask friends where they bank and if they are satisfied.

- Forge a relationship with a bank long before you will need a loan. You will find out how they treat you. Get to know some folks at the bank on a first-name basis. Start building a relationship. Believe it or not, banks want to talk to you even if they cannot lend you money.

- Scan your newspaper for evidence of who is making the kinds of loans you are seeking. Not all banks can be the best at everything. Some are better at business loans; some are better with consumer needs.

- Visit two to four banks to find your fit. Be upfront; tell them you are considering a loan and that you are talking with other banks. Then listen to their pitch.
- Consider working through the Small Business Administration or other economic-development groups to secure better terms. They are not only for businesses that cannot get funding any other way.

Chapter 7

SBA-guaranteed Loans

The Scoop

Definition Or Explanation: Term loans from a bank or commercial lending institution of up to 10 years, with the Small Business Administration (SBA) guaranteeing as much as 80 percent of the loan principal.

Appropriate For: Established small businesses capable of repaying a loan from cash flow but whose principals may be looking for a longer term to reduce payments or may have inadequate corporate or personal assets to collateralize the loan.

Supply: Vast. The SBA guarantees some $10 billion per year in loans. That is, because of SBA loan guarantees, more than $10 billion in loans are made annually by participating lenders.

Best Use: Purchasing equipment, financing the purchase of a business and in certain instances, working capital. The SBA guarantee can help borrowers overcome the problems of a weak loan application associated with inadequate collateral, or limited operating history.

Cost: Comparatively inexpensive. Maximum allowed interest rates range from highs of prime plus 4.75 percentage points to prime plus 2.75 percentage points, though lenders can and often do charge less. These rates may be higher or lower than rates on nonguaranteed loans. Even better, banks making SBA loans cannot charge fees (known as commitment fees) for agreeing to make a loan, or prepayment fees, which means the effective rates for SBA loans may be, in some instances, superior to those for conventional loans.

Ease Of Acquisition: Challenging. Although the SBA has created streamlined approaches to loan

applications, conventional SBA guarantee procedures and protocols pose a significant documentation and administrative challenge for most
borrowers.

Range Of Funds Typically Available: The SBA
guarantees $50,000 to $750,000 of loan principal.

The SBA Bridges The Gap . . .

The demands of a term loan are challenging for any business. The old banking adage "they only lend money when you
don't need it" is an old banking adage largely because it's true.
It should not come as any surprise then that term loans are particularly challenging for small businesses.

To understand why this is so, consider two of the three primary criteria banks use, cash flow and collateral, to evaluate
loan proposals. The third, incidentally, is the character of the
borrower—i.e., do they exhibit the kind of behavior, past and
present, that is consistent with the repayment of debts. While
the character test is easy to pass, cash flow and collateral are
more challenging for small businesses.

Take the issue of collateral. Many small businesses
cannot collateralize a loan be-
cause they are service businesses
without much in the way of tangible assets. Compounding the
problem, many small-business
owners are cash poor; whatever
assets they have are generally
sunk into the business, often
making their personal guarantee
inadequate.

That's why an SBA loan guarantee can be effective, according
to Michael Gallagher, a vice
president and manager of mar-

Shop Talk

Many balance
sheets have a lia-
bility item called
"current portion of long-term
debt." If you have an SBA
loan—or, for that matter, any
loan—with, say, a five-year
term, the amount of the loan
due in the coming year is the
current portion of long-term
debt.

ket development with Wells Fargo Bank. "Providing lenders with a government guarantee on as much as 80 percent of the principal bridges the gap between what is likely to be a borrower's available collateral and the collateral a lender would require to make such a loan."

... And Lowers The Cash Flow Hurdle

The other way that SBA loan guarantees can help is by extending the term of the loan, according to Gallagher.

SBA-guaranteed Loan Flowchart

1. Borrower files a loan application with an SBA lender. Lender analyzes loan application and approves it subject to an SBA guarantee.

2. Lender submits application and credit analysis to SBA, along with an application completed by the borrower.

3. SBA processes the guarantee request and, if approved, issues a guarantee on 75 percent of the loan proceeds (80 percent if the loan is less than $100,000).

4. Borrower pledges to SBA business assets as collateral, as well as provides a personal guarantee. If the loan is undercollateralized, liens on personal assets, such as the borrower's personal residence, are required.

5. Lender approves and authorizes loan, disburses funds to company.

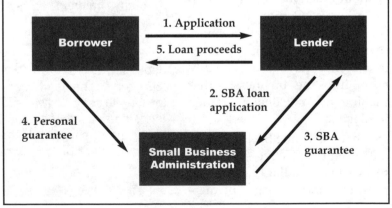

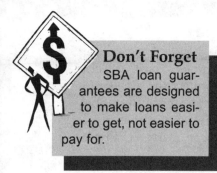

SBA-guaranteed business loans (as opposed to real estate loans) typically have seven-year terms, and in many cases, can even have 10-year terms. "For most term loans that are not guaranteed, the longest a bank will usually go is five years," he says.

The cash flow impact of extending the term of a loan can be compelling. For instance, a 9 percent, $300,000 loan paid monthly over five years costs $6,228 per month. But this same loan amortized over 10 years costs just $3,801 per month, $2,427 less. For the small-business owner with uncertain, or variable, cash flow, this is a material difference.

A Word On Posture

The flowchart on page 70 indicates a step in the sequence that sometimes surprises would-be borrowers: a pledge of the business's assets and a personal guarantee with liens on personal property. That's right. The principals of the business guarantee repayment to the Small Business Administration in the event the loan goes south, and the agency has to pay off the portion of the loan it guaranteed.

What's going on here? After all, one of the primary reasons to seek an SBA guarantee in the first place is to overcome inadequate collateral. In fact, if the SBA maintained the same rarefied collateral standards as most lenders, there would not be any compelling reason to seek an SBA guarantee to begin with.

But according to Wells Fargo's Gallagher, the SBA takes more risk on a personal guarantee than most lenders do. "In truth," Gallagher says, "the SBA tends not to turn down guarantees where insufficient collateral is the only unfavorable factor in the loan application."

But Gallagher's statement gets at the heart of the matter: Small Business Administration loan guarantees exist to facilitate the disbursement of a loan, not to protect the assets of a business and its owners in the event the loan runs into trouble. The guarantees and liens then serve an important role in the eyes of the SBA. Specifically, they motivate the borrower to perform financially and repay the loan.

How To Find An SBA Lender

While most banks, as well as select commercial finance companies, offer SBA loans, there are two specialized categories worth knowing about. These are Certified Lenders and Preferred Lenders, both of which have entered into contractual relationships with the SBA and officially participate in the Certified Lender/Preferred Lender programs (CLP/PLP).

Over Here . . . Over There

If you are planning to export, you should look into the SBA's Export Working Capital Program. This financing facility allows up to an 80 percent guarantee on private-sector loans of up to $750,000 for working capital. Loan maturities are typically 12 months and include two 12-month renewal options. Loans can be for single or multiple export sales and can be used for pre-shipment exposure coverage. They cannot, however, be used to purchase fixed assets.

Another source of export financing is the Export-Import Bank of the United States. Like the SBA, the Ex-Im Bank offers working-capital guarantees to small and medium-size businesses to cover 90 percent of the principal and interest on commercial loans. In addition, the Ex-Im Bank offers export-related insurance services that can protect entrepreneurs against foreign buyers who won't pay. For more information about the Ex-Im bank, or to find regional Ex-Im Bank offices, call (202) 565-3946.

SBA Business Loans At A Glance

	7(a) Business Loans	LowDoc Loans	FA$TRAK Loans
Use	Equipment, working capital, buy existing business	Equipment, working capital, buy existing business	Equipment, working capital
Term or line of credit	Term	Term	Both
Maximum guarantee amount	$750,000	$80,000	$50,000
Percentage of principal guaranteed	80% of loans under $100,000; 75% of loans over $100,000 to $1 million	80%	80%
Term	Up to 10 years	Up to 10 years	7-10 years, term loans; 5-year line of credit
Rates	Adjustable rate only; maximum of: P* + 2.75%	Adjustable rate only; maximum of: P + 4.75% for loans of less than $25,000; P + 3.75% for loans between $25,000 and $49,999; P+2.75% for loans between $50,000 and $100,000	Adjustable rate only; maximum of: P + 4.75% for loans of less than $25,000; P + 3.75% for loans between $25,000 and $49,999; P+2.75% for loans between $50,000 and $100,000
Speed of SBA processing	Up to 6 weeks for nonpreferred lenders	Up to 3 weeks	Within 3 days

Source: Wells Fargo Bank
*P=prime rate

A Good Deal

Not all banks that make SBA loans are created equal. Some are good and some are not so good. Therefore, choose your SBA lender carefully. What's the best criterion to go by? Experience. Generally speaking, the more SBA loans a lender has made, the better it is at it.

These lender programs were designed to provide better response to borrowers; they accomplish this goal by placing additional responsibilities on the lenders for analysis, structuring, approval, servicing and liquidation of loans, within SBA guidelines.

About 850 lenders qualify for the SBA's Certified Lender Program, having met certain criteria, the most important of which, from the borrower's perspective, is extensive experience in SBA loan-guarantee processing. Certified lenders account for about 9 percent of all SBA business-loan guarantees. Since the certified bank does much of the SBA's work, the agency offers turnaround times of three business days for processing the application.

Approximately 500 lenders meet preferred lender standards. This group processes approximately 30 percent of SBA loans. Preferred lenders have full lending authority and as a result can offer a one-day turnaround on completed loan applications.

If you are seeking an SBA loan, your best bet is to work with a certified or preferred lender. The SBA-guarantee process is tricky at best, and you want a lender who has been through it more than once. To find certified or preferred lenders, visit the SBA Web site at www.sba.gov. Click on "Listings & Directories" in the reading room, or click on "Local SBA Resources." As always, you can call your local SBA office for guidance.

Onerous But Unavoidable Features

Under the heading that there is no such thing as a free lunch, much less a free loan guarantee, the SBA loan–application process offers would-be borrowers a host of challenges with respect to documentation and administration. Gregg Mitchell, vice president of SBA lending with Wells Fargo, which lends $100 million per year to small businesses under various SBA programs, has seen literally thousands of SBA loan deals. Some aspects of the application process that tend to give borrowers a run for their money include the following:

- **Controlled disbursements:** When you get a 7(a) business loan, you usually don't get a check to deposit in your account and spend as your please. The SBA lender makes out checks to certain vendors that are described in the loan application. "Where this can get sticky," Mitchell says, "is when you start out applying for a loan, you may believe you will spend, say, $50,000 with one vendor for a certain piece of equipment. But when the time for the loan grows closer, that amount may have gone up or down." If the amount changes too much, the application may have to be reapproved. At the very least it must be changed, which of course chews up valuable time.

- **Hazard insurance:** To secure an SBA loan, you must have your insurance company provide the lender an endorsement, which, in the event of a disaster, such as a fire, tornado or theft, directs proceeds from the policy to the lender, not the borrower. If you have the right insurance, the endorsement is almost a no-brainer; it simply takes time and effort. If you don't have the right insurance, you'll find yourself shopping for it before the loan application process is completed.

- **Additional disclosures:** Mitchell says that many disclosures and documentation are generally unnecessary with conventional loans. Resumes, statements of personal history, disclosures on arrests and convictions, and interim financial statements all add to the mounting paperwork associated with the loan-guarantee application.

- **Landlord consents:** If you rent or lease your business's facilities, the landlord may be asked to provide his consent to allow the lender the right to enter the premises and retrieve the business collateral in the event of a default. Unfortunately, landlords don't always willingly sign these con-

A Good Deal

Time is money, and so-called certified or preferred SBA lenders, because of their relationship with the SBA, can turn around loans much faster than other lenders.

sents; in fact, sometimes they refuse to sign them. Their reluctance stems from a belief that if a tenant might default on a loan, he or she might also default on a lease. And if that's the case, then the landlord doesn't want the bank emptying the factory or office of the only valuable assets

Faster Track ... Smaller Guarantee

Certain lenders in the SBA's loan-guarantee program also make FA$TRAK loans. The application for a FA$TRAK is as streamlined as possible, according to Wells Fargo's Gallagher. In fact, he says, there is no SBA application. "With FA$TRAK," he says, "lenders use their own systems for analysis, approval and disbursement, and do not have to meet all the application requirements of a conventional 7(a) loan.

"If you are seeking an SBA loan and need $100,000 or less, you can save a lot of aggravation by going with a FA$TRAK loan," Gallagher says. If your lender can make FA$TRAK loans but is offering the 7(a), push for the FA$TRAK. "You'll be happy you did."

One of the differences between a FA$TRAK and regular SBA-guaranteed loan is that FA$TRAK can be used for lines of credit as well as term loans. "Many companies," Gallagher says, "prefer to access working capital by drawing on it as needed rather than being locked into a term loan with regular payments."

Another difference is the guarantee percentage. For conventional loans, the SBA guarantees 75 percent to 80 percent of the loan principal. For FA$TRAK, the guarantee extends to just 50 percent of loans of $100,000 or less.

For companies looking for a loan, the percentage of guarantee doesn't matter, except that the lower the guaranteed portion, the stronger the deal must be to get a nod from the lender. Maximum rates on FA$TRAK loans are the same as for 7(a) loans.

that may be left. "The land-lord consent can be a tough issue," Mitchell says. "I've seen it kill weaker deals."

- **Other insurances:** If a loan is undercollateralized—meaning that after all business and personal assets are pledged, there is still a gap between the loan principal and the assets behind it—then in all likelihood the SBA will require life insurance on the principals of the business. Wells Fargo's Mitchell says young entrepreneurs can easily obtain inex-pensive term insurance. But older entrepreneurs may face steep premiums, sometimes in excess of $12,000 per year. If a business owner is elderly, he or she may not even be able to buy life insurance. And cost aside, life insurance can take weeks, and in some case months, to put in place, further slowing down the loan process.

Another type of necessary insurance is flood insurance, which is required for any business that happens to reside in a flood plain. No big deal, you say? "Many entrepreneurs are surprised to learn their business is located in a flood plain," Mitchell notes. They are often also surprised by how difficult flood insurance is to get and how expensive it can be. Lenders must consult a geological database, and if it says the company is in a flood plain, it is in a flood plain.

- **Liens:** The SBA will not turn down a guarantee on a loan just because it is undercollateralized, Mitchell says. But it will take a firm stance on ensuring all the borrower's business and personal assets back the loan. And with regard to these assets, the agency will often go far beyond guarantees by placing a lien on business and personal assets. The upshot of this posture is that if the SBA puts a deed of trust against your home, and you default on it and eventually file for bankruptcy, your home could be at significant risk.

Wells Fargo's Gallagher, who acknowledges the difficulties the above terms and conditions can place on borrowers, remains pragmatic about them. "It is politically necessary that when the government becomes involved in lending that there are as many safety nets in place as possible. Without them, the government

Less Is More

Another streamlined approach to SBA loans are LowDoc loans. LowDoc refers to low-documentation loans. Rather than the voluminous and challenging 7(a) application, the LowDoc loan application is a simple one-page affair.

But for loans in excess of $50,000, borrowers must supply good old Schedule C of their federal income tax return and/or their business returns. In addition, LowDoc loans have a ceiling of $100,000, and borrowers are prevented from paying off certain kinds of debts with the proceeds from a LowDoc loan. Rates on LowDoc loans are variable and range from a high of prime plus 4.75 percentage points to a low of prime plus 2.75 percentage points.

While the LowDoc can overcome some of the headaches associated with the application process, it does nothing to alleviate some of the more restrictive terms associated with conventional SBA loans, which include controlled disbursements and flood, life and hazard insurance, among other items.

Overall, the LowDoc program provides some solutions for entrepreneurs, but where possible, FA$TRAK loans represent a better option, Wells Fargo's Gallagher maintains.

All lenders can offer LowDoc loans, although not all may choose to. The best bet for finding one that will is to call your local SBA office and ask for the names of institutions, as well as the names of bankers themselves making LowDoc loans. When you call, ask for a public information officer.

would get a PR black eye any-time something went wrong." What would happen if, he asks, a slew of SBA-backed businesses were wiped out by floods, and none of them had flood insurance? "These requirements," he says, "are simply a necessary part of the process."

SBA-guarantee Fees

Although SBA lenders are not allowed to charge application fees, points or prepayment penalties, there

Taking Action

To get a FA$TRAK loan, you must go to a selected preferred lender. These selected preferred lenders can be found at the "Local SBA Resources" section of www.sba.gov. However, since not all preferred lenders make FA$TRAK loans, it may be necessary to call more than one lending institution.

are guarantee fees to contend with. In actuality, these are charged to lenders by the SBA, and lenders almost always pass these fees on to the customer—i.e. you the borrower. If you get an SBA-guaranteed loan, the following are what you might face in terms of guarantee fees:

- Loans with maturities of one year or less carry a guarantee fee of 0.25 percent of the amount guaranteed. On a $200,000 guarantee, this works out to $500. Peanuts.
- Loans in excess of $80,000 with maturities of more than one year carry a fee of 3 percent for the first $250,000 guaranteed, 3.5 percent for the next $250,000 guaranteed, and 3.875 percent for any amount that exceeds $500,000.

Consider the following example:

Loan Amount	x	Percent Guaranteed	=	Guarantee Amount
$800,000		75%		$600,000

Fees		
1st $250,000	3.00%	$7,500
2nd $250,000	3.50%	$8,750
Remaining $100,000	3.875%	$3,875
Total Guarantee Fee		$20,125

It's important to note that fees generally don't come out of your pocket; they come from the loan proceeds. Though this is an easy way to go, it's important to understand that guarantee fees essentially jack up the effective rate of the loan.

How? Let's say you borrow $800,000 for five years at 9 percent. Your monthly payment on the loan is $16,608. Now assume that you pay a guarantee fee of $20,125, which is taken out of the loan proceeds. In truth, then, you only get $779,875 ($800,000 – $20,125). But you are making monthly payments on $800,000. The net result is that you are not really paying 9 percent interest. That is simply the contractually agreed upon rate. The effective rate that you as the borrower would be paying is almost 10.125 percent. This effective interest rate is almost 12.5 percent higher than the stated interest rate.

Chapter 8

Private Loan Guarantees

The Scoop

Definition Or Explanation: A guarantee of payment that stands behind an early stage company and enables it to take out a loan from a bank. Conceptually, private guarantees play the same role as a Small Business Administration loan guarantee.

Appropriate For: Early stage companies that within a year will turn the corner toward profitability, or commence product sales. The limited time frame stems from the fact that loan guarantees typically only last a year, and at the end of that period, the company must be able to raise equity capital to pay off the original loan, or be able to apply for and get a loan based on its own fundamentals.

Supply: Though this technique is uncommon, the supply is theoretically abundant. Specifically, any wealthy individual (i.e., angel investor) willing to consider an equity investment should also be willing to consider a loan guarantee.

Best Use: For companies that can put the borrowed funds to use and show an immediate result either in profitable product sales or the commercialization of a product or service concept. Loan guarantees work particularly well for very young companies that would end up selling a majority equity stake in the business if forced to use equity capital.

Cost: The fees and interest on a loan guarantee can be expensive compared with a traditional loan. However, loan guarantees make it possible for an entrepreneur to raise capital without surrendering control, which makes it cheap compared with most forms of equity financing.

Ease Of Acquisition: Loan guarantees are somewhat easier to negotiate than pure equity investments because the investor guaranteeing the loan never turns over any funds, unless, of course, the company does not perform as projected.

Range Of Funds Typically Available: No upper or lower limit.

Why Loan Guarantees Work

Whether you are raising debt or equity capital, you will run into the same behavior: Lenders and equity investors will be reluctant to let go of their money. While the attitude is the same, the motivations are different.

The bank would simply love to lend you the money. After all, the only way it makes an above-average return is by lending what customers deposit. But because a bank is lending other people's money, it operates in what is known as an "abundance of caution" mode. That is, banks by design are only allowed to make loans in situations of absolute safety. Working with emerging growth companies means few instances of absolute safety, hence the challenge of loan financing.

Equity investors would generally like to finance your company as well. But they too have problems. Emerging growth companies are not just risky; they're also illiquid. Once they swallow the risk, most equity investors are still reluctant to cut a check because they know that even if the company succeeds, it will be tough to recoup their money. To do so, the company generally must go public or be bought out. And if the company succeeds only on a marginal basis, their investment can remain trapped inside the company.

It's because of these emotions and constraints that loan guarantees can work so well. Specifically, when an angel investor stands behind a loan and guarantees it on behalf of a company, he doesn't have to shell out his own capital, at least not initially. And with a guarantee in the picture, the loan is

100 percent safe, meaning that almost any bank in the continental United States can make it .

According to Arthur Lipper III, chair of British Far East Holdings in Del Mar, California, which provides and arranges financing as well as advisory services, "To get such a deal done, entrepreneurs need three ingredients: two banks and one guarantor." Providing loan guarantees to high-octane growth companies is a subjective undertaking, Lipper says, and there are many ways a deal might be structured. However, he says, a typical one-year loan for $1 million might be put together as follows:

First, the investor purchases a letter of credit from his or her bank. It stipulates that the investor's bank will pay to the entrepreneur's bank $1 million on a certain date one year in the future.

Lipper says that to issue such a letter, a bank charges 1 percent to 2 percent of the amount of funds being guaranteed—in this case $10,000 to $20,000—as a fee. Because it's a bank, and banks tend to avoid risks, it will also require the investor to deposit $1 million in government securities or $2 million in marginal securities. (So-called marginable securities are those

Loan Guarantee Flowchart
For $1 Million Loan

1. Investor pays bank $20,000 to guarantee $1 million loan; deposits up to $2 million of securities into guaranteeing bank.

Angel investor/ guarantor

4. Entrepreneur repays angel $20,000 loan guarantee fee, plus consulting fee of $50,000.

Guaranteeing bank

Entrepreneur/ emerging growth company

2. Angel issues loan guarantee to entrepreneur's bank for $1 million.

Entrepreneur's hometown bank

3. Bank disburses $920,000, representing $1 million loan, less one year's interest.

A Good Deal
If you get a bank loan that is guaranteed by a third party, negotiate for a prime interest rate, since by virtue of the guarantee, your bank is not incurring any risk.

that can be borrowed against, a determination that is made by the Federal Reserve.) These assets collateralize the letter of credit the bank issues.

Now, with a rock-solid letter of credit for $1 million protecting it, Lipper says, the entrepreneur's bank will then lend him or her the $1 million needed to grow the business.

None of this comes cheap. In fact, when you add it up, it's darn expensive financing. Following are some of the costs the entrepreneur is expected to pay in such a transaction, according to Lipper:

First, there's the guarantee fee. Remember, the investor had to pay his bank a fee to get it to issue the letter of credit, in addition to depositing funds into the bank. "The way the investor tends to think," Lipper says, "is that it's the entrepreneur's loan that is being guaranteed, not mine; therefore, they should pay the fees."

Next, Lipper says, he typically collects 5 percent of the loan as a fee for putting the deal together. For our hypothetical $1 million deal, that's another $50,000.

Then there's the interest to the bank. For deals such as this, banks typically charge the prime rate, plus 1 percent according to Lipper. "It's absolutely outrageous for them to charge a premium like that," he maintains, "since there is no risk to the bank whatsoever." Moreover, to avoid any possibility of default, the bank issuing the letter of credit will probably stipulate that the interest on the loan be taken out of the proceeds upfront, as shown in the above example.

Don't Forget
The concept of a loan guarantee is not new. In fact, loan guarantees provide the underpinning of the Small Business Administration's 7(a) loan guarantee program. However, when loan guarantees are practiced in the private sector, they can be more flexible and deliver significant benefits to lenders, investors and, most important, entrepreneurs.

The only positive thing you can say about all these fees is that they generally don't come out of your pocket. In most deals, they come out of the loan fees, so you as the borrower end up paying them in the form of a higher effective interest rate.

It's important to understand that the effect of all these fees coming off the top of the loan proceeds is that they ratchet up the interest rate the company pays for its funds. In our example, the guarantee fee is, say, $20,000, the consulting fee is another 5 percent fee, or $50,000, and the bank's interest upfront of perhaps 8 percent is another $80,000, for a total of $150,000. So the entrepreneur is really paying $150,000 for the use of $850,000 ($1 million loan proceeds–$150,000 fees and interest). The true rate of interest then is 17.6 percent ($150,000/$850,000).

The disadvantages don't end there. The pièce de résistance comes in the form of a "carried interest" in the company, which, Lipper says, is either a percentage of the company's revenues—3 percent to 5 percent—or a hunk of the company's equity, the percentage of which is subject to negotiation. If you're a purist and don't want any outside owners of your company, give up some of the revenue and keep the equity.

This equity, by the way, can often be structured as warrants, which are options to purchase equity at a specified price for a specified period of time. "For the company, the advantage of warrants," according to Lipper, "is that the company does not surrender any equity immediately, and when the warrants are exercised, the company gets an additional infusion of capital."

Shop Talk

When guarantors start talking about a fee structure with a "carried interest," it means they want a piece of the action beyond consulting fees, such as a percentage of sales, options or even equity. It would be unimaginable for a guarantor not to request a carried interest. After all, he or she may be, for example, putting $1 million at risk, so would certainly want more upside than a $50,000 fee.

Silver Linings

Despite the seemingly prohibitive cost of such financing, there's a compelling benefit that makes it hard to dismiss out of hand, especially for early stage companies: By using guarantees to get a loan from a bank, a company can avoid surrendering any ownership that goes part and parcel with raising equity capital.

This is particularly important for young companies in the early stages of their growth. When companies need capital at the outset of their development, equity investors must acquire a disproportionately large piece of the company to justify the risk. The net effect is that an entrepreneur can be left with little more

Taking Action

If you have talked to angel investors about an equity investment and they have turned you down, contact them again and ask them to consider a loan guarantee instead. Remind them that if the deal goes as planned, all their liquid assets will remain intact and work for them.

than a grubstake before they leave the starting gate. By contrast, a loan, even an expensive one, leaves the founder with 100 percent of his company, a feat that presumably motivates him to work harder to make the venture a success.

Another benefit of loan guarantees is that it may be easier to get an investor to guarantee a loan than to buy equity. Whereas the latter requires the investor to cut a large check and put all of his money at risk, a guarantee only requires him or her to deposit securities into the bank issuing the letter of credit. The earning power of the common stock or bonds the investor uses to collateralize the guarantee is not impaired and continues to work for the investor, ideally growing in value. In essence, the investor is simply leveraging his own assets.

Lipper says it's a mistake for investors to guarantee a loan that they are not prepared to write a check for if things go south. "However, most investors are the same," he says. "They believe they can pick the deals that will work, and avoid those which will not." For better or worse, however, it's this mind-set that makes pitching a loan guarantee much easier than pitching the concept of direct investment.

End Game

Inquiring minds may wonder what happens in a loan guarantee deal at the end of the loan. After all, in our hypothetical example, the underlying $1 million loan was payable at the end of 12 months. To go from a standing start to $1 million in a year after taxes, liquid and unencumbered is a mighty, if nearly impossible, feat for most companies.

The object of the initial loan guarantee is not to pay off the loan. More accurately—and far more likely in a successful scenario—the company would, at the end of the loan period, be in a position to pay off the loan with another loan that it was able to negotiate without a guarantee or with an equity investment from another investor. Presumably, with the growth the company demonstrated and the potential it holds, one of the two alternatives becomes viable.

Looked at this way, a loan guarantee is designed for companies that can make a go of it with interim financing as opposed to permanent financing.

It is also for companies that have high profit margins. For instance, if a company's operating margin (sales less cost of goods sold less selling, general and administrative expenses) is 10 percent, and the investor's share of the revenues is 5 percent, then there's not much left. In fact, the remaining interest expense might convert a slim profit into a loss. "This kind of financing tends to work best for technology companies where there is some form of intellectual property that gives them a protected profit margin," explains Lipper.

In addition, loan guarantee financing tends to work best in situations in which the price of the company's product or service is elastic. That is, in which the price can be increased to cover the cost of the financing without driving away customers. For instance, a gas station could not do this, while a database-management company probably could.

Don't Forget
Private loan guarantees offer only a short-term solution. Generally, at the end of the year, you'll have to replace the guaranteed loan with another loan or equity financing.

Finally, a loan guarantee should be contemplated by entrepreneurs whose companies can generate predictable sales and earnings. "The nightmare for the company is that they make the revenue projection but do not hit the earnings projection," Lipper says. "Then they are left with high financing costs and likely little or no profit."

Chapter 9

504 Loans

The Scoop

Definition Or Explanation: Established in 1980, the 504 Loan Program provides long-term, fixed-rate financing for major fixed assets, such as real estate, facilities construction or expansion, or other fixed-asset needs. 504 loans are made through Certified Development Companies (CDCs).

Appropriate For: Businesses that fall into SBA-size ranges and whose owners are interested in reducing the costs of real estate and equipment loans.

Supply: Availability of funds is not a problem. In fiscal year 1997 alone, the 504 program produced 4,130 loans amounting to more than $1.44 billion. Access to funds is limited by CDC locations, since their mission is to fund businesses within their community or region. Thus, if there is no CDC in your area, availability of these funds may present a problem.

Best Use: Proceeds from these loans may be used for fixed-asset projects, such as purchasing land and improvements, including fixing up existing buildings, grading, making street improvements, upgrading utilities, adding parking lots and land-scaping; construction of new facilities; or modernizing, renovating or converting existing facilities; or purchasing long-term machinery and equipment.

Cost: Interest rates on 504 loans are tied to an increment above the current market rate for five- and 10-year U.S. Treasury issues. Fees total approximately 3 percent of the loan amount and may be financed by the loan. Generally, project assets are used as collateral, and personal guarantees from the principal owners are required.

Ease Of Acquisition: Challenging. Federal regulation combined with several parties involved in the transaction make for a complex application process.

Range Of Funds Typically Available: $50,000 to $750,000 for up to 10 years on equipment and 20 years for real estate. The maximum amount may increase to $1 million under certain circumstances. The private-lender contribution is unlimited.

Pros And Cons

The 504 Loan Program provides low-cost fixed-rate long-term financing to small businesses that cannot obtain funds from conventional sources. Lower down payments than traditional lenders require—usually 20 percent to 25 percent—and below-market rates allow small businesses to conserve working capital, and longer terms reduce monthly debt payments.

On the other hand, start-ups without adequate capitalization may find it difficult to obtain a 504 loan due to the equity requirements. Making it more difficult, if the borrower has been in operation for two years or less, the equity requirement increases from the 10 percent for more mature companies to 15 percent.

Companies considering refinancing or moving after a few years might rethink applying for a 504 loan due to prepayment penalties attached to the CDC portion of the financing. Finally, because of employment requirements, these loans are not for companies that are

Shop Talk

Loan-to-value ratios describe the percentage of an asset that can be financed with a loan. If a CDC lending policy requires a 90 percent loan-to-value ratio, that means it lends $90,000 for every $100,000 of assets the borrower purchases with the loan proceeds.

looking to reduce their staff through the acquisition of high-tech equipment, etc.

Certified Development Companies

"CDCs, which are licensed by the SBA, are the eyes and ears for this program," says Diane McDonald, deputy director for Alacom Finance in Memphis, Tennessee.

CDCs are nonprofit corporations sponsored by private interests or local governments. Their mission is to contribute to the economic development of their community or region through job creation; thus, a CDC portfolio must create or retain one job for every $35,000 of debenture proceeds provided by the SBA. These companies operate under the jurisdiction of a board that includes local government officials, private-sector lending institutions, and business and community organizations. There are about 300 CDCs nationwide.

CDCs also offer assistance to small-business borrowers in organizing the loan package and completing SBA paperwork. Since the CDC processes, closes and services the loan, a close relationship between the borrower and the CDC can develop, often to the benefit of the small business. Participants in the Premier Certified Lender Program (PCLP) enjoy additional authority and can approve loans on their own, which can cut the approval process time dramatically.

Premier Certified Lender status is a consideration for a borrower in a hurry. Eligibility for PCLP was recently extended after a 30-month pilot program, thus expanding the availability of this service.

Don't Forget
The SBA guarantee, which is embedded in the 504 loan process, increases the documentation you need to produce and increases the degree of difficulty associated with the application process.

Who's Involved, And What's Qualified?

The 504 Program generally provides an alternative source of long-term fixed-rate financing to established companies with a proven track record.

Typically, these loans are secured with a senior lien from a private-sector lender for up to 50 percent of the total loan amount. Forty percent is funded through the sale of 100 percent SBA-backed debentures sold in the capital bond market by the SBA and guaranteed by the SBA. The remaining 10 percent takes the form of an equity position required from the borrower.

Get Real

The SBA offers another alternative for real estate financing under the 7(a) loan program. This option differs from the 504 Program in a number of significant ways.

- The 7(a) program offers a longer term—25 years vs. 20 years with the 504 program.
- A 7(a) loan does not incur the level of prepayment penalties of the 504 loan.
- 7(a) loans offer an adjustable rate product (with interest caps available) vs. the fixed-rate-only feature of the 504 program.
- 7(a) loans are funded by lenders with SBA guarantees as opposed to the private debenture sale used in the 504 program.
- 504 borrowers are generally well-established businesses, while 7(a) borrowers may be newer businesses without a strong track record.
- Job creation is not a factor in obtaining 7(a) financing.
- In some cases, 7(a) loans can be used to refinance owner-occupied real estate. Check with your CDC.
- 7(a) rates are negotiable with the lender. For loans of less than seven years, the maximum is prime plus 2.25 percent or 2.75 percent for loans of longer than seven years. 504 loans are tied to market rates for five- and 10-year treasury issues.

A Good Deal

Financing through the 504 program is a good deal for borrowers because the required down payment is as little as 10 percent, compared with the 20 percent to 25 percent that would be required from a conventional lender. For a $200,000 property, a borrower seeking a CDC loan would need only $20,000 in equity, as opposed to $40,000 for a traditional real estate loan.

In terms of eligibility, the 504 program requires that financed machinery and equipment have a useful life of at least 10 years, and that real estate be primarily owner-occupied. Check with the CDC regarding specific occupancy percentages, which differ depending on whether the property is new construction or a renovated site.

It is important to note that the 504 program provides so-called permanent financing for long-term assets. As a result, temporary financing, such as a bridge or construction loan, is usually required to start a project. Once the project is under way, CDC financing can permanently replace the temporary financing.

Applying For A CDC Loan

Typically, 504 loan requests are initiated by a private lender. So if you think this is a viable option for your financing needs, it is in your best interest to find a banker familiar with 504 financings.

As is the case with all small-business loans, borrowers should have three years' worth of financial statements, plus personal financial statements for company principals. This is in addition to other qualitative information concerning management, the company, the market and usage of loan proceeds.

Taking Action

The first thing to find out about CDC loans is not whether you qualify, but if there is a Certified Development Company in your area. Start asking bankers, accountants or real estate attorneys. Or go to www.sba.gov and click on "Local SBA Resources." Select "CDC Lenders" and check your region for a list with contact information and area of operation.

504 Loan Program Overview

The chart below summarizes the most important features of a 504 loan.

	Private Lender	504 Financing	Equity
Percent of project	50%	40%	10%
Security	1st lien	2nd lien	NA
Dollar amount	No limit	$50,000-$750,000 ($1 million in some cases)	NA
Interest rate	Variable or fixed	Fixed	NA
Real estate terms	10+years	20 years	NA
Equipment terms	7 years	10 years	NA

Once a banker is convinced of the loan's viability and the company's creditworthiness, the bank may recommend the loan as a candidate for 504 financing. And, in fact, banks have real incentive to recommend this program. First, since the bank's portion of the loan is 50 percent, its exposure is lower. Also, since its investment is less than that of traditional financings, it can spread its investments out over a number of projects, reducing the bank's financial exposure, increasing its customer base and stimulating the local economy through job creation. Finally, this program gives the bank a senior lien position on 100 percent of the assets being financed. Thus, the 504 program offers benefits to both borrower and banker.

Once the bank has given preliminary approval on a 504 request, the prospective borrower is turned over to a local CDC, which works with the applicant on a true management level. The CDC may, for example, offer financial and technical assistance, or help businesses obtain such assistance from other sources. This is in addition to assisting the borrowers with the preparation of the application and the closing documentation.

The CDC then recommends the package to the SBA for approval (unless it is a PCLP and has approval authority). SBA approval means that the adminstration guarantees the CDC portion of the loan (roughly 40 percent). Funds are then raised through a monthly debenture sale and are guaranteed 100 percent by the SBA.

When the loan is approved, the funding process begins. A hypothetical example makes this process easier to understand. Assume there is a $1 million project, with proceeds to go toward purchasing land and constructing a building. The bank provides $500,000 and assumes a first mortgage. The CDC takes a second mortgage for $400,000. The remaining $100,000 comes from the borrower. Depending on the terms of the loan, in most cases the bank for an interim period actually assumes $900,000 (its $500,000, plus the CDC's $400,000). This period may extend from one month—if no construction is involved and the wait is just until the next debenture sale—up to six or eight months if there is construction. Longer interim terms are possible given extenuating circumstances. (Remember, these loans provide permanent financing and do not cover construction. But construction loans are not permanent, either. At some point they must be replaced with a longer-term vehicle, such as a CDC loan.)

Once the debentures are sold, funds are wired to the bank. It receives its $400,000 and retains its senior lien on the $500,000. Of course, this is not the end, and most CDCs remain involved with their loan customers, providing valuable and ongoing consultation even after the loan closes.

Chapter 10

Royalty Financing

The Scoop

Definition Or Explanation: Royalty financing is an advance against future product or service sales. The advance is paid back by diverting a percentage of the product or service sales to the investor who issued the advance.

Appropriate For: Established companies that have a product or service, or emerging companies about to launch a product with high gross and net margins. Also companies with elastic pricing (i.e., the ability to raise prices without impacting sales. In addition, royalty financing is most appropriate for companies that experience a quick cause and effect between marketing activity and sales increases.

Supply: Substantial. Royalty financing may appeal to investors who typically do not make investments in private companies. In addition, angel investors, venture capitalists and even state, city or regional economic-development agencies can be sold on the concept of royalty financing.

Best Use: Financing-intensive sales and marketing activities.

Cost: Inexpensive for companies with high-margin products or services.

Ease Of Acquisition: Relatively easy because the technique appeals to a wide variety of investors. In addition, because royalty financing is essentially a loan, it generally does not provoke state and federal securities laws.

Range Of Funds Typically Available: $50,000 to $1 million.

Royalty Financing: The Secret Weapon

Many companies still in their formative stages face a difficult dilemma when looking for equity capital. Equity investors, whether they are angels or venture capitalists, often demand a big piece of the company because of all the risk they incur. The dilemma is compounded by the fear that, if the company gives up 30 percent, 40 percent or even 50 percent of the company on the first round of outside financing, nothing but a grubstake is left by the time the company goes public.

Enter royalty financing, which eliminates the dilemmas of equity financing by removing them from the picture, according to Peter Moore, founder of Banking Dynamics, a consulting firm in Portland, Maine, that helps companies raise capital, and a proponent of the royalty financing technique. "Instead of selling equity," Moore says, "a company simply pledges a piece of its future sales against an advance provided by the investors."

A Case In Point

Here's how Moore structured a financing to help a software company turbocharge its sales. Rather than angel investors, Moore approached the Greater Portland Building Fund, and Coastal Enterprises Inc., quasi-public economic-development organizations charged with developing business in the state.

But instead of a loan or equity, Moore sought for his client an "advance" of $200,000 against its future sales. If the advance was made, each investor would get 3 percent of the software company's sales for 10 years, or until they received payments totaling $600,000. This $600,000 would represent the original $200,000 investment, plus $400,000.

A Good Deal

Royalty financing is a good deal for investors who typically do not invest in early-stage companies. They can taste the fruits of their investment almost immediately, and if the company prospers, they benefit every month or quarter thereafter.

At the broadest level, for the investors to earn the agreed-upon $600,000 within the maximum allowable time frame, the software company would have to generate total sales of $20 million over 10 years. Although the software company had less than $1 million in sales at the time, it had over the course of its three-year life doubled sales each year. "This was a big selling point," Moore says. Moreover, investors were comforted by the fact that the firm's software program, which helps companies manage hazardous-waste streams, meant there were 300,000 potential customers, he points out.

The deal was structured so that the time frame was flexible—up to 10 years to make repayment—but the return, $600,000, was not. Because of this, the return the investors could earn was variable as well, and ranged from pretty good to exceptional. Specifically, if the software company repaid the advance in 10 years, the investors would earn a compound annual return of 11.6 percent on their investment. If, however, the company's sales mushroomed, and $600,000 was paid to

The Bucks Pile Up Here

Royalty financing can provide some truly spectacular returns to investors, if sales take off like a jackrabbit. Here are rates of return associated with royalty financing, taking into account the amount of time it takes an investor to earn a twofold return on his or her investment.

Repayment at the end of:	Compound annual return
Year 1	200.0%
Year 2	73.1%
Year 3	44.2%
Year 4	31.6%
Year 5	24.5%
Year 6	20.1%
Year 7	17.0%
Year 8	14.7%
Year 9	13.0%
Year 10	11.6%

the investors in five years, their compound annual return also mushroomed to 24.5 percent—a rate that even an institutional venture capitalist would have to admire.

It took Moore and his client about four months to hammer out all the details of the deal. One of the key terms he negotiated was for a delay in the commencement of royalty payments. Specifically, royalties did not accrue until 90 days after the deal closed. In addition, the actual royalty payments did not have to be paid until 60 days after the revenues were recognized. "All in all, it was five months from the time the company received the financing until the first payment was due," Moore says. "This gave the owners the time they needed to put the capital to work and start producing sales."

It's A Good Thing

Royalty financing is extremely flexible and can be structured in myriad ways. But regardless of the final structure, the technique delivers a host of advantages that entrepreneurs should carefully consider before rushing to sell equity in their companies.

- **Attractive to individual investors:** Generally speaking, it's difficult for most individual investors to become involved in financing private companies. They often lack the capital to make a difference. Many times individual investors don't have the minimum net worth requirement established by state securities regulators. But perhaps one of the biggest barriers is that buying straight equity generally only provides a return if the company is acquired or goes public—two big ifs. Moore speculates that a monthly or quarterly return—which happens as long as sales occur— is more preferable to individual investors over the total

Shop Talk

The concept of "revenue recognition" takes on greater significance within the context of royalty financing because it defines the payments to the investor. Should revenue be recognized when the customer agrees to purchase the product, or when it's paid for, or perhaps after a 30-day return period has elapsed?

absence of a yield and zero liquidity so typical of early-stage venture deals.

- **May bypass securities laws:** Because the royalty advance is a loan, it may not, in plain vanilla form, bring state or federal securities laws into play. Most equity financing, in which companies sell shares to individual investors, requires complex filings that mean significant legal and accounting fees.

- **Increases future financing options:** A company funded by royalty payments increases its financeability down the road. If the funds do, in fact, ramp up sales, the company becomes a more attractive candidate for additional financing. In addition, sometimes the presence of one kind of equity investor precludes the participation of another. For instance, a company financed with institutional venture capital funds cannot, in most cases, ever go back to raising money from individuals. But by "saving" itself for outside investors to a later round of financing, a company keeps its options wide open.

- **Preserves equity:** The royalty structure preserves the founders' equity positions. Remember, there are only 100 percentage points to go around, and they begin to disappear with alarming ease once a company starts raising outside capital. In addition, when founders are able to hold on to a significant portion of the ownership, they may have greater incentive to make it successful than entrepreneurs who have given away most of the store.

Not For Everyone

It may sound as if royalty financing is a panacea. Unfortunately, it's not. There are several instances in which royalty financing will not work.

- **Thin margins:** If a company's gross margin (sales less cost of goods sold) is only 10 percent, and 6 percent goes to royalty payments, the remaining 4 percent doesn't leave much room for making any money. In the aforementioned example, the software company Moore financed had a gross margin of 90 percent. With margins this wide, it could comfortably give up 6 percent of the sale.

- **Noncompetitive pricing:** Royalty financing works best for companies whose pricing is fairly elastic. If you can raise your prices to cover the cost of financing the marketing of the product without losing customers, you are a better candidate than a company whose customers are price sensitive.

Taking Action

To receive a primer on royalty financing, send a self-addressed stamped envelope to Peter Moore, Banking Dynamics, 97 A Exchange St., Portland, ME 04101, or call (207) 772-2221.

- **Lengthy sales cycles:** Royalty financing won't work for companies that do not see an immediate cause and effect between marketing efforts and sales. "You've got to be able to turn on sales like a spigot," says consultant Moore. Otherwise, one of the primary benefits for which investors are in the deal—namely, a monthly royalty check—is seriously compromised. The one thing a growing company doesn't need is unhappy investors.

  This limitation goes even deeper. Royalty financing is not appropriate for financing product development. After all, making something new is tricky. Success may be elusive, or—and how often does this happen?—it may take much longer to develop the product or service than originally anticipated.

- **Bad marketing skills:** Obviously, just having a product can't win the day. For companies to effectively use this technique, they've got to be able to sell and market their wares. "Obviously," Moore says, "you must be able to inspire confidence among investors that you have the skills and experience to move products or services off the shelf frequently and quickly."

Chapter 11

Federal Government Venture Capital

The Scoop

Definition Or Explanation: Small Business Investment Companies (SBICs) and Specialized Small Business Investment Companies (SSBICs) are primarily lenders that are licensed by the Small Business Administration (SBA). These investment companies have their own private capital of several million dollars and may borrow additional funds from an SBA-sponsored trust at favorable rates. SBICs tend to specialize in an industry, making them more risk-tolerant than traditional bank lenders.

Appropriate For: Companies that are capable of repaying a loan. This typically means established to early-stage companies with good sales and earnings, or companies about to turn the corner toward profitability.

Supply: SBIC financing is abundant. According to the National Association of Small Business Investment Companies, there are 300 SBICs and SSBICs with more than $6 billion under management.

Best Use: For activities that generate cash flow in a relatively short period of time, such as product rollout, or for additional manufacturing or service capacity for which there is a demand.

Cost: Expensive. SBICs and SSBICs charge interest, but in addition, many look for some kind of equity compensation in the companies they finance. This equity compensation is usually in the form of stock, as well as options or warrants that allow the holder to buy stock at predetermined prices for a predetermined period of time.

Ease Of Acquisition: Challenging but attainable because the company must submit itself to traditional credit analysis to prove it can repay a loan. This difficulty is countered by the fact that these investment companies are hungry for new business and can be helpful in shepherding companies through the application and due diligence process. In addition, an SSBIC or SBIC generally represents a one-stop shop, and companies need only satisfy the requirements of this single investor to obtain funding.

Range Of Funds Typically Available: $150,000 to $5 million.

Is This Option Right For Me?

The affiliation SBICs and SSBICs have with the federal government through their SBA license tends to mislead many entrepreneurs. This is because many labor under the mistaken idea that there is an arm of the government that gives money to businesses that cannot secure financing from traditional sources of capital. Unfortunately, SBICs and SSBICs are not this elusive Holy Grail. Second, many entrepreneurs believe that the SBA, through a mechanism such as an SSBIC or SBIC, lends money to businesses with no visible source of repayment.

Unfortunately, this is not the case; SBA-licensed investment companies tend not to finance companies that do not exhibit an obvious source of repayment or that show a high degree of risk.

In fact, briefly exploring the financial structure of these SBA-licensed investment companies is helpful because it shows not only the kinds of deals they won't do, but the kinds they will, and what types of companies should spend their time pursuing this option.

For example, Freshstart Venture Capital Corp., an SSBIC in New York City, gets its money from two places. The first is equity capital, which Freshstart founder Zindel Zelmanovitch raised from public and private investors. But the second and far more substantial source of capital for Freshstart is funds from an SBA trust fund.

The interest Freshstart must pay on the funds it borrows, as all SSBICs and SBICs do, means the investment company must become involved in deals in which it receives interest as well. Otherwise, there is a massive mismatch between the investment company's sources and uses of funds. After all, how can an SBA-licensed investment company make investments in which it receives no interest but still pays interest on its own borrowings? The answer is investment companies can't because the difference between the interest they pay and interest they receive is precisely how it makes money.

> **Don't Forget**
>
> SBICs and SSBICs are primarily lenders. If your business can support a loan, an SBIC or SSBIC may be right for you.

And because their cost for funds can be quite low—from 4 percent to 7 percent—and the price SBICs and SSBICs charge on loans can be quite high—from 9 percent to 17 percent—these lenders can be pretty profitable. Freshstart, for instance, earned about $781,000 on about $1.8 million in interest income for the 12 months ending November 30, 1997.

More Verve Than A Lender

If SBA-licensed investment companies are primarily lenders, what makes them different from a bank? There are two

Davids Who Became Goliaths

The following companies were, at some point in their development, nurtured by SBIC funding.

Company	Year SBIC Invested	Current Number of Employees
Intel Corp.	1969	41,600
Federal Express	1973	110,000
Apple Computer	1977	13,191
Staples Inc.	1986	22,714

Source: National Association of Small Business Investment Companies

differences, really. First, SBICs and SSBICs tend to take slightly more risk than a bank in terms of collateral. That is, whereas a banker needs a loan to be fully collateralized, and/or guaranteed, at an amount that is equal to or greater than the loan value, an SSBIC or SBIC may not. Most investment companies specialize in a particular industry. As a result of their specialized focus, they tend to assign higher values to collateral than does a general commercial lender.

Second, SBICs and SSBICs take a larger interest in smaller loans that range from $150,000 to $1 million. Large commercial banks like to make large loans. It's that simple. The systems these banks have installed to analyze, disburse and monitor loans are so expensive that for many, a large loan is the only way they can hope to make money.

By contrast, many SBICs and SSBICs are smaller partnerships. They have limited capital and are careful not to make investments that will outstrip their financial resources. Some SBICs, however, are affiliated with large commercial banks. These SBICs are capable of making substantial loans, and many have investment minimums of $1 million.

Making Debt Behave Like Equity

Recognizing the inherent mismatch between emerging growth companies and loan financing, the SBA has taken steps to make financing from its investment companies more appropriate for younger companies.

Specifically, the agency has created what are known as participating securities, or debentures. These participating securities allow SBICs and SSBICs to borrow capital from the SBA trust fund and defer interest until their investments start to generate cash. The bottom line of this arrangement is that it allows investment companies to finance businesses that are not yet capable of paying interest, which presumably means earlier-stage companies.

A Good Deal

SSBICs and SBICs typically specialize in an industry and, as a result, assign more value to your specialized collateral.

Participating securities are creative and once again demonstrate the fiscal prudence within the SBA. For instance, while interest payments to the SBA trust fund are deferred, the

A Ticket To Ride

When Henrick Coriolan emigrated from Haiti in the late '70s, he had nothing but entrepreneurial verve and a vision for making himself into a successful businessman. "I came to learn and to be a professional," he says.

Today, with a small taxicab fleet and an auto service center in New York City, Coriolan has achieved success. It took not only hard work but capital. Coriolan got his thanks to a Specialized Small Business Investment Company.

After establishing his fleet, Coriolan decided to go into the auto service business as well, and in 1989 he opened his doors for business. Five years later he needed $350,000 to buy the building and some equipment.

Coriolan was summarily rejected for loans at banks for lack of collateral. In fact, he had collateral, his taxi medallions, but banks didn't recognize them. That's why an SSBIC that specialized in taxicab lending saw a way to finance Coriolan's deal when the large commercial banks would not.

"The bank generally would not consider them as collateral," says Freshstart's Zelmanovitch, whose SSBIC did the deal. "But we specialize in financing taxicabs, so I understand their value and can back a loan with them." Even if the loan went permanently south, Zelmanovitch could take possession of the medallions and easily have them resold at market prices. Not that lenders like to liquidate assets. They just like knowing that if they must, there will be enough left over to pay off the loan. "We look at every deal on a case-by-case basis," Zelmanovitch says. "Sure, we look for stability, but we also look the person in the eyes to see if we will be repaid."

agency actually makes the payments on behalf of the invest-ment company. But if the deal works out, the SBA takes 10 per-cent of the profits earned by the SBIC or SSBIC on its invest-ment. Of the 300 SBICs and SSBICs currently in operation, about 60 are licensed to issue participating securities and have approximately $1 billion in capital.

You can find SSBICs and SBICs fairly easily. The National Association of Investment Companies (NAIC) in Washington, DC, represents SSBICs as well as other investment companies focusing on minority investments. The NAIC does not have a referral service but sells its membership directory for $30. Write or call The National Association of Investment Companies at 1111 14th St. NW, #700, Washington, DC 20005, (202) 289-4336.

Or try the National Association of Small Business Investment Companies (NASBIC), a trade group that consists of SBICs and SSBICs exclusively. NASBIC also sells its mem-bership directory for $25. Write or call the National Association of Small Business Investment Companies at 666 11th St. NW, #750, Washington, DC 20001, (202) 628-5055.

Chapter 12

Angel Investors

The Scoop

Definition Or Explanation: Venture capital from individual investors. Angel investors look for companies that exhibit high-growth prospects, have a synergy with their own business or compete in an industry in which they have succeeded.

Appropriate For: Early-stage companies with no revenues, or established companies with sales and earnings. Companies seeking equity capital from angel investors must welcome the outside ownership, and perhaps the surrender of some control. In addition, to successfully accommodate angel investors, a company must be able to provide an "exit" to these investors in the form of an eventual public offering or buyout from a larger firm.

Supply: The supply of angel investors is large within a 150-mile radius of metropolitan areas. The more technology-driven an area's economy is, the more abundant these investors are. America's 250,000 angel investors pump $25 billion to $30 billion into growing businesses each year, according to Jeffrey Sohl, director of the Center for Venture Research at the University of New Hampshire.

Best Use: Runs the gamut, from companies developing a product to those with an established product or service for which they need additional funding to execute a marketing program. Also, for companies that have increasing product or service sales and need additional capital to bridge the gap between the sale and the receipt of funds from the customer.

Cost: Expensive. Capital from angel investors is likely to cost no less than 10 percent of a company's equity, and, for early-stage companies, perhaps more than 50 percent. In addition, many angel investors charge a management fee in the form of a monthly retainer.

Ease Of Acquisition: Angels are easy to find but sometimes difficult to negotiate with because they usually do not invest in concert and may demand different terms.

Range Of Funds Typically Available: $300,000 to $5 million.

Why Angels?

For most small or new businesses, so-called angel investors are the most appropriate source of financing. There are many reasons for this. Some of the more fundamental and important include:

- Angel investors are one of the most abundant sources of capital in the United States. America's 250,000 angels invest $25 billion to $30 billion each year in growing businesses.

- Angel investors typically provide equity capital. For most emerging growth businesses, equity capital is appropriate because it is permanent and does not require monthly or quarterly interest payments.

- Angel investors typically invest in business for reasons other than economics. A desire to help young entrepreneurs, and fill the role of the mentor they never had is the reason frequently cited by angels for why they invest.

- The amount of capital an emerging business needs, generally from $250,000 to $5 million, matches the commitments angels typically make.

Stalking Angels

Angel investors are at once difficult and easy to find. The situation is analogous to searching for gold. Generally, it's difficult to find, but once you hit a vein . . . all of your hard work

A Good Deal

Angel investors often add value in areas where new or emerging businesses need help, such as sales, marketing, strategic planning and finance. In addition, angel investors often prove to be an invaluable reservoir of contacts.

pays off in a big way. Here are the places to find angels:

- **Universities:** According to Bob Tosterud, executive director of the Council of Entrepreneurship Chairs, which consists of business schools with endowed entrepreneurship chairs, even schools with fledgling entrepreneurship programs generally have top-rated professors with ties to business and academia. Angel investors, Tosterud says, tend to hover near these programs because of the high level of new business activity they generate. He advises that if you are looking for money, call the nearest university that has an entrepreneurship program, and make an appointment to speak with the person running the program. Generally, he says, they can point you in the direction of angels.

- **Business incubators:** According to the National Business Incubation Association (NBIA), there are more than 550 business incubators in North America. At first blush, incubators appear to be the mere bricks and mortar that offer entrepreneurs reasonable rents, access to shared services, exposure to professional assistance and an atmosphere of entrepreneurial energy. But, according to NBIA executive director Dinah Adkins, many business incubators offer formal or informal access to angel investors. Call a business incubator and ask its director if he or she can put you in touch with an angel investor. But be forewarned, the incubator may only refer and help current tenants. To find a business incubator near you, see Chapter 14.

Shop Talk

The term "angel investor" derives from Broadway. The wealthy individuals who typically financed lavish productions were dubbed angels because of the small likelihood of ever realizing a return on their investment.

Taking Flight

Here are 10 actions steps you can take to find angel investors in your area:

1. Call your chamber of commerce and ask if it hosts a venture capital group. Many such groups have a chamber affiliation.
2. Call a Small Business Development Center near you and ask the executive director if he or she knows of any angel investor groups. Ask the SBA if you don't know where an SBDC is.
3. Ask your accountant. If your accountant does not know, call a Big Five Accounting Firm and ask for the partner handling entrepreneurial services. Ask him or her to point you in the right direction.
4. Ask your attorney. They always know who has money.
5. Call a professional venture capitalist and ask if he or she is aware of an angel investor group.
6. Contact a regional or state economic development agency and ask if anyone there knows of an angel investor group.
7. Call the editor of a local business publication and ask if he or she knows of any groups. These professionals often write about such activity.
8. Look at the "Principal Shareholders" section of initial public offering (IPO) prospectuses for companies in your area. This will tell you who has cashed out big.
9. Call the executive director of a trade association you belong to. Ask if there are any investors who specialize in your industry.
10. Ask your banker. If you do business at a small bank, ask the president of the institution. If yours is a larger commercial bank, ask your lender. If you do not have a lender, ask for a lender who works with loans of $1 million or less. A good small-business banker knows of such groups because companies that have received an equity investment are good candidates for a loan.

- **Venture capital clubs:** The tremendous wealth created through the commercialization of technology as well as a robust stock market for the past 15 years have resulted in a large number of angel investors who have begun to formalize their activities into groups or clubs. These clubs actively look for deals to invest in and want to hear from entrepreneurs looking for capital.

- **Angel confederacies:** Many angels band together in informal groups that share information and deals. Members of the group often invest independently or join together to fund a company. So-called confederacies are not easy to find, but once you locate one member, you gain access to them all, a number that could top 50 investors.

One word of caution: Formal venture capital groups come in two stripes—those that cater to individual investors or angels and those that target professional institutional venture capital funds. If you are pursuing angel investors, it's important to pursue the kinds of clubs that are aimed at your needs. For instance, the New York Venture Capital Group in Manhattan is a vibrant organization, but it caters mostly to professional venture capitalists. By contrast, the Western New York Venture Association in Amherst encourages memberships for individual investors.

Dealing With Federal Securities Laws

In 1982, Congress quite accurately recognized that many of the federal securities laws on the books represented an impediment to capital formation for smaller businesses. The result was the creation of Regulation D, which, among other things, offers small companies exemptions from federal securities laws for certain kinds of transactions. There are several wrinkles to "Reg D," as it is known, but three important rules that could influence any kind of deal you strike with an angel investor are:

Taking Action

Find at least one angel-oriented networking event in your area and attend. Try to collect at least 10 business cards and to give out at least 10 of your own.

- **Rule 504:** This rule is the least restrictive of all the federal securities laws exemptions, and allows issuers, i.e., companies, to sell up to $1 million of securities during a 12-month period, with no restrictions on the number or qualifications of investors. In addition, there are no information requirements, and general solicitation and advertising of the offering are permitted. In short, by using Rule 504, a company can sell securities to anyone without providing any information and still not provoke federal securities laws.

> **Don't Forget**
> Every state also has securities laws. Selling securities to investors in your state or in another may may bring into play two sets of securities laws. Find out if you fall under any state securities laws before you take an investor's check.

- **Rule 505:** This rule allows companies to raise up to $5 million from 35 "nonaccredited" investors and an unlimited number of accredited investors. Accredited investors are also defined by Reg D. Sixteen separate definitions range from banks and employee benefit plans to wealthy individuals. In the context of this discussion, accredited investors refer to individuals or angels. Individuals are considered accredited if they have joint or net worth of more than $1 million, or joint income in excess of $300,000.

  Rule 505 imposes some information-disclosure requirements on the issuer unless the securities are sold exclusively to accredited investors.

- **Rule 506:** Deals structured under Rule 506 are sometimes called unlimited private placements because Rule 506 can be used to raise any amount of capital. An unlimited private placement can be sold to as many as 35 nonaccredited investors and an unlimited number of accredited investors. Rule 506 does impose some so-called sophistication requirements on the nonaccredited investors. Specifically, the company must believe that the nonaccredited investors have the experience or counsel to evaluate the merits and risk of the offering.

Using rules 504, 505 and 506, companies can escape the burden of federal securities laws. However, all states have securities laws as well. What is exempt at the federal level may not be exempt at the state level. If your offering is not exempt at the state level, you may find you have to file the kind of registration statement with state securities authorities that you were trying to avoid at the federal level.

As with all securities matters, it's always best to check with a securities attorney before soliciting an offering or accepting money from investors.

Types Of Angels

The importance of the chemistry between entrepreneur and investor cannot be underestimated. "Ultimately," says angel investor Rich Bendis, who is also president of the Kansas Technology Enterprise Corp., "while economics play a big role in a deal, so too does personal chemistry." In fact, while a banker may completely trust and like an entrepreneur, he will not change his lending criteria because of these feelings. But with angel investors, the situation is completely opposite: If they develop a bond with an entrepreneur, angels can be convinced to make almost any deal.

Because of this phenomenon, Bendis says, entrepreneurs must understand the basic investor personality types. It will help them forge the bond that is so vital to closing the deal. While private investors come in many different shades, they can be broken down into five basic types: 1) corporate angels; 2) entrepreneurial angels; 3) enthusiast angels; 4) micromanagement angels; 5) professional angels.

- **Corporate types:** Typically, corporate angels are upper to senior management at Fortune 1000 corporations; they have been outplaced or taken

Don't Forget

Angels invest in companies for reasons that often go beyond just dollars and cents. As a result, your appeal must not only be financial but also emotional. Your appeal should be: "We need more than just dollars. We need you to bring your incredible wealth of experience to the table as well. In the long run, it may be even more important than capital."

early retirement. Stock options and a robust stock market have created a new generation of wealthy, or at least wealthier, corporate executives. Corporate angels may say they are looking for investment opportunities, but in reality, they are looking for another job. This doesn't mean they won't invest. These investors typically have about $1 million in cash and may invest as much as $200,000 in a deal, but some kind of position, usually unpaid at first, comes with the bargain, Bendis notes.

Corporate angels typically make just one investment, unless their last one didn't work out, he says. And with respect to the one investment they make, corporate angels tend to invest everything at once and to grow nervous when the hat is passed their way again.

- **Entrepreneurial angels:** These are the most prevalent investors, according to Bendis. Most own and operate highly successful businesses. Because these investors have another source of income, and perhaps significant wealth from an IPO or partial buyout, they take bigger risks and invest more capital. Whereas corporate angels are looking for a job, entrepreneurial angels are looking for: 1) synergy with their current business; 2) a way to diversify their portfolio; or, in rarer instances, 3) a way to prepare for life after their current business no longer requires their attention. As a result of this orientation, these investors seldom look at businesses outside of their area of expertise and will participate in no more than a handful of investments at a time.

  Entrepreneurial angels almost always take a seat on the board of directors but rarely take on any kind of management duties, Bendis says. They will make fair-sized investments, $200,000 to $500,000, and invest more as the company progresses. However, because of their agenda, when the synergy or the potential they initially perceived disappears, often they do as well.

- **Enthusiasts:** While entrepreneurial angels tend to be somewhat calculating, "enthusiast angels," as they are termed, simply like to be involved in deals. Most enthusiast angels are 65 or older, are independently wealthy from success in a business they started, and have abbreviated work schedules, Bendis says. For them, investing is a hobby, and as a result, they typically play no role in management and rarely seek board representation. But because they spread themselves across so many companies, the size of their investments tends to be small—from as little as $10,000 to perhaps a couple of hundred thousand dollars. "On the plus side, however," Bendis notes, "enthusiasts tend to have a difficult time saying no, and often will bring their friends into a deal."

- **Micromanagement angels:** "Micromanagers are serious investors," according to Bendis. "Some are born wealthy, but by far, the majority attained wealth through their own efforts." Unfortunately, this heritage makes them dangerous. Since they have successfully built a company, micromanagers attempt to impose the same tactics they used with their own companies. Though they do not seek an active management role, micromanagers usually demand a board seat. If the business is not going well, they will try to bring in new managers.

  It's possible to exploit the behavior patterns of micromanagers, but at a cost. "Specifically, they enjoy having as much control as possible," he says. "Many will gladly pay for it by putting more capital in the business."

- **Professionals:** The term "professional" in this context refers to the investor's occupation, such as doctor, lawyer and, in some rare instances, accountant. Professional angels like to invest in companies that offer a product or service with which they have some experience, Bendis notes. A doctor looks at medical instrumentation companies, a franchise attorney looks at franchise deals and so on.

  These investors generally do not need to know what's going on in the business day to day, and they do not micromanage their portfolio companies. In fact, professionals rarely seek

A Good Deal

Angel investors can often fill the role of de facto financial advisor and, as such, lead you to other financing sources. Once they're in your court, all you have to do is ask.

board representation. However, Bendis says, they can be unpleasant to deal with when the going gets rough, and may believe that a company is in trouble before it actually is.

Professional angels typically invest in several companies at once, and their capital contributions range from $25,000 to $200,000, Bendis says. "They are good for initial investments, but are less likely to make follow-up investments," he adds. Perhaps more than any other category of investor, professionals operate within loosely defined but clear networks, and tend to have more comfort investing alongside their peers. Thus, the first professional investor you find will probably offer a pathway to others. Finally, professionals can offer additional value when they bring to bear legal, accounting or financial expertise for which the company would otherwise have to pay hefty fees. Be forewarned, however, because some professionals want to be hired after they invest.

Chapter 13

Electronic Matching Services

The Scoop

Definition Or Explanation: The Angel Capital Electronic Network (ACE-Net), as well as other electronic matching services, are not a source but more accurately an efficient conduit to angel investors. Once these investors are located, deals can be structured in almost any fashion.

Appropriate For: Any company at any stage in its development

Supply: Several well-established electronic matching services are listed in Appendix A. And more are popping up every day.

Best Use: Electronic matching services such as ACE-Net can deliver significant value to entrepreneurs who, though savvy, perhaps do not know where to turn to find private, individual investors to invest in their company. Most matching services operate by having the investors reach out to the company if they are interested in its line of business, stage of development or offering. Therefore, matching services provide entrepreneurs with highly qualified leads. Even if none of these leads turns into investors, they provide a good starting point for referrals to other investors.

Cost: Most matching services are inexpensive. Fees to list a company range from free to several hundred dollars. However, the various debt and equity financings a company might structure with an investor who contacts them through a matching service can be expensive.

Ease Of Acquisition: It's easy to be listed on any electronic matching service. But it can be challenging to cut a deal with investors once they have found you. In addition, investors might contact a company simply because they are looking for technical information to help them with one of their other investments. Even this can lead to something. Specifically, if you are genuinely helpful to investors, they should be gracious enough to supply referrals to at least three other investors who should have an interest in your deal. They won't do this unsolicited, however. You'll have to ask for names.

Funds Typically Available: $25,000 and greater.

The Dawning Of A New Era

To understand why private companies have such a difficult time raising equity capital from individual investors, or angels, it helps to understand the concept of efficiency as it relates to raising capital.

This term is often applied to stock markets. Efficiency in this context refers to the speed and ease with which information is disseminated to investors. The theory: The more efficient a market is, the more capital it will attract. One glance at a stock quote terminal or the many investor-oriented Web sites proves beyond a shadow of a doubt that the U.S. stock markets are efficient with a capital E. Just a few clicks of the mouse produce quotes, historical quotes, news, comparative financial data, charts, graphs and Securities and Exchange Commission filings. Note that with the rise in efficiency has come a dramatic rise in trading volume on the U.S. markets.

By contrast, the capital markets for private companies are woefully inefficient. There is no centralized body of information. Whatever information exists about private companies is not uniform or created on a regular basis. The buyers do not know where all the sellers are, and the sellers do not know where the buyers are. Proof of this comes from the many small, private companies that scour the United States to find investors but never link up with the millionaire investor looking for deals in his or her own backyard.

So the degree of difficulty associated with raising capital is directly related to the inefficiency of the private capital market. Fortunately, however, the rise of the Internet as a powerful new communications medium is ushering in a new era of efficiency as well as providing new opportunities to raise money that simply did not exist only a few years ago.

The Network Revolution

One of the most visible signs of this new era is ACE-Net, which stands for the Angel Capital Electronic Network. ACE-Net is a project sponsored by the Small Business Administration, which, after years of public-policy debate, lobbying, and nurturing at universities and economic-development organizations, became operational in 1996.

ACE-Net is an "Internet-based network that will provide new options to small companies looking for capital and new opportunities for so-called 'accredited investors' looking for investment opportunities," according to Terry Bibbens of the Small Business Administration, who was one of the many architects of the program. ACE-Net removes many of the limitations entrepreneurs face when trying to link up with angel investors on a nationwide basis, he says.

How It Works

The mechanics of the network are wonderfully straightforward. Listings of offerings on ACE-Net can be found through online search engines that permit investors to find their desired type of company, technology, investment size or geography. Once located, the investor can review or download the forms filed by the listed companies. If the investor wishes to cut a deal, he or she can then contact the company directly. According to Bibbens, companies that want to be list-

A Good Deal

ACE-Net excels over other matching services because it offers access to accredited investors. That means if you contact an investor through ACE-Net, he or she probably has the financial wherewithal to make a deal with you.

ed on ACE-Net must do so through one of several nodes, which are listed below.

As for the investors, access to the deals listed on ACE-Net is limited to accredited investors. These are defined by the Securities and Exchange Commission's Regulation D as, among other criteria, individuals who have a net worth or joint net worth with a spouse in excess of $1 million; or have net income in excess of $200,000 or joint income with a spouse in excess of $300,000 in each of the last two years and who reasonably expect similar income in the current year.

Shop Talk

ACE-Net "nodes" are organizations that feed deals into the ACE-Net machine. Many of the nodes are well-established, well-organized regional or local electronic matching services with a wide array of services for entrepreneurs.

Since it became operational in 1996, ACE-Net has ironed out many of the wrinkles inherent in any project of this scope. Chief among these changes is a shortened filing form that increases the ease with which a company can post its offering on ACE-Net (see the "ACE-Net Short Form," starting on page 136). Previously, companies had to file what is known as Form U-7 or a SCOR Small Company Offering Registration) form. The 50 questions that make up the U-7 are challenging, and when completed, the form looks suspiciously like a full-blown prospectus.

The new filing, known as the ACE-Net Short Form, makes the use of ACE-Net a feasible alternative for any company raising money, according to Greg Dean, director of the Small Business Administration's Office of Advocacy. "With the short form and the nominal fee to post an offering," he says, entrepreneurs have absolutely nothing to lose through ACE-Net, but perhaps very much to gain."

Why is ACE-Net so important? It increases the efficiency of information distribution—dramatically. In fact, within the strictest constructs of the discipline, ACE-Net mirrors the mechanisms of any stock market or bourse by matching buyers and sellers with uniform information flowing between them. When this happens, capital moves more freely, which is precisely what cash-hungry entrepreneurs need.

ACE-Net Short Form

Below is the ACE-Net Short Form. If you intend to try ACE-Net, do not fill out this form. To register for ACE-Net, you must fill this form out online.

1. The federal and state small-business exemptions under which the securities are being offered/sold:_____
   _____

2. The state(s) where the securities may be offered/sold:
   _____

3. Whether the sale of securities is restricted solely to "accredited investors."_____

4. Whether there are any "restrictions" to be placed on secondary sales of the securities, (i.e., under NASAA's Model Accredited Investor Exemption stock must be "purchased for investment" and not for immediate resale):_____
   _____

With respect to the business of the Company and its properties:

- Describe in detail what business the Company does and proposes to do, including what products or goods are or will be produced or services that are or will be rendered.

> It is expected that you will copy and paste your executive summary or your business plan at this point in the document when you are filling it out online. The executive summary is the minimum required. The business plan is preferable for the amount of information it provides the investor.

- Exact name of Company as set forth in Articles of Incorporation or Charter:_____
  _____

- Type of securities offered:_____
  _____

- Maximum number of securities offered:_____
  _____

- Minimum number of securities offered:_____
  _____

ACE-Net Short Form

- Price per security: $_____
- Total proceeds: If maximum sold: $_____
                      If minimum sold: $_____
- State and date of incorporation:_____
- Street address of principal office:_____
  _____
- Company telephone number: (_____) _____
- Fiscal year: _____ (month) _____ (day)
- Person(s) to contact at Company with respect to offering:
  _____
- Telephone number (if different from above): (____) _____

The following table sets forth the use of the proceeds from this offering:

	If Minimum Sold Amount	%	If Maximum Sold Amount	%
Total Proceeds	$_____	100%	$_____	100%
Less: Offering Price	_____	____	_____	____
Commissions and Finder Fees	_____	____	_____	____
Legal & Accounting	_____	____	_____	____
Copying & Advertising	_____	____	_____	____
Other (Specify):_____	_____	____	_____	____
Net Proceeds From Offering	$_____	____	$_____	____
Use of Net Proceeds				
	_____	____	_____	____
	_____	____	_____	____
	_____	____	_____	____
	_____	____	_____	____
	_____	____	_____	____
	_____	____	_____	____
Total Use of Net Proceeds	$_____	100%	$_____	100%

ACE-Net Short Form (cont'd.)

Indicate the capitalization of the Company as of the most recent balance sheet (adjusted to reflect any subsequent stock splits, dividends, recapitalizations or refinancings) and as adjusted to reflect the sale of the minimum and maximum amount of securities in this offering and the use of the net proceeds therefrom:

Amount Outstanding

Debt:	As of: __/__/__ date	As Adjusted Minimum	Maximum
Short-term debt (average interest rate ____%)	$	$	$
Long-term debt (average interest rate ____%)	$	$	$
Total Debt	$	$	$

Stockholders equity (deficit):

Preferred stock—par or stated value (by class of preferred in order of preferences)	As of: __/__/__ date	As Adjusted Minimum	Maximum
_____	$	$	$
_____	$	$	$
_____	$	$	$
Common stock—par or stated value	$	$	$
Additional paid in capital	$	$	$
Retained earnings (deficit)	$	$	$
Total stockholders equity (deficit)	$	$	$
Total Capitalization	$	$	$

Number of preferred shares authorized to be outstanding:

Class of Preferred	Number of Shares Authorized	Par Value Per Share
_____	_____	_____
_____	_____	_____
_____	_____	_____

ACE-Net Short Form

Number of common shares authorized: _____ shares.

Par or stated value per share, if any: $_____.

Number of common shares reserved to meet conversion requirements or for the issuance upon exercise of options, warrants or rights: _____ shares.

Chief Executive Officer:

Name: _____

Title: _____ Age: _____

Name of employer's titles and dates of positions held during the past five years with indication of job responsibilities:

_____

_____

_____

_____

Education (degrees, schools and dates):_____

_____

_____

_____

Also a Director of the Company   [   ] Yes   [   ] No

Indicate amount of time to be spent on Company matters if less than full time:_____

_____

Number of Directors: _____. If Directors are not elected annually, or elected under a voting trust or other arrangement, explain:_____

_____

_____

_____

_____

How To Get Started

Getting your offering onto ACE-Net begins by contacting any one of the organizations listed in Appendix A. These so-called "nodes" are electronic investor networks in their own right but also act as feeders for ACE-Net. The organizations that operate these nodes can assist you with the completion of the ACE-Net Short Form and other details associated with using the system.

The federal government certainly doesn't have a lock on electronic matching services. In fact, they are popping up all over. See Appendix A for a sampling of networks with a national focus, as well as some with a regional focus.

The Limitations Of Cyberspace

Entrepreneurs seeking to raise capital should cast a wary eye on the Internet. Oh, it can help. But it is not a turnkey solution. In fact, the words "raising money on the Internet" are at best a misnomer and at worst downright inaccurate.

Having made such a bold and declarative statement, it's only fair to say that at least one company raised money on the Internet. This company was Spring Street Brewery. Spring Street was able to do this largely because it was the first company in history that tried to do so. The sheer volume of publicity Spring Street generated with its "Internet IPO" made its $1.6 million financing a self-fulfilling prophecy.

Don't Forget
The old Wall Street dictum that stocks are not bought but sold applies to early-stage companies raising money. Deals are not bought. More accurately, they are sold to investors. You will need more than the Internet to sell your idea to investors.

However, a company today posting a prospectus or offering circular on the Internet is not news at all. In fact, because all the hype has gone out of this tactic, the only thing left for entrepreneurs to bank on is hope—hope that investors find the posting of their deal, hope that investors are interested, hope that investors read and download all of the information that will be required for them to make an investment, hope investors will be excited enough about what they read that, unsolicited, they will send a check to the company, hope that the check doesn't bounce and hope that enough investors do this so that the company raises its desired amount of capital.

The upshot is the Internet is a powerful communications medium, but it is a weak selling medium. That is, it cannot provide an acceptably powerful selling mechanism to convert leads into buyers.

The networks mentioned in Appendix A escaped some of these pitfalls. After all, many are small intra-nets that represent investors who have made a conscious decision to list on the network, and in some instances, such as ACE-Net, have had to actually qualify to be accepted by the network. The underlying assumption then is that these investors are actually looking for deals and may call upon companies that interest them.

However, many Web sites that simply post deals, with access open to any browser, offer little hope for the kind of reaction required to raise a material amount of capital. Likewise, the simple act of posting an offering on your own Web site, though inexpensive, generally won't create the kind of buzz that will carry the day.

When shopping among electronic matching services, be sure to find out the kinds of investors who have access to the network, and what, if any, net worth or suitability requirements they meet.

Chapter 14

Business Incubators

The Scoop

Definition Or Explanation: Business incubators are a good path to capital from angel investors, state governments, economic-development coalitions and other investors. Business incubators house several businesses under one roof or in a campus setting, and offer resident companies reduced rents, shared services and, in many instances, formal or informal access financing.

Appropriate For: Pre-revenue-stage companies to early-stage companies that are selling products or services

Supply: More than 550 incubators in North America cater to high- and low-technology businesses. Of these, more than 80 percent report that they provide formal or informal access to capital.

Best Use: Many types of financing may be found through incubators, which may or may not be appropriate for your business. Generally speaking, however, incubators and the kinds of investors they lead a path to work best for companies at the earliest stages of their development.

Cost: There may be many kinds of financing found through incubators, from state-assistance funds based on matching private sector investments, which could be inexpensive, to straight equity investments from angel investors, which could be very expensive.

Ease Of Acquisition: Getting into an incubator can be easy or challenging. Simply being in an incubator offers value to investors. Incubator managers know this, and as a result, many carefully screen would-be tenants to see that they match certain criteria. The good news is that once in an incubator, the path to angels or other investors might be more direct since they tend to hover around easily identified centers of entrepreneurial activity.

Funds Typically Available: $25,000 and greater.

A Case In Point

Technology giant Teledyne has created a burgeoning cluster of high-tech businesses in and around Austin, Texas. The entrepreneurial culture there is so strong that it drew one-time English professor May Dammer into the data management business. Dammer formed her company, Revolutionary Technologies, in 1991 to help large companies with data-integration management and ensure that related data on different systems were consistent.

After doing basic research at the technology research firm Micro Electronics and Computer Technology Corp. in Austin, Dammer moved across town to the Austin Technology Incubator. According to Dammer, the founder of the incubator was George Kozmatsky, who also founded the region's font of it all, Teledyne. "George provided unbelievably helpful counsel and guidance," Dammer recalls.

But he also provided her with introductions to an informal network of angel investors affiliated with the incubator. One of these investors was retired admiral Bobby Inman. Inman, who had a real sense of the need to keep data consistent across a large enterprise, felt that Dammer was on to something. Inman committed $250,000 to the venture, which in turn anchored another $1.25 million from other area investors, for a total first-round financing of $1.5 million. "My acceptance in the incubator carried weight," Dammer says. "By being accepted there, it offered a third-party endorsement for investors."

Looking back at the experience, Dammer reflects that being in an incubator is one of the reasons that Revolutionary Technologies is a successful business today. Sure, all the goodies inside Austin Technology Incubator were important, but in the case of Revolutionary Technologies, Hammer suggests, there was a more subtle, though massively important, dynamic. In a word, it was control. In the incubator's nurturing environment, Dammer was actually able to turn down prohibitively expensive financing proposals on the basis of the percentage of the company it would cost her. "It's a huge problem when you lose control of the company in the first round of financing," Dammer says. "If the business goes through a false start or has some serious difficulties getting off the ground, which happens in start-up situations, and then the investors feel like they have to take over, they tend to push the company in one direction or another."

By contrast, at Revolutionary Technologies, Dammer held a majority position until the third round of financing. "I was lucky," she says. "I was able to build the foundation for the business according to my vision." Apparently, she built it right. Today, Revolutionary is profitable, with some $22 million in sales and more than 150 employees. The investors haven't fared bad, either. According to Dammer, for every $1 of capital invested, the company has generated more than $11 in sales.

> **Don't Forget**
> Lots of entrepreneurs suffer because of the isolation and loneliness that come with starting and growing a business. An incubator can help you overcome this challenge by providing a support group of similarly situated individuals.

> **A Good Deal**
> Incubators can do more than simply help blaze a trail to sources of capital. They also offer support in the form of reduced rents, flexible space, shared services, access to professional services and, perhaps most important, an environment of energy and entrepreneurial spirit.

Deep Roots, Lots Of Services

The roots of business incubation go back about 40 years, to a time when, not surprisingly, the industrial landscape was changing in fundamental ways.

It all started when heavy equipment manufacturer Massey Ferguson pulled out of Batavia,

New York, in 1959, leaving behind a hulking 850,000-square-foot facility. This catastrophic economic event seemed like the end of the line for the town. As it turned out, it was only the beginning, not just for Batavia, but for a new generation of emerging companies that would change the composition of the American economy.

After the ax fell in Batavia, local resident Joe Manucuso bought the building the company left behind. He hoped to use it to bring new businesses and new jobs to the area. His idea was right for the times and caught on rapidly, as businesses (including an actual incubator, hence the name) attracted by cheap rents, flexible space and shared services, filled the building. "Today," says Dinah Adkins, executive director of the National Business Incubation Association (NBIA), "business incubators offer comprehensive support to fledgling businesses."

But the other important benefit that business incubators often provide is access to the kind of early-stage capital that emerging companies need. For instance, according to Adkins, a recent survey of NBIA members shows 83 percent of incubator owners and directors provide formal or informal access to seed capital. Seventy-six percent provide assistance with obtaining federal grants; 74 percent assist with preparing financing proposals; 60 percent can help obtain royalty financing and 57 percent can lend a hand obtaining purchase-order financing.

Taking Action
If a business incubator sounds like it might be right for your business, and you want to find the one nearest you, send a self-addressed stamped envelope to the National Business Incubation Association at 20 E. Circle Dr., #190, Athens, OH 45701, or call (614) 593-4331.

Why Incubators Attract Investors

Adkins says it should not surprise anyone that angel

investors tend to hover over business incubators. First, she says, almost all "client companies," as they are called, are carefully prescreened for acceptance. "The fact that a business has been accepted into an incubator," Adkins notes, "offers due diligence value to potential investors. In a way they have already passed an important litmus test by simply being there."

Incubators attract sources of capital because of the simple economics of convenience. Rather than searching high and low for potential deals, investors can easily find a multitude of investment opportunities under one roof.

Finally, the businesses an investor is likely to find inside an incubator can make whatever dollars he or she is prepared to invest go much further. Says Adkins, "With low rents, shared services and access to professional services and training at low and sometimes no cost, investors can gain a real sense of comfort that their investment will last longer and take the business farther than might be true within a conventional business environment."

Only The Lonely

The benefits of an incubator aren't restricted to technology companies. Adkins says that's one of the great misconceptions about business incubators. In fact, the statistics tell just the opposite story. Of the incubators in business, she notes, 40 percent concentrate on service, 23 percent on light manufacturing, 22 percent on technology and 7 percent on basic research, while the remaining 8 percent support diverse businesses and industries.

Getting into an incubator may not be a slam dunk, Adkins cautions. "The best incubator programs have become adept at analyzing the company to see if their investment is worthwhile. They evaluate the deal the same way a professional venture capitalist might. Just like everyone else, they are looking for companies that will be successful."

Chapter 15

401(k) Financing

The Scoop

Definition Or Explanation: A 401(k) is a tax-deferred savings account that an employer establishes for its employees. This savings vehicle can be used for almost any kind of investment. The 401(k) stays intact even if the employee leaves the firm. If the employee leaves to start a new business, his or her 401(k) can be used to invest in, or even finance, the new venture.

Appropriate For: Any company at any stage of development. Since entrepreneurs fund the company with their own retirement savings, they need only convince themselves that the deal is worth the risk.

Supply: This option is for entrepreneurs who have been cut loose from corporate America, with their 401(k) plan. Beyond simply having a 401(k), the supply is further influenced by how much of their tax-deferred retirement savings entrepreneurs are willing to put at risk.

Best Use: Financing start-ups. When start-up companies are financed with equity from outside sources, it's the most expensive avenue of financing because the company is worth so little. A round of seed financing can cost 30 percent of the equity. Although 401(k) financing forces a company to surrender equity, it is surrendered to the firm's founders and, as such, is not really lost.

Cost: The fees can run high because several professionals are required to engineer the transaction. However, 401(k) financing does not cost the founders any equity in their business.

Ease Of Acquisition: Moderately challenging.

There are several legal and accounting issues that must be resolved for this technique to work properly.

Funds Typically Available: $100,000 and greater.

A Case In Point

After nearly 20 years in sales and sales management for a large manufacturer of printed forms, labels, and electronic printing systems, Jim Brien was growing antsy. The business plan he was writing in his head was getting more and more detailed. And when the future of the company he was working for seemed less certain, Brien, along with five fellow salespeople, formed Print Integration Partners, which not surprisingly, brokers printing and also offers forms-management services.

Brien's business plan showed that the company needed about $500,000 during the first two years of operation for office equipment, inventory (of forms) and receivables funding. Though Print Integration Partners was up and running, Brien wasn't ready for a grand opening until he knew that the business could be funded. "I thought it would be a big mistake for us to launch headlong into the business without any funding," he recalls.

"At the time," Brien says, "the biggest asset I had was the 401(k) plan from my previous employer, so naturally, my first reaction was to see what could be done with that." In fact, all the newly minted Print Integration Partners had 401(k) plans, and in the aggregate, there were more than enough assets to fund the business. The trick was unlocking these funds.

Brien and his partners could have liquidated their 401(k) plans. But, he says, there's a 20 percent penalty off the top, and the dis-

Shop Talk

An Employee Stock Ownership Plan (ESOP) is a legal and separate entity through which employees can collectively purchase equity in a business.

tribution from the liquidation must be taken as income in the year in which it is received. So, if it's a good-sized distribution, it will push the recipient into the higher end of the thirtysomething tax bracket. No thank you!

A simple and straightforward approach would be to simply have the 401(k) plans purchase shares directly in Print Integration Partners. This could be easily accomplished despite the widely held though mistaken belief that 401(k) plans can only make investments in publicly held companies.

However, Greg Brown, an attorney specializing in Employee Stock Ownership Plans (ESOPs) with Chicago law firm Seyfarth, Shaw, Fairweather & Geraldson, counseled Brien that there might be better approach. Specifically, Brown proposed that Brien establish a Print Integration ESOP from which the 401(k)s would purchase their shares in the company. Such a transaction would require a highly specialized team of financial professionals, according to Brown, but the structure would deliver several tax- and estate-planning benefits that most small businesses don't ever think about until it's too late. This team that Brien would need included an attorney, an accountant, a valuation specialist and a securities firm.

It took Brien about five months to assemble the team and put together the transaction. By April 1996, about five months after Print Integration Partners was incorporated, all the pieces were in place and the transaction could be executed. Brien and his partners then instructed Smith Barney, the custodian of their 401(k) plans, to purchase shares in the Print Integration Partners Employee Stock Option Plan, for which Smith Barney was also custodian. As a result, cash ($427,000 in total) went

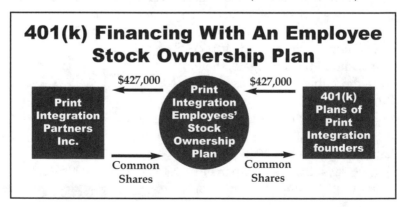

401(k) Financing With An Employee Stock Ownership Plan

$427,000 $427,000

Print Integration Partners Inc.   Print Integration Employees' Stock Ownership Plan   401(k) Plans of Print Integration founders

Common Shares   Common Shares

from the 401(k)s to the ESOP, and from the ESOP into the Print Integration Partners' bank account. Then stock certificates in Print Integration Partners were issued to the ESOP in the names of each of the employees making the investment.

Tricky, yes, but when it was all done, Brien and his partners had successfully tapped their 401(k) plans without any tax consequences, funded their new company without giving up equity or bringing in outsiders and kept the balance of their savings intact.

A Good Deal
If you finance your company with your own retirement savings, you do not surrender authority to outside parties. This is important for early-stage companies because outside investors often believe a company is in trouble before it really is and tend to cause difficulty with knee-jerk reactions to the company's problems.

Pros And Cons

When reviewing the transaction Brien is quick to point out that the structure Print Integration Partners and its team engineered had merit well beyond the initial financing. First, Brien says, the ESOP delivers built-in liquidity for founders' shares. "Most private businesses rarely last more than one generation," Brien says, "because there is nobody to buy out the founders or other stockholders when they are ready to retire or move on. But the ESOP means the exit strategy is already in place because when shareholders leave they have the option of selling their holdings to the ESOP at a fair price."

In addition to liquidity for founders shares, attorney Brown adds, there is also a compelling tax advantage. "Business owners can sell their shares to the ESOP and defer the capital gains tax on these shares by purchasing stock or bonds issued by U.S. corporations." Since at retirement most entrepreneurs must invest the money they take out of the business for income, this tax deferral meshes nicely with the business owner's life cycle.

Second, with an Employee Stock Ownership Plan in place, Print Integration Partners had an effective tool to attract, retain, motivate and reward employees, with several options on how it could accomplish any of these objectives. For instance, Brien says, "Commencing our second year in business, we issued ESOP stock to everyone in the company so that everybody had a stake in what the company did." That's the incentive. But as for the reward, says Brien, "we have the option of passing profits to stockholders via 401(k) matching, without it being taxed. Really, there are now several options we have to manage profits and pay a fair tax."

Third, and most important, Brien says, Print Integration Partners was able to fund its start-up operations without searching

Don't Forget
The valuation specialist needs a well-developed set of financial projections to do his or her job. Don't wait until the last minute to get this done because it adds weeks to the process while the other moving parts in the deal cool their heels.

for outside investors, who would have extracted a high price in terms of the ownership of the company they would demand. In the end, Print Integration Partners didn't give up a point of equity—no small feat for a start-up company.

Assembling The Team

The success of a 401(k) transaction depends largely on the team that is assembled to help implement the transaction. Here are the principal players:

- **Counsel:** You need an attorney to draft the documentation for the ESOP, as well as to define and engineer the relationship of the ESOP to the 401(k) plans. Although such a transaction is not beyond the ken of a general practitioner, its cutting-edge nature probably demands an ESOP specialist.

Don't Forget
Look at your 401(k) plan and evaluate whether it contains sufficient assets to fund your business. If the 401(k) contains less capital than you project will be necessary, but makes a sizable dent, contemplate the answer to the question: Am I willing to put all of this money at risk?

- **Valuation consultant:** Since at the end of the day, the ESOP is buying stock from a corporation, you need a qualified opinion about the value of the stock being purchased. There are lots of valuation specialists, and many concentrate on specific industries. Rather than just finding a specialist who understands a particular industry, it's also important to find a valuation specialist who can work with emerging or start-up companies. After all, traditional measures of value, such as assets, or book value, are often not available with start-up businesses.

- **Stock brokerage:** A brokerage firm is needed to act as the custodian for the ESOP stock. Care must be taken to choose a firm with the right size and capabilities. After all, current or future employees who participate in the plan need to establish or roll over their plan with the broker. As a result, you want a broker who can provide not just service but also investment options or access to investment options above and beyond the ESOP stock.

- **Accountant:** Everybody needs good tax advice, but with an ESOP, the tax issues are even more complex. After all, as was mentioned, the company's net income can be managed in part or whole through the ESOP. In addition, the 401(k) needs an administrator to keep track of stock purchases by employees. Some accountants, as well as brokerage firms, can fill this role.

Chapter 16

Direct Public Offerings

The Scoop

Definition Or Explanation: Direct public offerings (DPOs) are the direct sale of shares in a company to individual investors. After the shares are sold by the company, investors may or may not trade on a stock market or exchange.

Appropriate For: Direct public offerings work better with established companies, but they can also be used for start-up and emerging companies. One of the most important characteristics a company should possess for a successful direct public offering is a strong affinity for its customers, the surrounding community or the industry in which it does business. In a direct public offering, these affinity groups become the company's shareholders.

Supply: Vast. For years, individual investors have heard about the millions, and in some cases billions of dollars, being made by venture capitalists through investments in companies in their formative stages of development. These same investors would like the chance to play venture capitalist, and your direct public offering may give them that opportunity.

Best Use: Financing the expansion of profitable operations. Direct public offerings can be used to finance research and development, but public investors often become impatient during long periods of product development. When they are unhappy, they can cause problems for the company later as it tries to raise money to finance the marketing and rollout of the product or service.

Cost: Expensive. A direct public offering is less expensive than an initial public offering (IPO) with an investment banker, but only moderately so. The absence of an underwriter's commissions is sometimes more than offset by the marketing expenses a company must bear in a direct public offering. In addition, like a conventional initial public offering, the company must surrender a significant hunk of ownership to its direct public offering investors.

Ease Of Acquisition: Difficult. Any transaction that involves securities is challenging. The absence of an underwriter can make the process at once easier and harder. Easier because the company can call the shots without recrimination. Harder because an underwriter has experience with IPOs, and a company typically does not.

Funds Typically Available: $500,000 and greater.

The DPO Orientation

Direct public offerings are exactly like initial public offerings, yet at the same time completely different. Here's how the two are alike. A direct public offering and an initial public offering both involve the sale of a piece of a company's ownership to the public. A direct public offering and an initial public offering may be carried out under the same federal securities laws, specifically the Securities Act of 1933 and the Securities Exchange Act of 1934.

Direct public offerings are different because they are sold by the company, not by an intermediary such as a broker or investment banker. Unlike conventional IPOs, DPOs can, in addition to receiving full federal securities registration, be sold under myriad state laws and federal securities laws exemptions. Unlike conventional IPOs, which typically trade on a recognized stock market after they are completed, DPOs often do not trade at all. And finally, unlike IPOs which are typically bought by investors who are speculating, DPOs are bought by investors who have some natural affinity for a company. They invest in a company because they are somehow connected to it.

A Case In Point

After 10 years in business, Michael Flynn wanted to go national. But his Flynn Laboratories Inc., which manufactures homeopathic medicines, needed to become an FDA-licensed pharmaceutical manufacturer if it was to actively market product across state lines. Where would Flynn get the capital to make a new FDA-licensed facility?

"I went to a bank, and they said, 'definitely not,'" Flynn recalls. Investment bankers didn't offer much hope, either. But the light went on when Flynn realized that if just 200 of his more than 28,000 customers invested about $2,000 each, his Flynn Labs would have the patient equity capital it needed. Flynn avoided traditional brokerages and instead marketed common shares directly to individual investors.

While people interested in alternative medicine are not those typically interested in the stock market, Flynn says he had an unfair advantage. "Our deal, which in a way was an alternative public offering, was attractive to these investors."

Flynn sent out more than 35,000 offering announcements. They resulted in about 1,700 requests for prospectuses. He also fulfilled 400 requests for prospectuses from friends, family, associates, colleagues and peers. Of the initial 2,100 investors who received a prospectus, Flynn says, about 240 eventually invested.

None of this was quick or easy. It took Flynn more than 12 months to close his deal's $430,000 minimum. And of his 240 investors, Flynn says, only 15 percent mailed in a check after reading the prospectus. To get the other 200 or so, Flynn had to prospect over the telephone. He estimates that he called 700 to 800 investors. Nor was any of this cheap. Legal, audit, printing and marketing costs totaled $102,000, Flynn says.

Although the effort took time and money, Flynn says, there were side benefits. "Sure, there were days when I wished I would run into just one person

A Good Deal

If you are considering a DPO, make sure your offering memoranda are on the Internet. This distribution medium can save you a lot of money in printing and postage costs.

who had $500,000." But, he says, it was a real learning experience talking to so many customers. "Reaching out to so many people and telling your story is never bad for a business if it's done with the right heart and attitude."

In fact, sales during the year, when Flynn was most preoccupied with selling the deal, were about $100,000 higher than the previous year. And the momentum spilled into the next fiscal year, when sales had surged ahead by 15 percent at midyear.

DPO Limitations

According to Drew Field, an attorney and author of the book *Direct Public Offerings* (Sourcebooks), DPO deals are not easier or less complex than conventional IPOs. "But direct public offerings represent a more manageable way to go because you do not have to accommodate or rely upon others, such as investment bankers or brokers, who can prove to be difficult and dangerous. You can manage a direct public offering just as you would any other project."

But Field is quick to point out that DPOs are not for everyone. If you are considering such a deal, he says, you must be able to operate within the natural limitations of this financing technique. Specifically:

- **Little or no trading market for the common shares:** Remember, the reasons for going public are diverse. In addition to plain old raising money, entrepreneurs often take their company public to make estate planning easier, and also to provide an "exit" for people who invested during the company's development. Unfortunately, it's difficult for DPOs to serve these purposes because,

> **Shop Talk**
> Financiers sometimes refer to a "minimum offering." Many private transactions, as well as alternative public offerings, have a minimum and maximum amount they seek to raise. Once this minimum is raised, the funds are disbursed to the company, while it continues to try to raise the balance. It's not uncommon for the minimum on a $1 million deal to be $100,000 or $200,000. Why? Because no company wants to do part of the deal and have to return the money simply because it overestimated what it could raise.

Don't Forget

It's not where you start, but where you end up that counts. A DPO may seem like a humble way to raise capital, but if the company grows and prospers, it can open a gateway to the upper tiers of the market.

when they are completed, there is not an active market for a company's common stock.

- **The inability to use stock to acquire other companies:** Many companies go public to use their stock as a "currency" to acquire other companies. Unfortunately, without an active trading market, there's not much reason for a seller to take such stock in lieu of cash. Therefore, unless they have a whole lot of cash in the bank, companies that plan to achieve their growth through acquisitions should probably not consider using a direct public offering.

- **Little personal gain:** It's hard to get filthy rich on a direct public offering. It might help build a company that pays you a tremendous salary, but in terms of cashing out by selling your own holdings in the company to public investors, it just doesn't happen. What could happen is that a company financed with a DPO could grow to a size and scale where it "graduates" to a real stock market, and attracts new investors or an investment banking firm that wants to underwrite a real deal. But all of that happy activity is a long way off. Here and now, a DPO adds to your company's coffers, but not much else.

When you add it all up, direct public offerings are plain vanilla. They provide a financing solution for companies that need equity capital from investors who will give the company the room it needs to grow, frequently referred to as "patient" equity capital. When you have greater needs, like estate planning, acquisition strategies, personal wealth building or corporate prestige, the effectiveness of a DPO is compromised.

In truth, however, patient equity capital is all most companies need. The romance of a full-blown IPO, with its inevitable aftermarket trading, often turns out to be a hollow love. In fact, the time and effort spent kowtowing to public investors and analysts after the deal is done are precisely what cause many chief executives to run their businesses into the ground.

Characteristics Of DPO Candidates

If you can operate within these limitations, you are almost home. But not quite, since a DPO still may not be a viable technique for your business. According to author Field, not all companies possess the right mix of traits. He says DPO candidates should have some or all of the following characteristics:

Two Thumbs Up?

Following are some likely DPO candidates based on strong affinity relationships:

1. A manufacturer of unique home appliances (wood-burning stoves, solar panels)
2. An agricultural cooperative
3. A lawn-care company
4. A unique resort
5. A publisher
6. A microbrewery or winery
7. A catalog merchandiser
8. A training or educational concern
9. A pet-care service

Following are some unlikely DPO candidates, based on weak or inappropriate affinity relationships:

1. A biotechnology company conducting research and development
2. A prison-management company
3. A government contractor
4. A manufacturer of industrial abrasives
5. A funeral home
6. A fast-food restaurant
7. A personnel agency
8. A book distributor
9. An auto dealership
10. A money manager

- **Your business is easily understood.** Field says that individuals who participate in DPOs have a limited scope of interest. "They do not purchase shares in companies they do not understand. In addition, because individual investors are by definition individuals and not brokerages or institutions with research departments behind them, the scope of what they understand is much narrower."

- **Your business is profitable.** Make no mistake, start-up and unprofitable companies can successfully complete a direct public offering. After all, as was suggested earlier in this chapter, many individual investors want to be venture capitalists. But many more potential investors will be attracted to a profitable and established business. In many instances, institutional venture capitalists get their courage to invest in fledgling businesses from the OPM factor. That is, they are investing Other People's Money. Individuals, on the other hand, are investing their own money, and they are reluctant to turn it over to a business that might lose it.

- **Your business has some sizzle.** In a conventional public offering, the broker promotes a company's sizzle through his or her direct selling efforts. In a direct public offering, the selling and promotional efforts, which are usually conducted by a company's management and founders, are tightly regulated and constrained. Therefore, Field says, direct public offerings require much motivation on the part of the investors. Unfortunately, it's difficult for mundane enterprises to inspire the required level of action among investors.

- **There are easily identifiable groups that have an affinity for your company.** These include customers, clients, vendors, allied grassroots political organizations and the community in which the company does business. It's through these relationships that many of the direct

A Good Deal

Companies that make money always get better terms than those which are in the red. If possible, hold off on a DPO until you can show a profit. This strategy will save you precious points of equity when the time comes to raise funds.

public offering shares are sold. Entrepreneurs, however, must evaluate whether the affinity they perceive is mutual and strong enough to motivate prospective investors to consider their offering.

Regulatory Filings For A DPO

The legal aspects of a direct public offering are some of the most challenging, which is why hiring an attorney is typically one of the first steps in the DPO process.

If you want to go public by selling more than $1 million in securities in several states, and to trade on a recognized U.S. stock market, chances are you will need to file a federal registration statement under the Securities Act of 1933. These filings are done with:

- **Forms SB-1 and SB-2:** These federal filings for an initial public offering for a small-business issuer, though simplified from years past, are one of the most difficult hurdles of a conventional or direct public offering. The required audited financial statements that accompany these filings, and other financial disclosures add expensive accounting and legal fees.

- **Regulation A filings:** For offerings up to $5 million, issuers can take advantage of so-called Regulation A. Rather than a registration of securities, Regulation A is a "qualification" of securities and is designed to be a less rigorous and expensive filing process. For instance, there is a "testing the waters" provision whereby a company can discern if there is sufficient interest to proceed with an offering. Also, Regulation A does not require audited financial statements, though most states require them for offerings of a certain size.

There are exemptions to federal securities laws that companies can take advantage of for the DPO. Specifically:

- **Rule 504, Regulation D:** Offerings of less than $1 million are exempt from registration under the Securities Act of 1933 through the SEC's Rule 504 of Regulation D.

- **Intrastate offerings:** Offerings sold to investors within a single state do not have to file under the '33 Act, in recognition of the state's rights.

If you are considering a direct public offering that will take advantage of federal exemptions, you still must deal with state securities laws. Each state sports its own laws, and coordinating an offering that is exempt from federal securities laws but tries to comply with the securities laws of say, 10 states, would prove to be a challenging, perhaps even impossible, task. Below are some choices for overcoming the challenge of state securities laws:

- **State exemptions:** Just as the feds let you structure an offering so that you do not have to register under federal securities laws, you can structure an offering so that it is exempt from filing under state securities laws. The exemptions typically relate to the size of the offering, generally $1 million or less, and the number of investors who can participate, generally between five and 50. Since many states' exemptions are different, it's difficult to sell securities in an exempt offering in more than one state, but it can, and has been, done.

- **SCOR offerings:** Small Company Offering Registrations, or SCOR deals, represent a quantum leap in unifying the myriad state securities laws into one, almost universally accepted, filing. With a SCOR filing, a company can sell up to $1 million of securities to investors in a public offering. Even though most states have agreed to accept the SCOR filing, predictably, differing requirements among the separate state securities regulators can make the approval process frustrating. The recently enacted "coordinated review" process, whereby a group of states airs their comments among themselves rather than having the company that is issuing the shares interact separately with each state, is proving successful.

A Good Deal

Exemptions from state and federal securities laws are a great deal for companies seeking capital. Many of the securities laws date back to the 1930s, are difficult to understand, possess vast gray areas and, worst of all, require significant legal fees to negotiate. By taking advantage of exemptions at the state and federal level simultaneously, you can avoid the onerous state and federal filing requirements that can and do stifle the capital-formation process.

Planning A Trading Market

Almost every investor wants to know how to sell shares. In truth, this is an unfortunate and in some ways irresponsible desire on the part of the investor. After all, when a professional venture capitalist puts capital in a company, he or she often has a five- to seven-year time frame for the investment to reach fruition. The criteria for a direct public offering, which is often called public venture capital, shouldn't be any different. In truth, trading shouldn't even enter into the picture. If the company truly succeeds, then, in one fashion or another, the investors will be rewarded.

The above issue notwithstanding, you must plan for the resale mechanism of your direct public offering. Following are your options:

- **Order matching systems:** This is the best choice for a tiny public company that has completed a direct public offering. In essence, with an order matching system, a stockbroker at a brokerage firm gets referrals from the DPO company of investors who have expressed interest in buying shares, and sellers who have expressed interest in selling shares. If there appears to be a match between a buyer and a seller in terms of price and quantity, the broker then facilitates the transaction.

  The resale of shares may be regulated in the state where the sale takes place. With an order matching system, there doesn't have to be, but there generally is, a published bid or asking price. The liquidity, or the ease with which shares can be turned into cash, is not high with an order matching system; however, such systems represent the kind of accommodation that can make a big difference to individual investors considering an investment in your company.

- **Nasdaq stock markets:** The National Association of Securities Dealers (NASD) operates the Nasdaq National Market System for larger companies and the Nasdaq SmallCap Market for smaller companies. These are sophisticated markets for trading securities. Companies that have completed a direct public offering can trade on Nasdaq, but they must register shares under the

Securities Act of 1933 and the Securities Exchange Act of 1934, which covers periodic reporting requirements.

Since these are the complex legal and accounting documents that many companies sought to avoid in the first place with their direct public offering, Nasdaq trading may be impractical. In addition, trading on any of the Nasdaq markets requires at least two brokers who are willing to be market makers—that is, middlemen to match buyers and sellers—for a company's securities.

- **Bulletin Board and Pink Sheets:** Companies that have not registered their shares under the 1933 and 1934 Securities Acts can still trade on the NASD's Bulletin Board. The Bulletin Board also requires at least two brokerage firms to make a market in a company's shares. Bid and ask prices are distributed electronically on almost any quote terminal, giving Bulletin Board companies the appearance of a real public company.

  A more obscure trading venue is the "Pink Sheets." In truth, Pink Sheet companies trade exactly as Bulletin Board companies do, with the primary difference being that bid and ask quotes are not distributed electronically. Instead, they are printed daily by the National Quotation Bureau on—you guessed it—pink paper.

- **The stock exchanges:** The New York and American Stock Exchange listing requirements make them an unrealistic choice for most direct public offerings. Of the regional stock exchanges, Boston, Chicago, Pacific and Philadelphia, the latter three have a tier for smaller companies. However, registration under the Securities Exchange Act of 1934 is required for exchange trading, making it impractical for many DPO candidates.

Don't Forget

When mailing information to investors, always include a response mechanism, such as a business reply card or toll-free number. A couple of interested investors contacting you can be worth as many as 500 cold calls.

How To Get Started With A DPO

A direct public offering is not for the faint of heart. It takes time, money and persistence.

Entrepreneur Michael Flynn at Flynn Labs talked to more than 700 potential investors in the course of finishing his DPO. In addition, he spent more than $100,000 in the process. Entrepreneurs must evaluate whether they have the chutzpah to see a DPO through. If you think you do:

A Good Deal

A good accountant can be one of your strongest allies in a direct public offering. Make sure yours has experience in this area.

- **Ensure that you have a way to corral your affinity groups.** Direct public offerings don't work well without a large group of investors that has some sort of connection with the company, its product or its service. A publishing company, for instance, not only has a large base of customers but also has a lot of information about them and can easily contact them by mail or e-mail, through its own media, or via the telephone. On the other hand, in a somewhat frustrating arrangement, successful restaurants have a steady stream of customers but almost no information on them.

  For companies facing this dilemma, salvation depends on whether or there is a way to access rudimentary information about members of the affinity group, and, once accessed, whether the affinity is strong enough to make a deal. For instance, a restaurateur can easily purchase the names of people who have dined at fine restaurants. So what? Just because someone has dined at a restaurant doesn't mean he or she has is an affinity for a specific restaurant.

  However, there are lots of ways a company can find information about people who would be naturally interested in them. Flynn, for instance, was able to buy the names of people who had purchased homeopathic medicines from list brokers. Other possible scenarios:

  1. A pet-care company might fruitfully prospect among the members of PETA, or People for the Ethical Treatment of Animals.
  2. An environmental-services company might pitch the members of the Sierra Club.

3. A company making sailboats could send direct mail to the readers of *Sail* magazine.

- **Hire an accountant.** If you don't have one, get one. If you do have one, start negotiating for some extra work. To raise money, you need a set of financial statements, period. Internally generated financial statements are helpful, but to bring in outside investors, you must have financial statements prepared by an outsider as well.

Even though many companies have long-standing relationships with accountants, the production of a full set of financial statements, with notes, is often the kind of thing that falls through the cracks. This can be debilitating when you're talking to outside investors.

The beauty of most direct public offerings is that they do not require audited financial statements. If your plan is to start in the lower depths of the market and eventually "graduate" to the Nasdaq stock market or the American or New York Stock Exchange, you will eventually need them anyway. (To understand the various levels of review an accountant offers and the kind of financings that require them, see "On The Level" on page 173.)

Finally, owners of start-up businesses often think they don't need financial statements. Here's why, in most cases they do. First, if there has been some kind of lump-sum investment either from the founder or some other investor—a strong selling point for meeting with new investors—the financial statements will irrefutably document its existence.

Second, if the founder is forgoing salary he hopes to recapture when the company gets on its feet, the financial statements are the perfect place to document the company's growing liability to its founder. To raise such an issue three or five years down the road and out of the blue

Taking Action

Not only do you need financial statements, but you must also be able to discuss their content with authority and clarity. Try a little question-and-answer role-playing with your CPA before talking to investors.

On The Level

Here are the different levels of financial statements that companies should consider, according to Steven Mayer, a partner with accounting firm Goldstein Golub Kessler & Co. in New York City. "First there's a compilation, which is where the accounting firm creates financial statements out of the figures that are supplied by management. In some cases, the accounting firm simply retypes numbers supplied to them by the company and might suggest that the numbers 'appear' reasonable," Mayer says.

The next level is generally known as an analytical review. "In addition to compiling the numbers that are supplied by management, some testing is done," Mayer reports. The accountants want to ensure that everything lines up properly. "For example, if sales are up and commissions are down, that's a signal that something may be wrong with the way the numbers were put together."

The most intensive review is the audit. "Here," says Mayer, "in addition to all the testing, third-party assurances are given that the figures presented are accurate." This is why an audit takes so long. For example, if a firm reports it has, say, 25 microcomputers for sale in its inventory, the auditor will want to count them. If they say they have 25,000, the auditor will want to count the average number of computers stacked on a palette.

Mayer says the cost of an audit might start at $7,500. But that would be for a service business, which has no inventory to verify. If there are lots of inventory and receivables, Mayer says, there's almost no fee ceiling.

There's also a time commitment. First, the accounting firm camps out in your conference room for a couple of weeks. But because it's an audit, and because they issue an opinion and there is a great deal of liability behind that opinion, the accountants might be more conservative on certain matters, such as recognizing revenue, than you are likely to be. "So," Mayer says, "you often spend [a lot of] time negotiating."

might strain relations between a company and its shareholders. Putting items such as forgone salary or loans to the company on the table at the outset can save trouble down the road. And there's no better way to put them on the table than by putting them in a set of financial statements.

By now the message should be clear: Without financial statements, you won't get far along the path to raising money.

Taking Action

Purchase the book *Direct Public Offerings* (Sourcebooks). Author Drew Field offers the most comprehensive step-by-step guide to structuring a direct public offering, from assembling the team of professionals to launching a direct marketing effort.

- **Hire an attorney.** Securities laws are perhaps the most complicated laws in the land. There are three reasons for this: They are antiquated, they exist at the state and federal level, and they are carried out by perhaps the most tenacious of all bureaucrats.

Even if you decide to take advantage of the many exemptions from state and federal securities laws, you still need an attorney to make sure you are in compliance with these exemptions. And, of course, if you structure your offering so that state and federal securities laws come into play, hiring an attorney is also standard operating procedure.

Shop Talk

Did you ever wonder why, at the dawn of the 21st century, most of the significant securities laws were written in 1933 and 1934? These laws were put in place by Congress to prevent another stock market crash like the one in 1929, and today, they still represent the great divide between commercial and investment banking.

According to Flynn Labs' owner, "It's important that you seek an attorney with not just experience in securities matters, but with some facility in the direct public offering arena as well."

As for the attorneys, according to Joel Marks, a director of corporate finance for J.W. Charles & Company/CSG, an investment banking and brokerage firm concentrating on emerging growth companies, the attorney you hire should have a minimum experience of five deals. If these offerings are more than five years old, then it makes sense to find another attorney or, if you can afford it, bring in co-counsel, he adds.

In addition to experience, Marks says, look at the firm's Martindale Hubbell ratings. Martindale Hubbell, a publishing firm, produces the most prominent directory of law firms in the United States. Rankings, according to Marks, have a Legal Ability component (A for preeminent, B for very high and C for fair to high) and a General Recommendation component (V for very high, or unrated).

Chapter 17

Reverse Mergers

The Scoop

Definition Or Explanation: In a reverse merger, a privately held company buys a publicly traded, but usually dormant, company. By doing so, the private company becomes public.

Appropriate For: Reverse mergers are appropriate for companies that do not need capital quickly and that will experience enough growth to reach a size and scale at which they can succeed as a public entity. Minimum sales and earnings to reach this plateau are $20 million and $2 million, respectively.

Supply: There are thousands of dormant public companies, sometimes called shells, that might be viable merger candidates. By becoming public, a company becomes a more attractive investment opportunity to a wider range of investors. The supply of equity capital is more abundant for public companies than for private ones.

Best Use: Reverse mergers can be used to finance anything from product development to working capital needs. However, they work best for companies that do not need capital quickly. Not that reverse mergers take long to consummate, but the initial transaction is usually just the halfway point. Once public, a company generally must still find capital. Also, this financing technique works better for companies that will experience substantial enough growth to develop into a "real" public company.

Cost: Expensive. Compared with a conventional initial public offering (IPO), fees and expenses are not that high for a reverse merger. Deals can be completed for $50,000 to $100,000, which might be 25 percent of the out-of-pocket costs that come with a full-blown IPO. In the process of making the deal, however, the acquiring company might give up 10 percent to 20 percent of its equity. This is very expensive. After all, it means a company is surrendering ownership just for the privilege of being public. More equity will probably disappear when the company actually raises money.

Ease Of Acquisition: Difficult but not as difficult as a conventional initial public offering. Perhaps the most challenging aspect of a reverse merger is trying to create a real trading market for the company's shares once the deal is done.

Funds Typically Available: $500,000 and greater.

The Reality Of The Situation

Though initial public offerings (IPOs) are perhaps the most sought-after form of financing, the fact is, surprisingly few companies can hope to successfully negotiate their way through the tortuous process.

This truth leads to a nasty little Catch-22. Many promising small companies cannot obtain funding because they are private. However, without funding, they can't hope to grow to the size and scale that would allow them to go public.

Why is being a private company anathema to the capital-formation process? Because many investors believe that even if the company does well, without an exit strategy for the investors to get their money out of the company, they will never realize a substantial return on their investment. There might be some merit to this thinking. However, the other side of the coin is that the company, which is patiently funded so it is able to realize its true potential, has numerous options for rewarding its shareholders.

A Case In Point

Perhaps the best use of a reverse merger was made by LVA Group. The company's founder, Jerry Stephens, already had a profitable hospital-management business. But he saw an opportunity in free-standing centers offering laser refractive eye surgery to correct myopia, also known as nearsightedness. However, the process was awaiting FDA approval, according to Stephens. "The United States was a multibillion-dollar market."

Shop Talk

Investors frequently talk about "exit strategies," a fancy way to say "cashing out." Specifically, once investors put money into a company, they want to know how they can get their money back—at a profit.

To get ready, the company laid plans for financing the roll-out of centers in the United States and bought part of a laser surgery center in Toronto, where the process was already legal.

Considering financing alternatives, Stephens believed he could cobble together an IPO but concluded that it was highly unlikely for a new and untested concept. What if FDA approval were delayed?

But with a reverse merger, Stephens only had to convince the controlling shareholder of a public shell that the reward was worth the risk. And the controlling shareholder of a shell company Stephens was talking with happened to agree.

In the resulting deal, he bought stock in the shell company in exchange for LVA Group's assets. At the end of the day, Stephens had a majority position in the shell company, and the shell company had the operating assets of his company. The public company then changed its name to LVA-Vision to reflect the deal and the future course of the business.

Don't Forget

A reverse merger is not an end in itself. It is a technique or tool that makes a company more financeable.

Two months after the deal, the FDA approved the laser refractive procedure used by LVA, and Stephens was off and running. Almost immediately, he raised nearly $500,000 privately. He also used his publicly traded common stock to buy the remaining interest in the Toronto facility. The private capital he'd raised, combined with favorable lease terms on surgical laser equipment, helped Stephens roll out seven new surgery centers in the South and Midwest. After a brief honeymoon on the National Association of Securities Dealers' Bulletin Board, LVA-Vision moved up to Nasdaq's SmallCap.

In a climaxing deal, LVA used its stock to purchase a chain of refractive surgery centers from another company. To acquire the company, LVA issued several million of its own shares and in return got the other company's 19 wholly owned and operated refractive surgery centers around the country. As a final bonus, the company that LVA bought had $10 million in the bank when the deal was inked.

Today, LVA-Vision is the largest provider of vision treatment procedures in the United States.

The Benefits Of Going In Reverse

Following are some of the primary benefits entrepreneurs and their companies can reap with a reverse merger transaction:

- **Imperviousness to market conditions:** Conventional IPOs are risky for companies to undertake because the deal depends on market conditions over which senior management has absolutely no control. That is, if the market is off, the underwriter may pull the offering. The market doesn't even need to plunge wholesale. If a company in registration participates in an industry that's making unfavorable headlines, investors may shy away from the deal, causing it to run out of gas on the runway.

    But with a reverse merger, the deal rests on whether the people who control the shell like the

A Good Deal

Even if the market crashes while you're working on your reverse merger, it probably won't kill your deal. For the shell company with few assets and little or no story to tell, a good merger is good news and worth pursuing, no matter what market conditions are.

private company and desire to be acquired by it. Market conditions have almost no bearing on the situation.

- **Compressed timetable:** Regular initial public offerings can drag on for a year or more, from when the idea pops into the chief executive's head until he or she actually gets a check. Unfortunately, when a company transitions from an entrepreneurial venture to a real public company fit for outside ownership, senior management's time is at its most valuable. Time spent in seemingly endless meetings and drafting sessions can have a disastrous effect on the growth upon which the offering is predicated, and even nullify it. In addition, during the many months it takes to put together an IPO, market conditions can deteriorate, closing the "IPO window" on a company.

  By contrast, conditions permitting—which means, among other things, two interested and willing parties—a reverse merger can be completed in 45 days.

- **Reduced expenses:** For a real IPO, it can cost as much as $200,000 just to get a preliminary prospectus on the street. To actually bring the deal to the closing table, the costs increase. A reverse merger, however, can be done for $50,000 to $100,000.

- **Corporate income tax shelter:** Many shell companies have what is known as a tax-loss carryforward. This means that a loss incurred in previous years can be applied to income in future years. When this occurs, the future income is sheltered from income taxes. Since most active public companies become dormant public companies through a string of losses, or at least one large one,

Theoretical Exercise Of Warrants To Raise $2.4 Million For A Newly Public Company

Exercise right to purchase 300,000 additional shares of stock at $8/share

Private company

Payment of $2.4 million

Stock certificates for 300,000 common shares

Public investors with warrants

there's a better than average chance the shell you meet will offer this opportunity.

(As discussed in the next section, however, the shell company's previous history can rub off on you, which turns out to be one of the biggest drawbacks to reverse mergers.)

Don't Forget
In addition to fees, a reverse merger will also cost you precious points of equity in your company. The shareholders of the public company get a stake, and the deal makers who control the shell get a stake as well.

- **More ways to raise money:**
  The primary reason to do a reverse merger is the greater number of financing options that become available to companies once they are public. Some of these include:

  1. The issuance of additional shares in a secondary offering.

  2. Exercise of warrants. Warrants are options that give the holder the right to purchase additional shares in a company at predetermined prices. When many shareholders with warrants—which a public company can easily issue—exercise their option to purchase additional shares, the company receives an infusion of capital, as shown in the chart on page 182.

  3. Private Offerings. Many, many more investors will step up to the plate for a private offering of shares once they know there is some sort of mechanism in place for them to resell their shares if the company succeeds. Most investors realize that even a successful company may not be able to go public if market conditions are off. But a company that is already public . . . that's a different story. If it succeeds, there is a greater likelihood of developing a market for its common stock that accurately represents the company and lets investors sell their shares.

The Drawbacks Of A Reverse Merger

Reverse mergers aren't for everyone, however. There are several drawbacks to this financing technique. Among the disadvantages:

Theory Into Practice

In the diagram below, the hypothetical public company has 1 million common shares outstanding prior to any sort of transaction with a private company. Of these 1 million shares, half are owned by public investors and half are owned by the person or people who control the public company. Once a deal is struck, for the private company to acquire the public one, it might be consummated in this three-step process:

1. The public company issues 9 million shares of common stock to the person or people who own the private company. What is the ownership structure of the public company? There are now 10 million shares outstanding. Of these, 9 million, or 90 percent of the company, are held by the owner of the private company. Another 500,000 shares, or 5 percent ownership of the company, are held by the person or people who controlled the public company. And the public investors hold the remaining 500,000 shares, or 5 percent of the company. Note that prior to merger, the public owned 50 percent of the public company, but after the merger, it owned just 5 percent.

2. The 9 million shares of common stock are usually issued to the shareholders of the private company in exchange for something. In most reverse merger transactions, the private company: a) contributes all of its assets to the public company, b) issues shares of its own to the public company, or c) buys the shares outright from the public company at a nominal price.

3. The public company then changes its name, usually to the name used by the private company, to reflect the change in it business.

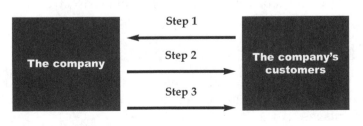

- **Image:** Reverse mergers have accumulated their share of controversy over the years for a few reasons. First, most reverse mergers start with dormant public companies. Usually, they fell into dormancy because of failure in their line of business. As a result, there may be an angry group of shareholders somewhere in the deal. Second, the chances of some irregularity occurring in the trading, most likely unknown to the company, are high. That's because most reverse transactions initially trade on the Pink Sheets or the OTC Bulletin Board, the least regulated tiers of the market.

- **Unknown shareholders:** At the end of the day, the private company that acquires a public one is left with an unfamiliar shareholder base with which it has no previous interaction. These shareholders can place significant downward pressure on a company's stock by continually selling their shares as a new trading market develops. Also, creditors or other parties that suffered because of the failure of the predecessor company can come out of the woodwork and make claims against the new management.

- **Indirect route to capital:** Reverse mergers represent a way to make a company financeable without actually financing it. Though they are theoretically quick and easy, like any securities transaction, reverse mergers contain enough wrinkles to draw out the process. But in most instances, just consummating the reverse merger transaction is only the halfway point in a company's pilgrimage to growth capital. When it's done, the company must still go out and beat the bushes for the cash it needs.

- **Difficulty becoming a real public company:** An exciting private company may have taken control of dormant public company, but that doesn't mean other investors will sit up

Shop Talk
The controlling shareholders of a shell corporation will most likely insist on owning a small stake in the deal going forward. This "trailing interest" is simply a cost of doing business.

and take notice. In fact, the only investors who tend to care about the change of control are those who invested in the original company. Often, their interest is mercenary: They simply want to know when the new company will succeed to the point where they can recoup their money.

As a result of this relative obscurity, most reverse mergers find that their stock doesn't trade much. Moreover, company executives and principals have a hard time attracting investors to their stock to create the kind of trading and liquidity that is the benchmark of a real public company.

Next Steps For A Reverse Merger

If a reverse merger still sounds like a good idea to you, here are the steps you need to take:

- **Find a shell company.** You can find one by contacting the usual suspects. As a first stop, ask an attorney. Every metropolitan area has a law firm with a securities practice. Often, these firms have a dormant public company sitting on one of the partners' bookshelves.

  Another alternative is an accountant. People who control shell companies tend to keep the financial statements, such as they are, up to date. This brings accountants into the loop. Like attorneys, they know where the bodies are.

  Another source is financing consultants. In fact, many actually have a couple of shell corporations and, upon request, can manufacture a clean public shell. A made-to-order shell without the baggage of a business failure in its background can sometimes be the way to go.

  But there's often a cost involved. That is, you will most likely end up with the financing consultants as minority shareholders in the new company, holding between 2 percent and 5 percent. However, in almost any reverse merger transaction, the principals of the shell company keep a small equity position in the company going forward. Therefore, this surrender of equity is simply a cost of doing business.

- **Devise your financing strategy.** As was mentioned several times already in this chapter, a reverse merger is an indirect route to raising capital. Entrepreneurs must first consider how additional capital will be raised after the deal is done.

As was mentioned above, a public company can issue and exercise warrants. Some public shell companies already have warrants issued and outstanding; some have previously registered the underlying common stock shares with the Securities and Exchange Commission—which is a significant benefit. This is much easier and much more valuable to a company that wants to raise capital with warrants. If the newly public company must create and issue warrants, the road to getting them exercised will be trickier but still possible. In short, exercising warrants where the underlying common shares are not registered requires the assistance of a brokerage firm and must occur in a state where there is no registration requirement for issuance of shares of up to $1 million.

Don't Forget

If you need all the bells and whistles of a true public company, you can spend as much time and money on the back end of a reverse merger as you would on the front end of a conventional initial public offering.

If you are going the private-offering route (i.e., an offering sold to select individuals rather than through a sale directly to the public at large), the deal must be carefully structured. Specifically, the amount of stock owned by investors that the new owners do not know and cannot influence must be diminished so that a stable quote can be established. Usually, this is done by reducing the percentage of the total number of shares these investors own (see "Theory Into Practice" on page 184). By doing so, as an added incentive, the private investors can be offered stock at a discount to the market price.

For example, if the stock costs $7, private investors are offered the opportunity to purchase common stock at $5. This incentive evaporates when sell orders flood the market and the market price of the stock drops to $5.

Of course, smart investors know they can't simply load up on $5 stock in a private placement and turn

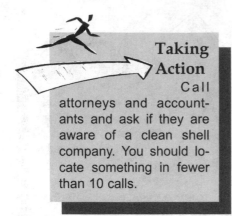

Taking Action
Call attorneys and accountants and ask if they are aware of a clean shell company. You should locate something in fewer than 10 calls.

around and sell it on the public market at $7. There simply aren't that many buyers to support that kind of selling. But the point is, it's much easier to sell common stock to investors at $5 in a private offering when the market price is $7 than it is to sell common stock privately at $5 when the market price is $4.

- **Clean up your act.** Unfortunately, there's a stigma attached to reverse mergers. LVA-Vision's Stephens, who used the technique to brilliant effect, said that although it worked for his company, "there's definitely another side to these deals. If it wasn't for my long-standing reputation in the medical community, our deal might have been perceived differently." Largely, the bad rap stems from the fact that reverse mergers are not understood, Stephens says.

  Entrepreneurs contemplating such a transaction can and should take steps to elevate the profile of their "new" company. Specifically:

1. **Hire a national accounting firm.** One of the reasons the Big Five fees are high is because they inspire a lot of comfort among investors, traders, and regulators. If you saved a lot on fees at the front end, this might be worth investing in on the back end.

2. **Hire a prestigious law firm.** It's almost a certainty that the attorney who initially helps you with your reverse merger transaction, if he or she is an expert in these kinds of deals, will not be with a prestigious downtown law firm. However, after the offering is completed, you should consider retaining one of these firms. Why? When deciding whether to get involved in your offering, many investors and brokers will judge your firm by the company it keeps. An unknown law firm makes a neutral to negative impression. But a well-known and powerful law firm sends an unmistakable message.

- **Start with a clean shell.** As was mentioned, many shells are created for the express purpose of merging with a private company. These shells have no predecessor entities and, as a result, little baggage in the way of a business failure or other skeletons in the closets.

- **Check your greed.** The great rallying cry of the 1980s, popularized by the Hollywood oily takeover artist Gordon Gekko, "Greed is good," doesn't apply with a reverse merger. It's possible to structure a reverse merger so that at the end of the day, the public owns 2 percent of the company and the remaining 98 percent is controlled by the owners of the private company that acquired the shell. Unfortunately, there's almost no incentive for any other investors to become involved if the only people who truly benefit are the insiders. The lesson is, if you plan to involve the public with the intention of engaging in a truly symbiotic relationship, you simply must leave some value on the table.

In many ways, the reputation of reverse mergers is similar to the notoriety junk bonds had during the 1980s. Junk was used by corporate raiders to buy companies and break them up. But junk bonds also nurtured an entire generation of exciting growth companies and had a material and profound impact on the economy in terms of wealth and employment.

Remember, a reverse merger is simply a technique. The ultimate quality of the deal depends on how wisely it is deployed.

Chapter 18

Initial Public Offerings

The Scoop

Definition Or Explanation: An initial public offering (IPO) is the sale of equity in a company, generally in the form of shares of common stock, through an investment banking firm. These shares trade on a recognized stock market. For smaller, emerging companies, that will probably be the Nasdaq SmallCap market or the Nasdaq National Market System.

Appropriate For: Start-up to established companies. Start-up companies must demonstrate the potential to develop into profitable enterprises that will deliver significant annual increases in sales and earnings. Established companies must also demonstrate significant future growth potential. In either case, minimum earnings growth potential is 20 percent per year, and the company should be able to achieve a valuation (total shares outstanding times their price) of at least $100 million to be truly successful as a publicly held corporation.

Supply: Theoretically abundant. In the United States, investors pour billions of dollars into the equity markets each month, and several billion dollars find their way into smaller initial public offerings. However, for conventional IPOs, the true supply is much smaller and is ultimately governed by the number and willingness of investment banking firms to underwrite the offering.

Best Use: Financing the expansion of manufacturing or service capacity or marketing activities that have an immediate impact on earnings. Also to provide a company with increasing sales, as a layer of working capital to fund growing inventory (if there is any) or accounts receivable. IPO funds can be used to finance research and development, but stock prices tend to decline during prolonged periods of product development, which in turn generates a new set of challenges for founders or senior management.

Cost: Perhaps the most expensive way to finance a company. Not only will an initial public offering cost a significant chunk of the company's equity—no less than 25 percent and perhaps a great deal more—but fees and expenses can climb to as much as 20 percent of the deal. For a $5 million offering, that's $1 million.

Ease Of Acquisition: Unreasonably difficult. Going public is one of the most difficult transactions. Perhaps 750 to 1,000 companies go public each year in offerings underwritten by investment banking firms. Many more try but fail during the process.

Funds Typically Available: $5 million and greater.

Why Go Public?

There are many benefits to going public. But those aside, what are the strategic reasons a company should consider an initial public offering? Here are some:

- A company cannot reasonably expect to raise venture capital from institutional funds.
- A company needs to raise more than $5 million. At this point, stalking angel investors can be too time consuming.
- A company needs a significant amount of permanent capital it won't have to pay back to a bank or other lender.
- A company seeks growth through acquisitions, and needs a "currency" other than cash to attract and consummate deals.

In addition to strategic considerations, being a public corporation often confers the following benefits:

- A public company has direct access to the capital markets and can raise more capital by issuing additional stock in a secondary offering. Public companies can also more easily raise funds privately.
- Public companies can use their common stock to attract and retain good employees.
- Being a public company is more prestigious than being a private company.
- Going public provides owners and founders an exit for selling their ownership holdings in the business.
- Public companies are worth more than private companies. The public companies that compose the Standard & Poor's 500 are valued at about 17 times their earnings (i.e., a company earning $1 million would be worth $17 million), while private companies are typically bought and sold at one to five times cash flow.
- Going public makes you rich—at least on paper. And make no mistake, none of the lawyers, accountants or investment bankers involved in the process gets the least bit squeamish about their client's desire for riches. After all, your success means their success.

For entrepreneurs who want to go public, their first, most important, fundamental task is to find an investment banking firm that will underwrite the offering. Once that task is completed, with a little luck, a strong market and a lot of determination, everything else will fall into place. Accordingly, the bal-

Terms Of Endearment

Throughout this chapter, reference is continually made to "going public." In the context of this chapter, the words refer to a conventional initial public offering, which is underwritten by an investment banking firm. After the offering, it trades on a recognized stock market such as Nasdaq's SmallCap or the Nasdaq National Market System, the American Stock Exchange, the New York Stock Exchange or any of the regional stock exchanges.

ance of this chapter is dedicated to assisting entrepreneurs in finding the investment banker who can do their deal.

Broad Brush: Finding The Investment Banker

As times go, 1997 was a fairly typical year for IPOs: 624 offerings raised $43 billion.

But like any other year, a select few firms dominated the business. In fact, just 25 firms did 408 of the offerings that accounted for $39 billion of the $43 billion raised that year. The average-sized offering for the 408 deals done by the 25 dominant firms was $95 million ($39 billion/408 offerings). Going back a little further in the history books, the average size of the 545 deals done by the larger and national firms during 1996 was $81 million ($44.6 billion/545 offerings).

However, published rankings do not reveal who is doing all the other deals. If you are considering an initial public offering, you must find out. During 1997, for instance, these other deals represented 35 percent of the IPO market. More important, their average size, $19.9 million, is more in tune with the needs of a wider variety of entrepreneurs. And to show that history does provide a guide in this regard, in 1996, these other deals represented 40 percent of the IPO market, and their average size was $16 million.

> **Shop Talk**
> Micro-cap companies are those in which the total shares outstanding times the price equals $100 million or less. Some money managers use a benchmark of $250 million to define micro-caps.

What do these numbers mean? If you are trying to raise between $5 million and $15 million through an initial public offering—the range this book was designed to cover—the would-be underwriter who will do your deal is probably unknown to you at this point. The sad fact is, unless you are a student of the business, if you recognize the name of an investment banking firm, it's probably too big to show any interest in your initial public offering.

The problem comes down to money. Your tiny IPO won't generate the requisite level of fees to make any meaningful impact on the investment bank's bottom line. And, with little trading profits, it simply doesn't make sense to provide research coverage.

If you are doing a smaller IPO, and in Wall Street parlance, anything less than $20 million is little (in some rarefied circles, anything below $100 million is little), you need to find an investment banking firm that also specializes in smaller IPOs.

Pilgrim's Progress To An IPO

Here is a typical timetable for an initial public offering from when an entrepreneur commits to the process to when he collects the big check at the closing table.

Week 1: Conduct organizational meeting.

Week 5: Distribute Securities and Exchange Commission (SEC) registration statement; additional drafting sessions.

Week 6: Distribute second draft of registration statement; additional drafting session.

Week 7: Distribute third draft of registration statement; additional drafting session.

Week 8: File registration statement with the Securities and Exchange Commission; begin preparation of road-show presentations; begin getting clearances in states where the offering is to be sold.

Week 12: Get comments from SEC on registrations statement.

Week 13: File first amendment to registration statement with SEC, addressing comments. Prepare and distribute preliminary prospectus; commence road-show meetings.

Week 15: SEC declares offering effective; company and underwriter agree on final price; prepare, file and distribute final prospectus.

Week 16: Close and deliver offering proceeds.

Fine-Tooth Comb: Finding Your Investment Banker

To find the right investment banker, you must conduct some research. Specifically, you must discern which firms in the past two years have consistently done initial public offerings similar in size and scope to the one that fit your needs.

There are three good sources of historical information on initial public offerings:

- www.ipocentral.com
- *Going Public: The IPO Reporter,* published by IDD Enterprises, LPs in New York City
- *The SEC New Registrations Report,* published by CCH Washington Service Bureau in Washington, DC

Going Public: The IPO Reporter is expensive but can be reviewed at any corporate or public library that subscribes. *The SEC New Registrations Report,* also expensive, can be found in libraries as well. Sometimes the circulation director at these publications will tell you which libraries subscribe to the publication. Barring those two resources, the Web site ipocentral.com is free and can be viewed by anyone with a computer and access to the Internet.

From a qualitative standpoint, *Going Public* is the best source. *The SEC New Registrations Report* and ipocentral.com, though good, are oriented toward initial public offering filings rather than the process at large. In addition, *Going Public* provides pre- and post-offering data, which are necessary to evaluate the skills and expertise of the investment bankers who appear to be appropriate candidates.

Whichever source you use, however, your research will identify 50 to 75 investment banking firms that appear to underwrite initial public offerings similar in size to the deal you want, namely $5 million to $15 million. Of these

Don't Forget

The so-called window for IPOs can open and shut without warning. To take full advantage of openings when they occur, you need good financial statements and an ongoing dialogue with an investment banker.

firms, the following algorithm will indicate which are the best candidates to pursue and which might be better left alone.

- Investment bankers with one IPO to their credit over the past two years are probably not good candidates. Often, an investment banking firm makes an initial public offering not because it wants to but because it must. Or the low IPO count may be attributable to the fact that the one IPO that turned up in your research was a disaster, and the firm won't return to that well. Or, and unfortunately this happens all too often, the underwriter may have gone out of business since the IPO, due to events that may not be unrelated. Whichever of the above set of circumstances applies, underwriters with an IPO count this low are probably not worth your effort to pursue, unless the firm happens to be in your own backyard.

- Investment bankers that have done one IPO per year over the past two years may be viable candidates. Granted, one deal per year is low, but it also says a number of good things. First, it means the firm can put all of its resources behind the offering to get it done. Second, it means that once the offering is trading, the firm won't be stretched so thin it cannot support the deal.

- However, the investment banking firm that does just one IPO a year is probably pretty picky about its deals. Look at the thumbnail financials of the companies the firm underwrote. If:

  1. all of their underwritings are for profitable companies, or

  2. all of their underwritings are for companies in one industry, or

Don't Forget

Filing a registration statement and going on a road show is just the tip of the iceberg. Many companies spend a year finding an investment banker, negotiating with him or her, and drafting the registration statement to be filed.

Taking Action

Plot the share prices of public companies similar to yours over the past six months. An investment banker's interest in meeting with you will be positively correlated to the trend in these share prices.

3. all of their underwritings are for companies with substantial revenues, and you possess none of these characteristics, this probably isn't a match.

- Underwriters that have completed four to eight deals over the past two years are good candidates for your IPO. One or two deals per quarter is a brisk clip for a small investment banking firm. In fact, it's a pace that, in most cases, will ultimately destabilize the firm—a factor you as the company must keep in mind if you progress to the negotiation stage. But business risks aside, a firm doing four to eight IPOs a year is clearly looking for deals and is probably worth pursuing. Keep in mind, however, the principals of these firms are always on overload. Second, it is almost unheard of for a firm to take any interest in deals that simply come in off the street. You must get a face-to-face introduction, which is discussed below.

Getting Introductions

Even though your research may have helped you identify the underwriters you believe are the best candidates to take you public, that doesn't mean they want to hear from you. According to John Lane, an investment banker in Westport, Connecticut, with 20 years of experience, "Most people in our business will not even look at a business plan that has not been in some way personally referred to them."

Lane's comment underscores a tough reality for entrepreneurs: If you are not plugged into the financial community, your row is a tougher one to hoe. His insight also helps explain why, if investment bankers

Taking Action

Purchase the membership directory of the Regional Investment Bankers Association. This trade group, based in Charleston, South Carolina, consists primarily of boutique investment banking firms focusing on IPOs of $5 million to $15 million. The membership directory offers contact names, telephone numbers and other pertinent information about investment bankers. To order, call (803) 577-2000. However, don't cold-call the listed firms. Find a way to get an introduction first.

National Accounting Firms Ranked By IPO Offerings

Company	Dollar Volume of IPOs	Numbers of IPOs 1997
Ernst & Young	8,317.7	121
KPMG Peat Marwick	8,312.9	82
Arthur Andersen & Co.	7,383.4	118
Deloitte & Touche	5,516.6	61
Price Waterhouse*	5,244.3	67
Coopers & Lybrand*	4,096.6	61

Source: Securities Data Co.
*Coopers & Lybrand and Price Waterhouse merged operations in 1998.

are so choosy about their deals, so many incredibly unworthy companies make it through the IPO gauntlet.

You can be plugged into a referral by making a connection between yourself and the underwriter. Listed are some ways to do this:

- **Accounting firms:** If you are considering an initial public offering, experts frequently advise hiring a national accounting firm. National firms do the audit work for most IPOs (as the above chart illustrates). And because IPOs are driven by financial issues, it also means that the accountants at these firms know investment bankers and can make the kind of introductions that will get your business plan to the top of the consideration pile.

    But it's not just the national accounting firms that do IPOs and know investment bankers. Any accounting firm that has handled six or more IPOs in one year for companies that look like yours is worth talking to. They can give you the kind of introduction to an investment banker that might just pan out. Of course, no accountant will ask an underwriter he or she knows to look at a deal simply because you call and ask them to. There must be a quid pro quo in the form of a working relationship. But working toward an IPO can be the foundation of that relationship, as long as you are paying for services along the way.

Finally, your existing accountant is worth asking about other accountants he or she knows who specialize in IPOs. This might eventually mean a parting of the ways with your accountant, but if an IPO is beyond the sphere of his or her practice, you may have outgrown your trusted advisor.

- **Attorneys:** The only professionals who probably rival accountants in terms of the investment banker's mind share are lawyers. Every financing transaction, whether an IPO, a venture capital financing or a fair-sized term loan, has two attorneys. One works for the capital seeker, one for the capital provider. Consequently, capital providers, such as investment banks, often view lawyers as valuable counselors. As a result, a referral from an attorney can make an investment banker pay attention to your business plan.

There are several ways to find attorneys who specialize in initial public offerings:

1. *Going Public: The IPO Reporter* discloses the underwriter and *c*ompany counsel for every IPO. A single pass through a year of back issues will generate a fairly comprehensive list.

2. *The SEC New Registrations Report* lists the attorneys for every initial public offering filed during any given month.

3. CCH Washington Service Bureau also publishes an annual report, called the *Law Firm Activity Report*, which provides a detailed listing of IPO law firms.

Like an accountant, an attorney will not open his or her phone list simply because you ask. You can only seek a referral in the context of an engagement. But the engagement can be light, such as the review of issues relevant to an

Shop Talk

In a "firm commitment" IPO, the underwriter agrees to buy shares from a company and resell them. In a "best efforts" IPO, the underwriter agrees only to try to sell the shares to investors. If, after using its best efforts to place the shares, the underwriter fails, there is no IPO.

upcoming IPO. These might relate to patents, employment agreements, covenants on bank loans or client contracts. With a common objective between you and your attorney—sorting out some important business issues so that your company can pursue a public offering—referrals to an investment banker become a natural, proper event.

Selling The Underwriter

When you meet with an underwriter, it's likely that you will be expected to make a formal presentation. (See Chapter 23 for advice on how to prepare and present your business plan.) However, in addition to presenting your company, there are other important points to keep in mind to ensure that your first discussion with the investment banker is not your last.

- **Demonstrate that you can drive the deal home.** Investment bankers know how difficult an IPO is. Consequently, they won't bet on a weak horse. You must be able to demonstrate that if a mountain is in your way, you will move it.

- **Don't negotiate fees.** If you are contemplating an IPO of $15 million or less, the investment banking firm will take the maximum allowable compensation by law. No amount of negotiating will change this fact, and it may even strain the relationship.

- **Show your warts.** If there's something lurking in your background, such as a bankruptcy or a legal problem, it's better to disclose it upfront. If it comes out during the course of the underwriter's due diligence, with the resulting perception that you tried to conceal it, whatever deal you thought you had with the underwriter is dead.

- **Prove your salesmanship.** Your would-be underwriter must have a sense of confidence that you can excite others about your company and its growth prospects. After

A Good Deal

Many underwriters will provide companies with bridge financing to help them finance the costs of the IPO. Bridge financing can be a godsend, but if the deal fails, the company must still pay the bridge investors back.

all, the underwriter depends on other underwriters, brokers and traders to make the offering a success. If you look like the kind of person who will put everyone to sleep, that presents an insurmountable challenge to your investment banker.

- **Don't be too noble.** IPOs are a game of greed. And like everyone else in the deal, you want to get rich. Trying to hide this fact only raises doubts about your character.

- **Show that you are committed to the company**. Investment bankers are wary of promoters who only want to take a company public and then move on. Granted, few people are capable of such a feat, but even the appearance of being such a character undermines you during your initial meeting with the investment banker.

- **Don't be ridiculous.** Your business plan might suggest that sales will be $200 million in three years, but few companies achieve such meteoric growth. Investment bankers know this. They also know, at the very least, if you are smart enough to pull off such a feat, you must be at least smart enough to raise more than the $5 million, $10 million or $15 million such action requires.

- **Forget about selling your shares in the IPO.** In all but the most established companies, a founder selling his shares in the initial public offering is unheard of. The underwriter simply can't sell a deal if the founders aren't tied to the company. And if you are a millionaire the day the company goes public, you are not longer tied to the company.

- **Be gracious.** Investment bankers typically say no. They rarely utter the word "no," however; instead they simply say "not at this point." If you have done a poor job at targeting, though, they will in fact say no, or simply never return your phone calls. But those who say not yet, ironically, really seem to mean it. Often, an initial public offering takes so long to shop that many of the details that turned the underwriter off at the first meeting—no profits, no sales, incomplete management, unproven product—fix themselves over time. And when fixed, you can go back to the investment bankers you have met along the way and ask again. Unless, of course, you were less than gracious after the first meeting and walked out in a huff.

Shop Talk

If you go public and trade on the Nasdaq stock market, your investment banker will be your primary "market maker" alongside other brokerage firms. The market maker matches buyers and sellers and helps maintain an orderly trading market. The market makers are perhaps a public company's most important constituency after it goes public.

Common Deal Breakers

Most companies that attempt an initial public offering fail. The most dramatic failures occur when a company is in registration, getting ready to take the leap, and market conditions deteriorate, shutting the IPO window—tight.

In truth, however, those are the lucky ones because they actually succeeded in filing their offering. Most initial public offerings die on the drawing board, which is the period of time between when an investment banker issues a letter of intent and the day the offering is filed with the Securities and Exchange Commission. Following are the top 10 reasons offerings die on the drawing board:

1. The investment banker tells the company founders they must lock up their shares and agree not to sell them for a period of 24 to 36 months. The founders refuse to do this.

2. The company's founders hide legal or financial problems that the underwriter eventually finds out about.

3. The company's financial reporting is aggressive. Upon further analysis of the company's financial statements, it turns out that under more conservative accounting policies, the company could actually report a loss.

4. The company dickers too much on the fees the investment banker is charging.

5. The company's founders and the underwriter are too far apart on what they think the company is worth and what public investors will pay for it.

6. The company's owners' or founders' lack of salesmanship proves they are unable to excite anyone about the deal.

7. The company is in an industry that "falls out of bed" with Wall Street. Remember conglomerates?

8. Some wrinkle about the company or the offering prevents it from getting clearance in a state that contains several or all of the investment banker's customers.

9. The company cannot afford the $250,000 it will cost to put a preliminary prospectus on the Street.

10. The deal structuring drags on for a long period of time and sales and earnings begin to fall. Unfortunately, the decline may be directly attributable to the amount of time senior management spent cooped up with accountants, lawyers and investment bankers.

Evaluating Investment Bankers

When investment banking firms are good, they tend to be very, very good. But when investment bankers are bad, the quality of their services can be downright scandalous. Following is a litmus test for getting some sense of your would-be underwriter's skill with regard to initial public offerings. It's important to keep this information in mind as you court an underwriter. After all, you want to be on your best behavior for the investment banking firms that know their craft when it comes to IPOs. And for the others whose past performance shows them to be somewhat lacking, you might want to test your swagger.

As you research your IPO underwriters, collect the following information for each offering the underwriter puts into registration to go public.

- The initial price range. When IPOs are filed, they are often stated in a range, such as 1 million common shares to be offered at $6 to $8 per share

- The actual offering price. Although IPOs are filed with a range of prices, the company goes public at just one price. For the above

A Good Deal

Your underwriter's research analyst is responsible for taking your company's story to the Street before and after the deal. Therefore, make sure your would-be investment banking firm has a strong in-house research function.

example, the final deal might end up to be 1 million shares at $7

- The difference, negative or positive, between the filing range and the initial offering price
- The number of days each underwriter's offering was spent in registration before the Securities and Exchange Commission declared it effective—i.e., ready to be offered to the public
- The price of the shares or units three months after the offering
- The difference, positive or negative, between the IPO price and the price of the stock three months later.

Armed with this information, evaluate each of your candidates with the following framework:

- **Aftermarket performance:** If every offering done by an underwriter is way, way up after the initial public offering, that is a red flag. First, it indicates that this underwriter prices offerings too low. Assume an investment banker sells 25 percent of your company and raises $7.5 million by selling 1 million shares of common stock at $7.50. If the share prices subsequently rise to $15, the underwriter underpriced the deal. This can hurt the founder of the company. After all, if the market would bear $15 per share, it means the underwriter, theoretically, could have raised the same $7.5 million by selling just 12.5 percent of the company. The investment banker's miscalculation cost the founders 12.5 percent of their company.

On the other hand, if the share prices are way up, that could indicate outright manipulation of the aftermarket trading. Remember, in the public stock market, if a number is too far out of kilter with reality, there's something wrong. Ideally, you want to see about a 15 percent to 20 percent increase from the initial offering share price within

Don't Forget

Going public is only part of the battle. Once you do, you must devote substantial human and financial resources to ensuring there is a continuous flow of new buyers for your company's stock.

three months after the offering. That is, an offering that came to market at $10 would trade up to $11.50 to $12 per share.

A Good Deal

Investment banking firms with lots of capital are more likely to support their IPOs once they begin trading. When interviewing investment bankers, ask them how much capital they have and how much they dedicate to over-the-counter trading. Evaluate this number in light of the number of IPOs the firm did in the past two years to get a sense of whether the firm's capital is stretched too thin.

- **Filing range differentials:** What is the percentage difference between what an underwriter files a deal at and the price at which the company actually goes public? If you uncover a number that is consistently negative, it could mean two things, neither of them particularly good. First, it may signal that the underwriter plays hardball. That is, filing at one price and then, close to the effective date, lowering the price, practically forcing senior management's hand to do the deal anyway because of all the time and money they put into the deal.

The other indication might be that the underwriter is weak and unable to generate enough support for the deal internally and externally at the filing price. The only acceptable excuse for a pattern of underpricing IPOs would be if they all occurred during a period of market decline, in which case the investment banker deserves kudos for getting any deal at all.

- **Number of days in registration:** How many days do an underwriter's deals typically spend in registration? If it's more than 90, it may be a sign that the underwriter is not skilled in IPOs. At the very least, this indicates you'll incur more risk with this underwriter than with a speedier one. After all, nothing good can come from stretching out a deal. In fact, it increases the chances that something bad will happen—market crash, declining financial performance, bad news in your industry—to scuttle the deal altogether.

- **Died in registration: Does** the underwriter show a pattern of filing IPOs but never completing them? Remember, it may cost as much as $250,000 to get your preliminary prospectus on the Street. You don't want to spend that kind of time and money with an investment banker who can't deliver the goods.

Chapter 19

Institutional Venture Capital

The Scoop

Definition Or Explanation: Institutional venture capital comes from professionally managed funds that have $25 million to $1 billion to invest in emerging growth companies.

Appropriate For: High-growth companies that are capable of reaching at least $25 million in sales in five years.

Supply: Limited. According to recent surveys from the National Venture Capital Association, U.S. venture capital firms annually invest between $5 billion and $7 billion. Many of these investment dollars go to companies already in the institutional venture capitalist's portfolio.

Best Use: Varied. From financing product development to expansion of a proven and profitable product or service.

Cost: Expensive. Institutional venture capitalists demand significant equity in a business. The earlier the investment stage, the more equity is required to convince an institutional venture capitalist to invest.

Ease Of Acquisition: Difficult. Institutional venture capitalists are choosy. Compounding the degree of difficulty is the fact that institutional venture capital is an appropriate source of funding for a limited number of companies.

Range Of Funds Typically Available: $500,000 to $10 million.

Take This Test

Does your business qualify for institutional venture capital? Run through this diagnostic test developed through an interview with John Martinson, general partner of Edison Ventures, a Lawrenceville, New Jersey, venture capital firm with more than $200 million under its management.

1. **Are you a technology company?** Technology is the stuff of gods for venture capitalists. With proprietary technology, a company can dominate a market and protect its profit margins. Institutional venture outfits do invest in low- or no-tech deals, just not as often. This means that competition among nontechnology companies is keener than among technology companies.

2. **Can you be a market leader?** Martinson says that institutional venture capital firms are hesitant to throw money at a company that is going up against a market leader with a me-too product or service. It's too difficult and too unlikely to succeed simply by stealing market share from the leader, he notes.

   There are exceptions, however. In particular, this is where technology can play a role by shattering the existing paradigm of how a product or service is offered, as well as by providing entree for an upstart.

3. **Will it be expensive to make this company?** Of course, what's expensive to one is cheap to another. But in most venture capitalists' terms, cheap is a company that can be put together and establish significant profitability on $10 million to $15 million. According to Martinson, this preference stems from the fact that most institutional venture capitalists do not want to rely on other sources of capital to make the venture work. They want to be able to help the company reach a profitable plateau with the funds they are able to commit to the deal.

4. **Is there a clear distribution channel?** Entrepreneurs often come up with great products and services but no clear or easy way to sell them, Martinson says. And, consistent with overall cost containment, can the distribution channel be accessed fairly inexpensively? For instance, the existence of mass-market retailers appears to offer inexpensive and wide distribution for many consumer products, and even some technology products. However, hidden costs often make these channels prohibitive, such as the requirement to supply possibly thousands of stores with inventory, the right to return unsold product, "slotting" fees or mandatory cooperative advertising costs. Companies that have joint-venture marketing opportunities—that is, the opportunity to move product through someone else's distribution—or that have direct and proven access to the market—are typically more attractive to venture capitalists than those that must invent their distribution or pay high fees to use someone else's, Martinson says.

5. **Does this product require significant support?** Complex products or services usually require customer-support organizations that are expensive and sometimes difficult to establish and maintain. For instance, given rising concern over security, a relatively low-tech home alarm system sold via mass-market distribution channels might appeal to an investor, Martinson says. But can customers install it themselves, or must a third party be involved? "If so, it's a much harder business to orchestrate, and much less appealing because of the involved costs and their impact on the margins," he says. But the need for customer support need not kill a deal. Sometimes a third party wants to get involved because it spells opportunity. For instance, SAP, one of the world's largest applications software companies, relies heavily on Big Five Accounting Firms to install and support its products. For SAP, funds that might otherwise go to a massive customer-support organization go instead to the bottom line, Martinson says.

6. **Can the product or service generate gross margins of more than 50 percent?** Gross margin is defined as sales

less cost of sales. If that number is less than 50 percent, it's a turnoff for most institutional venture investors. Why? Because it's difficult to pay all the selling, general, and administrative expenses and generate a healthy profit at this level. It's much more likely that a company will deliver the required high-operating or net margins if its gross margin is above 50 percent to begin with.

7. **Can the company go public or be acquired?** If neither of these events occurs, there's little chance of a real payday for the venture capitalists. The requirement also represents a double-edged sword. First, are the company's founders willing to go this route? People who want to run family businesses don't go public or get acquired. Second, does the company have the ability to go public? A desire to do so is just that, but actually getting such a deal done requires a great business, guts, some luck, and a lot of money upfront.

8. **Can the company achieve $25 million in sales, and are there prospects for $50 million to $100 million in sales?** With $25 million in sales, a company can generate the level of profits that makes the business worth enough so that a venture capitalist can become involved. Let's say, for instance, that a $25 million business brings $5 million to the bottom line and that the venture capitalist invests $10 million and owns 50 percent. Let's assume that the company goes public at 20 times its earnings, suggesting a value of $100 million. The venture capitalist who owns 50 percent of the company—hence 50 percent of the value, or $50 million—records a return of five times the original investment. That is generally considered a successful investment for most venture capitalists.

If you answered "no" to any of the preceding questions, with possible exceptions for numbers 1 and 6,

> **Don't Forget**
>
> Once an institutional venture capitalist invests in your business, there's only one way for him or her to make a profit: through an initial public offering or through the outright sale of the company. Therefore, if you want to pass the business on to the next generation, forget about institutional venture capital.

institutional venture capital is probably not an option for your company. Edison Ventures' Martinson is particularly firm on question 8. "If there's no possibility you'll hit the $25 million benchmark within five years, pursuing institutional venture capital is simply a waste of time."

Given these kinds of hurdles, it's no wonder few companies land institutional venture capital. The supplicants beating a path to Edison Ventures' door seem to bear this out. "We see 2,000 plans each year," Martinson says. "We might visit 300, seriously consider and conduct due diligence on 50, and invest in eight to 12."

If your plan does qualify for venture capital, by all means start looking. Generally speaking, there are two approaches: shotgun and rifle.

Using A Shotgun Approach

Using a shotgun approach means you send your business plan or some derivative thereof to as many venture capitalists

To The Source

If you decide to take the shotgun approach, you will need names and addresses. Here are two directories, published annually, that list the names of most U.S. institutional venture capital firms:

- **Pratt's Guide to Venture Capital Sources.** Pratt's has been published almost as long as there has been a venture capital business. This directory provides detailed information on more than 1,200 sources of institutional venture capital. Available in print or on CD-ROM. Call Securities Data Co. at (212) 765-5311.

- **Galante's Venture Capital Directory & Private Equity Directory.** This directory provides comprehensive profiles of venture capital and buyout firms. Also offers monthly updates on new sources. Available in print, on disk or on CD-ROM. Call Asset Alternatives at (781) 431-7353.

as possible and hope that the numbers alone will strike one that has been looking for a deal such as yours.

The shotgun approach has its proponents and its critics. For instance, Gordon Baty, a partner with Cambridge, Massachusetts-based venture outfit Zero Stage Capital, says, "Of every 100 plans that we get, 90 are completely irrelevant because they do not match our investment criteria regarding the industry, stage of development, geographic location, or the amount of capital we typically invest." Of this misguided bunch, Baty says, "our receptionist can weed out their business plans."

Taking Action

Talk to at least one chief executive in your industry who has raised venture capital. Ask him or her about the pitfalls of the process; this will help you decide whether to pursue institutional venture capital.

Fair comment. But the shotgun approach has one significant advantage over the rifle perspective. The latter relies on intensive research that is based on a venture fund's past investment patterns. What your research will fail to turn up is all the available venture capital funds that have now decided to focus their energies on restaurant deals, business service companies, publishing companies or Internet-content businesses.

If you are committed to institutional venture capital and the shotgun approach, you should cover all possible sources. Your initial correspondence should include the following items:

- Cover letter
- Executive summary from your business plan. (For strategies on how to write a business plan, including the executive summary, see Chapter 23.)

For the best response:

- Include a business reply card.
- Personalize your letter with name, address and salutation.
- Use a direct imprint rather than address labels on your envelope.
- Use a stamp rather than metered postage.

(For a sample letter and business reply card, see pages 218 and 219, repectively.)

September 17, 1999

Joe Investor
123 Money St.
Greendale, NY 45678

Dear Investor:

Please find enclosed the executive summary from our business plan.

As you can see from the summary statement, we have developed a new software product that helps sales personnel in the field increase productivity. Our product has been developed and beta-tested and we seek an equity investment of $1 million to conduct an initial rollout of the product.

The market potential for our product is more than $5 billion. During the course of development we have spoken with hundreds of potential customers, which, based on their estimates and responses to our questions, represent approximately $1 billion in sales. Based on a $1 million equity capital infusion, we believe we can generate product sales of more than $14 million, or just slightly more than 1 percent of identified sales.

The other sections of the executive summary briefly describe our markets, key personnel, proposed marketing operations, and summary historical and projected financial performance.

Please review this material at your earliest convenience and, if you are interested in our company, contact me via telephone, or by returning the enclosed business reply card. We anxiously await further word from you.

Sincerely,

Art Beroff

Sample cover letter

Name_____

Venture Firm_____

Address_____

City_____State_____ZIP_____

Telephone_____

Check all that apply:

__ We would like to see your entire business plan; please
    send it to us at the above address.

__ Please call me to discuss further.

__ We are not interested in investing, but you might call:
    Name_____ Phone_____

__ We are not interested in investing; please remove us
    from your mailing list.

Sample business reply card

In many cases, your mail will be well off the mark, and your letter will be weeded out by the receptionist—or the college intern sorting the mail. For instance, some venture capital firms might specialize in wireless communications companies from the so-called first stage on, while your company, which makes disposable medical devices is in the development stage.

A more reasonable approach might be to take at least one pass through your institutional venture capital sources and weed out the obvious misses for your particular line of business. Even a quick screen prevents many obvious misses. Of course, such an effort, while seemingly logical, undermines one of the chief benefits of the shotgun approach to begin with. That is, it lets you reach investors who may have changed their historical investment criteria and are now looking for companies like yours.

If you can mail your letter, business plan summary and business reply card for 50 cents each, it's worth going after the 1,200 to 1,800 traditional sources of institutional venture capital.

The Rifle Approach

The rifle approach, which favors limiting your search to 15 to 20 well-researched targets, is the one favored by most attorneys, accountants, consultants and other assorted experts. Venture capitalists seem to favor it because a highly targeted approach by entrepreneurs replaces an abundance of irrelevant opportunities with a manageable number of interesting ones.

The rifle approach is simple but time consuming. Basically, you search by five variables and then rank your candidates by how well they meet these criteria. The five key search variables are:

1. By line of business
2. By geographic preference
3. By investment stage
4. By leadership status
5. By deal size

A Good Deal

Many venture capitalists consider themselves value-added investors who help their portfolio companies with advice, contacts and mentoring. Ask your venture capital candidates what, if any, value they can add to your company above and beyond capital.

- **Searching by line of business:** Most venture capitalists specialize in one or more industries. It's the focus on a particular technology, industry or business that supposedly allows them to pick winners in their formative stages. This specialization is good news because it lets you easily identify venture capitalists who should be interested and those who should not. Review the reference guides listed in the "To The Source" on page 216, and select the venture capitalists who invest in your industry.

- **Searching by geographic preference:** The very hands-on approach of institutional venture capital investing makes distance a factor. That is, to be a board member, and perhaps be intimately involved in a company's development, a venture capitalist would find it difficult to invest in companies that are 2,000 or 3,000 miles away. Many do, mind you. But more venture capitalists stick to well-defined geographic regions such as the mid-Atlantic region, the Northwest, the Southeast or perhaps a particular state. Search your source material and weed out venture capital investors who do not look at deals where you are located.

- **Searching by stage of development:** In the same way that venture capital investors specialize in one industry or another, they also specialize in differing stages of development. That is, some companies invest in early-stage companies, while others invest in more mature companies. This should intuitively make sense. After all, from a venture capitalist's standpoint, a company that is trying to make a better mousetrap requires much different care and feeding than one that has already figured this out and is on the brink of national distribution.

  The chart on page 222 lists the generally accepted stages of development in the world of venture capital investment. Figure out where you fit on the continuum, and weed out the institutional venture capital investors who do not invest in companies at your stage of development.

- **Searching by leadership status:** In the world of venture capital investing there are leaders and there are followers. The leaders, also known as "lead" firms, are those that have recognized expertise, and who conduct extensive due diligence on their prospective portfolio companies. The followers, known as "follow-on" investors, are more passive. They simply invest alongside the lead firms. Lead firms can be helpful when you are trying to raise your second, third or fourth round of venture capital because their presence alone can attract other investors for these later rounds. They are no help when you are trying to raise your first round of venture capital. Review your source material and weed out the firms

Taking Action

Many states recognize the economic-development potential of venture capital and provide seed and development-stage funds to companies within the state. To find a fund in your state, call or write the National Organization of State Venture Funds at 301 NW 63rd St., Oklahoma City, OK 73116, (405) 848-8570.

Financing	Company Characteristics
Seed financing	Small amount of capital to prove a business concept or technology
Start-up financing	Funding of $500,000 to as much as $3 million; appropriate for companies that have developed a product or service and are now ready to start building and/or selling
First-stage financing	Can range from $500,000 to $5 million; for companies that have proven they can manufacture or deliver a product or service successfully and are now ready to expand the base of their operations
Second-stage financing	Ranges from $3 million to $10 million; generally for companies with a proven and profitable business model that need working capital funds
Mezzanine financing	Ranges from $5 million to $15 million; generally for companies about to go public; assists them in expanding operations and perhaps defraying some of the costs of the pending IPO

that do not act as the lead investors in deals.

- **Searching by deal size:** Institutional venture capitalists generally place upper and lower limits on the sizes of their investments. These limits are closely related to the overall size of the fund the venture capitalist is managing. venture capitalists with $250 million to invest typically don't want to look at your $500,000 deal. Why? Because to invest the entire fund in $500,000 increments means the firm would have to invest in 1,000 deals. Consider this number in the context of venture capitalist John Martinson's experience cited at the beginning of this chapter. Specifically, Martinson looks at 2,000 business plans each year to invest in an average of 10 companies. To do 1,000 deals, he would have to look at 200,000 business plans.

However, a $10 million venture fund probably does not want to take your $3 million deal, either. It's just too big for the portfolio.

Generally, you don't have to figure out a venture capitalist's preferred investment range. Because it's an important feature of the firm, the preferred deal size is often published in a venture capitalist's own promotional literature, and is a common line item in almost any directory listing.

Don't Forget
Venture capitalists frequently specialize in a particular industry. This means they may have an investment in or sit on a competitor's board. Before you talk with a venture capitalist and disclose potentially sensitive information, find out if this is the case.

If you follow the above methodology, your list of prospective venture capitalists should be short—perhaps 15 or fewer.

The following system was developed by G. Jackson Tankersley, a general partner of The Centennial Funds, the largest institutional venture capital pool in the Rocky Mountain region, to rank candidates from the best match to the least likely. Use it by assigning a score such as 2=good match, 1=acceptable match and 0=poor match, for each search variable. Then total the score for each fund. For example:

	Fund 1	Fund 2	Fund 3
Stage of development	1	2	1
Investment size	1	1	0
Geography	2	2	1
Industry	1	2	1
Leadership	0	2	0
Score	5	9	3

By this ranking, Fund 2 appears to be the most viable. Not that Fund 1 and Fund 3 should be discarded. After all, they were also carefully researched. It's just that Fund 2, along with any other fund that scored similarly, should grab your best effort.

A Good Deal

When a venture capital investor says he or she is not interested in investing in your company, ask for the names of venture firms he or she thinks might be interested. Remember, venture capital investors tend to be specialists in a particular area and may have valuable insights on where to turn for potential investors.

What does your "best effort" mean? One of the canons of the rifle approach is that you never cold-call a venture capitalist. Never. So your best effort means finding a way to get a referral or warm-body introduction to a venture capitalist so that he or she will take your call and/or actually look at your business plan. "The most credible deals, to me, come from the chief executives of companies we have already invested in," Tankersley says.

Finding some of the companies a venture firm has invested in can be fairly straightforward. Simply call the firm and ask for a brochure or a list of its investments. Many willingly and proudly disclose this information.

If they have invested in a firm you know or do business with, or they're a vendor (or a vendee), or belong to your trade association or chamber of commerce, or are located in your building, or have an employee whom you know, there's a viable path to the chief executive. You must get to and meet that person, and get his or her help in getting a referral to the venture capitalist you have targeted.

The venture capitalist's brochure, if one exists, also provides information that could yield a referral. Sometimes these brochures disclose, in addition to portfolio companies, the venture fund's:

- attorneys
- accountants
- investors
- advisory board members
- key employees and educational backgrounds
- technical consultants

All this information provides invaluable bits of data you can use to reduce the degrees of separation between you and the venture capitalists whom you want to read and consider your business plan.

PART 2

TECHNIQUES

Chapter 20

Preparing A Loan Request

Imagine you're a commercial lending officer. You have limited funds, unlimited discretion as to where the funds go and, let's not forget, ultimate accountability to a bank executive who holds your livelihood in her hands. Now, whom do you want to lend money to?

The bottom line is that lending institutions select those borrowers they deem as having the best likelihood of repayment. Like most of us, lenders have a risk-tolerance level that hovers in a conservative, self-protective midrange. As a potential borrower, your goal should be to increase your banker's "sleep factor" by providing the information she needs to make a positive decision with confidence that the bank's money—and her job—won't be on the line.

Financial statements form the backbone of the loan request and must be complete and professionally presented. According to Alan J. Candell, president of Gladwyne Capital in Gladwyne, Pennsylvania, a firm specializing in placing debt financing for emerging and middle-market companies, all lenders require a:

Shop Talk

An aging of receivables schedule shows money is owed to a company by its customers and is grouped into brackets of time. That is, all the money that is currently owed is in one bracket; money owed for between 30 and 45 days is grouped in another bracket; money owed for 60 days or more is grouped into another bracket. A company with chronically older receivables can often dramatically improve its cash flow simply by tightening up its collection process.

- balance sheet that shows the company's assets, liabilities and equity.

- cash flow statement that shows how much cash the business throws off each month, quarter or year.

- income statement that shows the company's revenues, expenses and net income.

(Note: audited financials are generally required for loans of more than a threshold of roughly $2 million.)

Depending on the nature of the loan, lenders may also require:

- a complete description of all collateral.

- a receivables aging that shows the funds owed to the company by its customers. Accounts are typically aged in current, 30-day, 60-day, 90-day and 120+-day categories. This item is essential for asset-based loans that are made according to a company's receivables.

- a description of all real estate, including photos (may not be necessary for loans that do not rely on real estate as collateral).

- a description of all machinery and equipment (not previously described under collateral).

- financial projections.

- personal and corporate tax returns for the past two years.

- an inventory listing (under certain circumstances).

More Than Just Numbers

Much like the business plan (although in a much briefer format), a loan request includes qualitative information about the company, its management and the industry. These items are particularly important for newer companies without a strong financial track record. Each topic should be covered in no more than two or three pages. Why? Because bankers, whose main interest is in the financial information, and whose schedules are as busy as yours, simply won't read much more. So if writing isn't your strong suit, consider hiring a business writer to help write the following elements:

- **Company description:** In the company section, include a brief history, short product and/or service descriptions and plans for the future.

- **Key personnel:** A management profile section should include brief (two to three paragraphs) bios of each principal and/or executive. These bios should include education, pertinent work experience, managerial experience, industry knowledge and applicable outside activities (such as membership or activity in trade or professional organizations). Note: Lenders do not want or need to know about part-time jobs you had in school or your job as a camp counselor unless the experience is relevant. They do want to know which facets of your background and education will ensure your success.

Don't be shy. Be specific with regard to skills and accomplishments. The goal is to inspire confidence and put an intelligent, experienced, successful person behind the numbers on the loan request.

- **Industry analysis:** An industry description includes a competitive analysis as well as a market analysis. Talk about industry trends and why they will support business growth. This section should make it clear that you understand your position in the market. One way to accomplish this is to do your homework in terms of the industry in which your business operates. This includes understanding the ratios—such as debt to equity—that can help to formulate a picture of how the business fits in with others of its ilk.

- **Use of proceeds:** The use of proceeds section should tell the lender what the loan proceeds will be used for. Be specific about whether the funds will pay for inventory, working capital, staffing, etc.

Taking Action

You can get a "statement study" report that details financial norms for your industry through banking trade group Robert Morris Associates in Philadelphia, Pennsylvania. To order, call (215) 446-4000.

A Good Deal

If you don't have time to chase down a lender—and it does take time—consider using a loan broker. A good one with experience can accomplish in an hour what it might take you three months to find on your own. Remember, when it comes to loan brokers, there are no professional standards except satisfied customers. So check references carefully before hiring anyone. (Also see "Loan Rangers" on page 236.)

Doing The Legwork

Before beginning your quest for a lender, understand some of your options in terms of types of loans and what you—as a borrower—bring to the table. For example, are you in the market for an asset-based loan? These loans are based on collateral other than real estate, often accounts receivable and inventory. Asset-based loans are usually of a shorter duration and can be accompanied by various covenants.

Lines of credit, on the other hand, provide funds on a revolving, as-needed basis and work well for businesses with seasonal markets that result in large peaks and valleys of cash flow.

Term loans can be secured by real estate or large machinery or equipment. These loans are typically made for longer than five years.

For a description of these and other types of available loans in today's lending environment, check out our "The Scoop" sections at the start of each chapter to get a handle on which type is appropriate for your circumstances. There may be more than one that appears applicable to your circumstances. Always discuss your actions with an accountant, a banker or a loan broker.

"There are so many lenders with so much flexibility that finding the right lender has become a science," Candell says. "Pricing and covenants can be substantially different, so it is critical to match the right loan package with the right lender."

Bank On It

The Office of Advocacy of the Small Business Administration publishes an annual study called Small Business Lending in the United States, a comprehensive state-by-state ranking of all 9,670 U.S. banks regarding their lending performance for business loans of less than $250,000.

It also publishes *The Bank Holding Company Study* which profiles the small-business lending activities of the nation's larger banks. It includes a listing of the top three lenders in small-business loan volume in each state.

These publications, among others, are available through the Office of Advocacy's Web site at www.sba.gov/advo/stats. Or contact the National Technical Information Service at 5285 Port Royal Rd., Springfield, VA 22161, (800) 553-NTIS.

Don' t Forget

Consolidation in the banking industry presents a risk. If your lender is acquired, the new parent may not want to do business with you and may interrupt loan agreements so strictly that it causes default. Choose your lender carefully and assess the risk of an acquisition upfront.

So don't waste time and money sending your loan proposal to every bank in town. Instead, do your homework. Call the banks in your area—both big and small. Ask to speak to a loan officer. Ask if they have done other loans for businesses at similar stages and in similar industries. Remember, every lending institution and every lender has a personality, and even major regional banks have likes and dislikes in terms of the types of investments they will approve.

Finding the right lender not only improves your chances of approval but also provide better leverage when it comes to the terms of the loan. "It's more than interest rate alone," Candell says. For example, a lender might generally allow receivables of 60 days or less as collateral. In certain industries, in which turnaround on receivables tends to be longer, however—such as health care, which relies in large part on insurance payments—the lender who is familiar with this aspect of the industry might allow 60- to 90-day receivables. Certain lenders might allow a higher advance rate—say, 80 percent vs. 65 percent against collateral if they're familiar with the intricacies of an industry.

Candell describes a client who was in the specialty finance business—an area that can be perceived as risky. However, because the loan was placed with a lender who understood the nature of the business, Candell was able to obtain a higher advance rate than might otherwise have been offered. Another of his clients needed funds to purchase vacant unzoned land— typically a tough sell to a bank that wants good collateral. But, remembers Candell, his client received an informal commitment in a day. "Quick responses and favorable terms can be the norm if you know where to place a loan," he says.

What Do Banks Really Want?

Dominic DiMao, assistant vice president of FirstTrust Bank, a family-owned bank with 19 branches in southeastern

Anatomy Of A Loan Proposal

There's nothing like a table of contents to get to the heart of the matter. Following is a sample table of contents from a loan proposal prepared for a health-care company that was interested in obtaining funds for a property acquisition and a refinancing. The components of a loan proposal should be geared to the specific loan. Thus, in this case, many items pertain to real estate. If the loan were to be used for a different purpose—to purchase equipment or hire additional personnel, for example—the components would change, particularly under the "use of loan proceeds" section.

Table Of Contents

I. Behavioral health care in the 1990s—An overview
II. Company profile—Past, present and future
    Exhibit A—Consolidated income statement (xx/xx/xx to xx/xx/xx)
    Exhibit B—Satellite locations
    Exhibit C—Consolidated income statement (fiscal year xxxx)
III. Management (including biographies)
IV. Use of loan proceeds
  A. Acquisition
    Exhibit D—Agreement of sale
    Exhibit E—Pro forma operating statement
    Exhibit F—Appraisal letter (for real estate)
    Exhibit G—Photos (real estate, property, etc.)
  B. Refinanced property
    Exhibit H—Statement of operations
    Exhibit I—Pro forma operating statement (FY xxxx)
    Exhibit J—Introductory brochure (marketing piece for property)
    Exhibit K—List of improvements
    Exhibit L—List of inventory
V. Audited financial statements for each of the three years ending mm/dd/yy, as prepared by (name of accounting firm)
VI. Financial statements for the period ending mm/dd/yy
VII. Budget for the fiscal year ending mm/dd/yy
VIII. Summary of note purchase agreement (relevant in real estate)

Pennsylvania, says that for small, individually owned companies, banks want proprietors to "stand behind their company." Small-business owners should have a financial stake in their business. For new businesses without a financial track record, the principals' background and experience are what sells them.

Loan Rangers

Loan brokers exist to assist businesses in obtaining appropriate financing. They can, of course, help prepare proper documentation, but perhaps the biggest advantage in using their services may be realized through their formal and informal lending network. "You can save about 98 percent of your time if you go to a lender that understands your business," Gladwyne Capital's Candell says. "You don't obtain funding by educating bankers, lenders or investors. People who understand your business and industry are more likely to make a financial commitment based on the true worth of your company."

Loan brokers charge a percentage of the loan proceeds for their efforts: typically 1 percent to 2 percent for loans greater than $1 million and 3 percent to 5 percent for loans less than $1 million. They often also charge an upfront fee. While this is not unusual, borrowers should be wary, Candell cautions. The industry has seen problems with these arrangements, and there has been much litigation. Check at least two references, Candell advises, no matter what the financial arrangement.

You can find a loan broker in your area by checking the Yellow Pages under "Financing/Businesses." Better yet, as you canvass lenders, ask if they're aware of any good loan brokers who have approached them over the years. Finally, your accountant may have a relationship with a loan broker, since, when clients have problems, they often turn to their trusty accountant, who in turn might turn to a broker to run interference with lenders.

In these cases, a "package" takes on a greater significance, as well as shows a commitment and professionalism, DiMao says.

For larger loans—$2 million plus, DiMao says that reporting ability becomes an important issue. That is, does the borrower have the systems in place to produce timely and accurate financial reports? Banks often require quarterly, even monthly, data, so it is to a borrower's benefit to have the systems in place to provide this information in a timely, professional manner.

> **Don' t Forget**
> A loan proposal is only packaging. You are really selling yourself, which means that to get a loan of any size, you have to look the banker in the eye and give her a sense of confidence that the bank will recoup all its money.

The bottom line? Borrowers must understand their own business and their position in the market and be able to clearly defend the purpose of the loan. A borrower must be able to explain how the loan will advance their business, as well as be able to show they have the ability to repay it.

Loan Proposals

While most lenders don't require formal documents, a loan proposal can help set a borrower apart from the pack. "They show that the borrower is professional, with an organized and businesslike approach, which makes the lender's job easier by providing the necessary documentation in a succinct format," Candell says. "This can also help speed up the loan process."

The loan proposal does not have to be an imposing and formal document. It must, however, be neat and professional.

A three-ring binder works well, as do the plastic bindings available from most office-supply stores (they have the machines to put them on as well). Use tabs to separate and clearly mark each section. Don't rely on your own proofreading skills—you're too close to the project. Have someone else check your spelling and grammar.

In today's high-tech environment, many banks use an automated credit-scoring system to say yea or nay to loans of less than $100,000. More and more banks are using these systems, and it appears that the dollar threshold will rise as banks gain confidence in these systems. Credit scoring can save both the borrower and lender a tremendous amount of time, so you may consider approaching a bank that utilizes these systems.

While the process may differ, all banks are looking for the same thing—the ability to repay. Beyond this, different factors may be given different emphasis depending on the personality of the lender.

In conclusion, remember, lenders have many loan requests to choose from, some of which are obviously stronger than others. But it's not their job to make the case for approving your loan. It's yours.

Chapter 21

How Investors Use Your Financial Statements

Financial statements shed light on the beast. That is, they help shareholders and investors stop groping with a shape in the dark and gain an understanding of what the creature as a whole looks like. Is it a cash cow? Or is it a dog?

And while everybody understands why creditors and investors need these statements, there is considerably less information about how they use them to make their investment decisions. In other words, what do your financial statements tell investors and creditors about your company?

Lenders Vs. Equity Investors

There is an immediate, important distinction between how lenders and equity investors use these statements.

To understand the behavior of your commercial lender, you need only visit the branch offices where the tellers are. There you'll see some people putting money in the bank and others taking it out. Those who put it in have every expectation the money will be there when they return to get it—regardless of where it's been. And the bank, as the custodian of the deposits, simply cannot afford to lose these customers. The bank runs a nice little spread business between what they pay you for your deposit and what they can get for lending it. As a financial institution, a bank is more accurately characterized as an intermediary than a risk taker. That is, the bank mediates the period of time that people want to borrow money vs. the time people are willing to lend it. They don't exist to lose money.

Once you understand these principles, it speaks volumes to the behavior of your garden-variety commercial lender. Loans are generally fully collateralized. If not, they are personally guaranteed. Most likely, they are both. Where fixed assets are thin or nonexistent, look for accounts receivable financing to be offered in place of term loans.

Little of this applies to equity investors. For instance, rather than the characteristics that demonstrate the ability to repay a loan,

Don't Forget

Lenders look at your financial statement to understand the company's ability to repay debt. Equity investors look at your financial statements to understand your company's ability to grow.

equity investors look for growth. After all, that and an oil well underneath the shop floor are the only things that will create an increase in value. In addition, equity investors try to understand the amount of capital the company requires as it grows. If the company requires substantially more equity capital than the investor is able or prepared to provide, perhaps it's not such a good investment.

> ### Don't Forget
> Raising money is fundamentally an act of financial communications. To give investors—debt or equity—the confidence to cut you a check, you must speak knowledgeably and confidently about your company's historical and projected financial performance.

The difference between the two can be summed up as follows: If a bank lends money, and that company subsequently triples sales and quadruples earnings, the return the bank enjoys is the same as if the company never grew a percentage point. In fact, such growth may even alarm the bank since the earnings could ultimately destabilize the company and undermine the ability to repay the loan. But for the equity investor, meteoric growth spells success, even if in the near term it leads to significant variance in earnings and cash flow.

These investors approach your financial statements with unique perspectives. Let's take a close look at the precise analysis each one undertakes.

How Lenders Analyze Financial Statements

Don Fracchia, a lender and senior vice president with Wells Fargo Bank, explains his approach. Though Wells Fargo has more than $52 billion in assets and serves middle-market as well as multibillion-dollar corporations, the bank also has a significant commitment to small business. The company's business-financing division focuses on small businesses with needs ranging from $50,000 to $2 million.

Large or small, however, Fracchia explains, banking credit analysis has three components.

- The behavior or character of the company and its principals

- The primary source or repayment for a loan
- The secondary source of repayment for a loan

While character can't be deduced from financial statements, it's a critical part of the analysis, Fracchia explains. "Do the owners exhibit the type of character to pay back debts?" he asks.

Interviews with principals, personal credit checks and public record searches, taken in the aggregate, yield important clues about how the company handles payment responsibilities.

> **Taking Action**
>
> Review your personal credit record and remove any unwarranted blemishes. Many lenders include a review of the borrower's personal credit history as a part of their analysis.

Assuming it passes this hurdle, Fracchia turns his attention to the financial statements, specifically the notes to the financial statements. These would seem rather pedestrian compared with the actual numbers, but in reality they provide inquiring minds like Fracchia's a deep well of information. "This is where I gain a brief history of the company, a detailed description of its debts, its current loan pricing, off-balance sheet items, pending litigation and details regarding affiliated relationships."

Determining Sources Of Repayment

In the three-part credit analysis, Fracchia tries to determine the primary source of repayment for the requested loan. That is, he looks at the company's performance to see what kind of debt it can support.

It's important to note that if you're losing money, it won't necessarily scuttle the deal, Fracchia says. "Small-business owners make a conscious decision to carry the wealth in the business or to carry it personally," he says. "In effect, they manage the bottom line. Salary, pension, profit sharing and any real estate that may be owned are all discretionary. A loss does not end the game. You have to see where it's coming from."

Margin Analysis

But before reconstructing the income statement to see what kind of debt the company can support, Fracchia says, most lenders look at the gross, operating and net margins. The following paragraphs provide insight about what these are and what they mean.

Mathematically the gross margin is calculated as follows:

$$\frac{\text{gross profit}}{\text{total sales}} = \text{gross margin percent}$$

The gross profit is: sales–cost of sales. That is, if you sold lemonade, the primary cost of the sales would be the lemons. For example, if you sold $500 in lemonade and the lemons cost $200, the latter figure is the cost of sales and the $300 ($500–$200) is the gross profit. When the gross profit is divided by the total sales, it is referred to as the gross profit margin. The gross profit margin tells you and the lender how much of your profits are eaten up by simply making the product or offering the service.

Next, there's the operating margin, which is calculated as follows:

$$\frac{\text{operating profit}}{\text{total sales}} = \text{operating margin percent}$$

Operating profit is the gross profit (see above) less what are known as the selling, general and administrative costs. Again, harking back to the lemonade stand, the lemons represent the cost of sales. But if your expenses for the stand, signs, uniforms and permits are $200, the operating profit is $100 ($300–$200). The operating profit, or margin, tells the lender what the company makes in its base business.

Finally, there's the net margin, which is calculated as follows:

$$\frac{\text{net profit}}{\text{sales}} = \text{net margin percent}$$

What is the net profit? It's the operating profit less gains and losses that might occur but which are not part of the normal course of business, less taxes. For instance, your lemonade stand might show an operating profit of $100. But if during the course of the year you sold a fully depreciated lemon squeezer for, say, $25, you would have a gain of $25. Now the total income before taxes is $125. If the tax bite is $50, your final net profit is $75. When this $75 is expressed as a percentage of the original $500 in sales ($75/$500), it indicates a net margin of 15 percent.

At the first cut, Fracchia says, he compares the margins with industry averages, which are published by banking trade group Robert Morris Associates to discern if the company is up to snuff. For example, if restaurant chains on average have 65 percent gross margins and you're only delivering a 50 percent margin, this sends up a red flag. (You can see how you stack up against financial norms in your industry by purchasing a statement study from banking trade group Robert Morris Associates at 215-446-4000.)

The most important of these performance margins, Fracchia says, is the operating margin, which consists of sales, less cost of goods sold, less selling, general and administrative expenses. "That tells me if the company is making money in its base business. If it's not, it's definitely a sign of trouble."

Even if there's a loss, the deal's not completely dead, Fracchia points out. Salaries are discretionary. If the owner is drawing an exceptionally healthy salary, and that is causing a loss at the operating level, there's still hope—if he or she is willing to compromise. Compromise in this context means the business owner would, going forward, be willing to leave in the business the cash he or she has historically taken out. This cash then becomes available to service the debt.

Net Flow Of Funds Calculation

Now comes the acid test: the net flow of funds calculation. In formula fashion, net flow of funds is as follows:

Net flow of funds = net income + depreciation + amortization ± extraordinary items

Depreciation is the amount by which a company's assets are devalued each year for wear and tear, while amortization represents the assignment of expenses to several intangible assets, such as patents, trademarks or customer lists. These items are added back in because, even though they are shown on the income statement as an expense, they do not consume a company's cash. For instance, if your company's truck is depreciated every year by $500, it's counted as an expense, but this

Shop Talk
The "coverage ratio" is the net flow of funds divided by the annual debt service. It shows how many times the debt service is covered by the net flow of funds.

expense has no influence on cash flow. That's why it's added back to the net flow of funds.

Extraordinary gains and losses—insurance settlements from a fire, or the sale of an asset, such as a truck, or damage to a facility—are added or subtracted from the net funds flow figure, according to Fracchia, because he wants to understand the average net funds flow. "If an extraordinary gain or a loss is just that, extraordinary," Fracchia says, "then we want to remove it from the picture."

Sometimes net discretionary income, which is the amount of personal income a principal or officer takes from the company over and above personal and living expenses, is added to the net flow of funds. It's used, Fracchia says, because if the individual is willing to kick some salary or bonus back into the corporation, those funds can help support the loan.

To pull all these concepts together into an example, consider a company with $65,000 in net income. If the company has total depreciation and amortization expenses of $25,000, a flood loss of $15,000 (where such losses have occurred more than once over the past few years), and the company owner has agreed to take $25,000 less in salary, then the company's net flow of funds is:

$$\text{net flow of funds} = \$65,000 + \$25,000 - \$15,000 + \$25,000$$
$$= \$100,000$$

In practice, Fracchia says, the bank uses an average net funds flow for two years. So what kind of a loan can a company secure, assuming its average net funds flow is $100,000? "For secured loans, which are loans collateralized or backed up by a company's assets," Fracchia says, "we want the ratio of net funds flow to annual debt service (i.e., net funds flow/annual debt service) to be at least 1.25." Formulaically:

$$\frac{\text{net flow of funds}}{\text{annual debt service}} >= 1.25$$

For the above hypothetical company, with annual net flow of funds of $100,000, the annual debt service must be $80,000 or less to meet the coverage ratio of 1.25.

$$\frac{\$100,000}{\$80,000} > = 1.25$$

In other words, if you owe the bank $80,000 per year for a loan, the bank wants you to show historical cash flow of at least $100,000 per year.

On a monthly basis, this $80,000 of debt service is about $6,700. Assuming a five-year term loan at 12 percent interest, the $6,700 translates into a $300,000 loan.

Balance Sheet Analysis

Next, Fracchia turns to the balance sheet. While the income statement analysis is fairly unequivocal in its purpose—to determine the primary source of repayment—the balance sheet is a little fuzzier. Part of the analysis is devoted to understanding the working capital needs of the business, and part of it is devoted to seeing if there are sufficient assets so that the loan can be recovered in the event of financial deterioration.

Calculating Working-capital Needs

If you seek a loan to cover your cash needs rather than, say, an equipment loan, Fracchia looks at your company's trading cycle. That is, he analyzes the creation of accounts payable (i.e., the purchase of materials) to make inventory, which is transformed, with any luck, into sales and accounts receivable. The speed with which the cycle occurs determines the company's working-capital needs.

To determine the actual need, Fracchia looks at the trend in turnover among the receivables, inventory and payable accounts. That is, how many days of sales are tied up in accounts receivable? Formulaically:

$$\frac{\textbf{average receivables balance}}{\textbf{average daily sales}} = \textbf{days of sales in receivables}$$

The average receivable balance is what, on average, is owed to the company at any time. And the average daily sales is the total sales divided by 365—the number of days in a year.

For example:

$$\frac{\$100,000 \text{ in average receivables}}{\$5,000 \text{ in sales per day}} = 20 \text{ days of sales in receivables}$$

At the basic level, if a company has 20 days worth of sales tied up in receivables, such as in the above example, it has a working-capital need equivalent to $100,000. But if the days of sales in receivables increase, say, by 15 days, because the length of collections increases, the working-capital needs increase by 15 days. In the above example, the working-capital needs increase by $75,000 (15 days x $5,000)

What about inventory?

$$\frac{\text{average inventory}}{\text{average daily sales}} = \text{days of sales in inventory}$$

For example:

$$\frac{\$300,000 \text{ in average inventory}}{\$5,000 \text{ average daily sales}} = 60 \text{ days of sales in receivables}$$

Suppose the company turned over its inventory every 60 days last year, but currently does so every 90 days. In reality, this means the company keeps on hand more of its product before it sells it. In this case, the amount of additional product the company has on hand is equivalent to the amount it sells every 30 days. As a result, it has a cash need equal to 30 days worth of sales.

Fracchia triangulates the trend in these accounts to determine the company's working-capital needs. Such needs are often addressed by what is commonly known as asset-based financing. (For more information on this topic, see Chapter 5.)

By industry convention, there are limits to what lenders like Fracchia lend against these assets. For example, if he's lending against your accounts receivable, about the most

A Good Deal

Many investors, debt and equity, prefer to finance working-capital needs. Rather than putting funds at risk for product development, working-capital investments allow them to participate in a company's cash flow.

he can offer is 70 percent of the average receivables. "That would be very aggressive," he notes. If Fracchia is financing inventory, he might fund up to 50 percent, but again, he cautions, the latter figure is on the aggressive end.

Finally, Fracchia turns his attention to the right-hand side of the balance sheet, where the liabilities and shareholder equity are. First, he'll look at the debts. By going to the notes, he sees who the lender is. If some of the debt comes from founders in the form of loans, that's good and bad news. It's good because banks tend to count loans from founders as equity instead of debt, thereby increasing the company's ability to secure more debt. It's bad news because they do this by subordinating loans from shareholders to their loan. If your company needs cash, the bank's treatment of your loans to the company offers greater benefit.

Fracchia compares remaining debt to the company's equity

When Things Go South

To see how the secondary source of repayment stacks up, banks typically assign the following values to assets:

- **Accounts receivable:** Generally speaking, lenders assign a value to the accounts receivable of about 60 percent of what a company shows on its books.

- **Inventory:** Figure from 0 percent to 50 percent. The greater a commodity inventory is, the more value it is assigned. If you have rolled steel and aluminum ingots, you're probably looking at the 50 percent end of the spectrum. Then again, if you have test tubes full of antigens, you might be looking at the other end.

- **Equipment:** Equipment is generally worth about 60 percent of the net book value, which is cost less accumulated depreciation.

to gain a sense of how leveraged the company is. This is the debt-to-equity ratio, or total liabilities, divided by total equity. For example, your company has $2 million in debts and $1 million in shareholder equity. Its debt-to-equity ratio is 2 to 1 ($2 million/$1 million). Depending on the industry, Fracchia says, banks generally goes as high as 4 to 1 on the debt-to-equity ratio—that is, $1 of equity for every $4 of debt. "Anything over four is pushing the envelope," he says.

Shop Talk

A company's operating cycle is equal to its days' sales in inventory, plus its days' sales in receivables. A company with 45 days in inventory and 30 days in receivables has a 75-day operating cycle.

Determining The Secondary Source Of Repayment

When you seek a term loan, say, for equipment or other fixed-asset purchases, the balance sheet analysis takes on a different character. In this scenario, it's done to determine the secondary source of repayment, which is the final phase of the bank's three-part analysis. Determining the secondary source of repayment, by the way, is a nice way of saying that the bank is trying to figure out if there are sufficient assets to liquidate and recover its principal in the event the borrower cannot recover from a tailspin.

This is why most banks are not good collateral lenders, Fracchia says. "If you can only lend to businesses where you will make a complete recovery in liquidation, then you're not going to be making many loans." But lending without 100 percent coverage goes against a bank's grain. The funds are, after all, not the bank's but depositors'. That's why personal guarantees are standard on almost every small-business loan. Still, liquidating a business owner's personal assets to recover a loan can be a rather sticky affair that banks would rather avoid. It's much easier and probably more pleasant when companies default on loans to be a cash flow lender, providing funds against accounts receivable or inventory.

But this doesn't keep banks from seeing if the business can repay a loan in a liquidation scenario. Liquidation is not necessarily standard operating procedure, Fracchia points out. "Banks aren't just looking at assets to see if they can be liquidated to pay off a loan," he says. "We also want to see how much equity there might be in the company's assets so that we can lend them more [money] in the event their situation temporarily deteriorates and they have cash needs."

How Equity Investors Analyze Financial Statements

If you're an established company—that is, you actually have a track record of sales and perhaps earnings—and you are seeking an equity investor in the form of a venture capitalist, an angel investor, or a corporate partner, the person on the other side of the table will look at your financial statements much differently, according to Peter Ligeti, a partner at Keystone Venture Capital Management. Keystone finances primarily established firms, which in venture capital parlance means companies with products and revenues, but are perhaps a long

The Disappearing Equity Investment

Many equity investors look closely at the accounts payable section of the balance sheet before making an investment. Why? They want to see how much of their equity investment will be eaten by creditors. Sometimes a $500,000 investment is whittled down to $250,000 after the creditors stake their claim. The accounts payable are so important that many equity investors sometimes contact creditors to see if they will hang in there a little longer.

To the equity investor who balks at paying off accounts payable, you can argue that for the company to continue to grow, it must be on good footing with its suppliers. Specifically: "They got the company to where it is today. But they're not investors. We have to replace their investment with real investment dollars before we can grow the company any further."

way from profitability. As a result, Ligeti has seen a lot of financial statements.

Equity Investor Balance Sheet Analysis

To get an idea of the differences between lenders and equity investors at the broad-brush level, consider Ligeti's general outlook on the balance sheet. "We are much less concerned with the presence of assets to pay us out if there are problems," he says. "Existing hard assets are likely pledged to the bank anyway. Our agenda is to invest regardless of the asset characteristics, if there's the opportunity to generate a large increase in value."

So rather than looking at hard assets, Ligeti zeros in on the intangible assets. Whereas these aren't important to a lender, they are to an equity investor, especially for a growing technology company. For instance, if a company is capitalizing research and development (that is, treating R&D expenditures as if an asset were bought), that's good. It shows a significant commitment to product development and improvement, which ideally will fuel future sales. But if it is too aggressive in its allocation of R&D expenditures to assets rather than expense accounts, that's bad. A more conservative look at the company's overall financial position might cause a reclassification of expenditures as expenses, and deliver a charge to earnings.

Next, Ligeti looks at the inventory to see if it's in sync with revenues. "If the inventory account is high relative to the revenues, or has been creeping up over time, that's a big question mark for us," he says. Maybe there's a big sale on the horizon. Maybe, however, the company is simply mismanaged.

On the accounts receivable, Ligeti takes great interest in the revenue recognition policies—that is, the company's policy on when during the sales cycle it actually

A Good Deal

Financial statements prepared by a CPA represent an excellent value in raising money because he or she can offer the perspective of an outside investor and help you strengthen the presentation to appeal to an investor's needs. Don't try to save on expenses by preparing financial statements on your own!

books its revenues. Growing companies, he says, sometimes push sales out the door. This is bad for investors because it makes profits look high, when in truth the cash flow might be poor because customers are not paying as quickly as the company counts its sales. In general, Ligeti looks at the sales to ensure that a high percentage of what are booked as sales are indeed done deals.

As for liabilities, most equity investors are looking for term loans. Most equity investors would prefer longer rather than shorter term loans, Ligeti says. Why? Short-term loans require much more cash than long-term loans because the payment is divided by more periods. Also, some term loans are interested only in a big balloon payment. The equity investor wants that balloon payment to come due as far into the future as possible

Moving along, accrued salaries payable to the owners can signal trouble for the equity investor, Ligeti says. The same is true for loans from the company's owners. The problem is that while bankers simply subordinate these debts to their own loans and then call them equity, a venture capital investor will not. "We don't want to put in equity just so the shareholders can be paid," he says. It's the same with notes, or loans by the shareholders to the company. "We don't want to be in a position where we make an investment and [shareholders] walk away with their loans paid."

What principals often call loans, venture capital investors call sweat equity, Ligeti notes. "It's not always a constructive use of proceeds to pay off the owners of the business. They have a large stake in the company, which will more than make up for accrued salary, or loans through appreciation in the value of their holdings." That is, if this appreciation occurs.

Even if equity investors won't pay off your loans, it may not be a bad idea to have them on your balance sheet. In particular, if you are underpaid from the start of your business, the difference between what you should be paid and what you are paid should be logged as a loan to the company because if down the road, the company prospers on a grand scale and it can afford to pay you back, with the loan documented from the get-go, there's ammunition to make a case. If, on the other hand, five years down the road you tell your equity investors that you feel the company owes you salary from the lean years, they will tell you to go "pound sand." This highly likely set of circumstances is one good reason why all companies, even young ones, should have a set of financial statements prepared early on.

> **Shop Talk**
> The income statement shows performance over a quarter or a year. The balance sheet, by contrast, takes a financial snapshot of the company at a single moment in time.

Finally, Ligeti looks at the balance sheet's equity section. He wants the lowest debt-to-equity ratio possible. It's not that he has any aversion to bank debt or financial leverage; he just wants to be sure that the company founders are his equity partners and are motivated to create an increase in value. After all, if the only real money in the business comes from lenders, it's easier for the owners to walk away when the going gets tough.

Income Statement Analysis For The Equity Investor

Next, Ligeti digs into the statements of income and cash flow. Of these, the cash-flow statement provides more information. In the world of equity investing, especially with growth companies, the concept of profit becomes slippery. "If a company is increasing its sales dramatically and operates in a slow-paying industry, such as health care, they could be cash flow negative the whole year. More often than not, companies go out of business not because they lack profitability but because they run out of cash."

If that's the case, what good are profits? That's the point precisely, and the reason Ligeti, like most other equity investors, has a decided preference for the cash flow statement.

Still, there are a few items he looks for on the income statement. First, like a banker, Ligeti looks at gross, operating and net margins to see if they are in line with industry averages. And he looks at the trends in contributions to revenues, if the company has more than one product or line. "Ideally, we'd like to see the revenues moving toward the higher margin products over time," he says.

Also, Ligeti wants to know whether the revenues are recurring, meaning, Is there a lot of repeat business, or must the company constantly find new customers? "Obviously, it's much less expensive to generate revenues from existing customers than it is to go out and find new ones," Ligeti says. "If the revenue structure is a recurring one, the company can substantially increase its earnings over a period of time."

Ligeti looks at the general and administrative expenses. Though high general and administrative expenses are not viewed favorably, perhaps they are high because the owner wants to break even rather than show a profit. Many business owners engage in this management of income to reduce or avoid paying corporate income taxes. Then again, maybe expenses are high because the owner is not on top of the company.

If Ligeti doesn't see R&D on the balance sheet in the form of capitalized expenditures, he'll look for R&D expenses on the income statement. This only applies to technology companies, for which innovation is the key to future profits. For most service or manufacturing companies, a commitment to R&D does not matter to equity investors.

In addition to the value of expenses, Ligeti says, most equity investors also examine the trend relative to revenues. "They're looking for operating leverage," he says. "Ideally, the company is engaged in a business where general and administrative expenses, as a percentage of sales, decrease as sales increase." That's a significant benefit, since under those conditions, the company becomes more profitable, hence more valuable, the larger it gets.

Cash Flow Analysis For
The Equity Investor

That would be a first cut at the income statement. For a closer look, Ligeti, like most equity investors, analyzes the cash flow statement. "Overall, I want to see how capital-intensive the business is," he says, referring to financial capital as well as plant and equipment.

There's nothing wrong with capital intensity. It's just that if the business needs a lot of money to grow, the equity investor must know this upfront. Seasonality, for instance, leads to capital intensity because a company must bulk up on inventory and endure carrying costs.

He's also checking out the rate at which accounts receivable turn over. Remember, accounts receivable eat cash. And the longer a receivable is outstanding, the more cash it eats. For growth companies, lengthy collection periods, in conjunction with an overall increase in the volume of receivable, mean that the company is really being squeezed. In fact, says Ligeti, it's possible for a growth company to be highly profitable but have negative cash flow every month.

Though receivables financing from banks would seem to solve capital-intensity issues, it's not always available. For instance, young companies often cannot get receivables financing. Also, companies that have new or untested products have a tough time landing receivables financing. And service companies' receivables always cause problems because there is no exchange of a physical product, and therefore nothing the seller can take back if the buyer fails to pay. It's often the equity investor who must step up to the plate to provide the extra layer of capital so that the operation can catch its breath. But the question on his or her mind, Ligeti says, is, Just how much capital is this going to take?

The answer to this question requires more than an analysis of what's happening with various balance sheet accounts and how they affect cash. There are also things like the principal portion of loan payments and capitalized lease obligations (i.e., when you own the equipment when the lease is over) that never show up on an income statement but are nonetheless vital and often require voluminous outlays for any company that is ramping up for the future. Ergo the preference for the cash flow statement over the income statement for most equity investors.

Taking Action

Analyze your own financial statements the way investors do. What do they tell you about the strengths and weaknesses of your own business? Address these weaknesses in your presentation to investors and how—once the company is funded—they can be remedied.

Chapter 22

Raising Equity Capital

Most new business ideas are viable, yet most new businesses fail. Many do so because the entrepreneur does not properly execute the idea. Others fail because they lack capital. There are two primary reasons businesses fail to raise the capital they need:

- The entrepreneur pursues the wrong sources of capital.
- The entrepreneur fails to adequately plan for his or her search for capital.

"Ready, fire, aim," unfortunately, is a formula for disaster when it comes to raising money. Chiefly because most companies have few viable investor candidates and getting in front of one ill-prepared dramatically increases the likelihood that they will pass on your deal.

The following paragraphs offer an algorithm for planning and meeting with angel investors. But in truth, the advice applies to any equity investor, including institutional venture capitalists, investment bankers and reverse merger candidates.

At the broad-brush level the sequence of your tactics for raising equity capital are as follows:

- Business planning: Much of business planning involves writing a business plan. For reasons discussed below, this is fundamental to your search. But on a pragmatic level, you can't set appointments until would-be investors have looked at your business plan. (See Chapter 23 for strategies for writing a business plan.)

- Lead generation: You must find the kind of people who typically invest in early-stage deals. Once you learn where they are, you must qualify them.
- Follow up, follow up, follow up.
- Close the deal.

Don't Forget

You must take the time and effort to plan your strategy. If you are starting a business or raising money for one in its early stages, you may only get one opportunity to do it. Failure to raise capital may mean the failure of the business.

Business Planning

Here are the planning steps to follow even before you make that first phone call to investors:

- **Prepare a business plan.** You must have a business plan for two very good reasons. First, if your initial contact with an investor is successful, he or she will request one. When an investor asks to see a plan, or even a plan summary, it must be on his or her desk the next morning. At the very least, it must go out first-class mail that day. If there is a delay of, say, three to six weeks

Taking Action

Consider using off-the-shelf business plan software. These programs can stimulate your thinking by confronting you with the kinds of questions an investor would ask.

between the request for a plan and its arrival, you can pretty much kiss that investor good-bye.

Second, investors ask a lot of questions. That's all they seem to do. And it's only by writing a business plan that you can possibly hope to answer the kinds of questions an investor will ask, with the kind of conviction and authority that will win the day. Remember, there is not an entrepreneur on the face of this earth who raised a single penny simply by writing a business plan. Entrepreneurs raise money by presenting their plan, and using the thinking that went into its writing to defend their ideas, strategies and tactics before investors. Flip ahead to the chapter titled "Writing A Business Plan," which discusses how to prepare one.

- **Determine your sizzle.** The business plan is the steak. Now what is the sizzle? What is the one-line answer to the first question the investor will ask: "What does your business do?" The response must be brief, understandable and memorable.

  For instance, if your business resells deep-discount travel packages for unused vacations at luxury resorts to Fortune 1000 consumer-products companies to use as fulfillment premiums, don't say that. The investor's eyes will glaze over at the word "unused." Say: "We are the business that makes luxury travel affordable for 50 million middle-income Americans." Then the investor will say, "I see," giving you the opportunity to say, "Travel in the Unites States is a $60 billion market annually. With a

Shop Talk
Investors and entrepreneurs often talk about the "lead investor." This is the person or institution that makes the most significant financial contribution to the deal. Also, because a large investment by one entity can often attract other dollars, the lead investor is the one that is sought first.

market this size, there are lots of niches, and we are operating in one that has little competition and high margins. . . ."

Or, let's say that your business offers physicians marketing services for elective surgical procedures, which helps them overcome the ceilings on fees imposed by HMOs and other third-party payers. Don't say that right out of the box. Instead, say, "We are the new breed of marketing agency that every physician now knows that she needs if she hopes to survive the changes in medicine. . ."

Such statements are your sizzle. They are succinct, memorable and, perhaps most important, repeatable. You want a sound bite an investor can easily repeat to his or her fellow investors. Even Wall Street uses this trick. When venerable motorcycle maker Harley-Davidson went public, the pitch to investors was: "Own a piece of an American icon."

- **Form an advisory board.** Every industry has people who have succeeded. Reach out to these people and ask for their help in the form of serving on your advisory board. There's a lot of psychology in why people readily agree to such a proposition. Many appreciate being recognized as successful. Others have that natural mentoring orientation that comes from being a successful businessperson. Some want to relive their previous success, while others would simply like to be part of a support system they wish they had when they were starting out.

But one of the real purposes of forming an advisory board is to help generate leads. When you ask advisory board members about sources of financing, if those requests have been properly initiated, you find that many willingly share their contacts. To a lesser extent, the purpose of forming an advisory board is to increase the comfort level outside investors have with your team.

- **Focus on getting a lead investor.** If you are privately raising equity capital, there's little likelihood that you will run into one sugar daddy who will cut a check for the entire deal. It's more likely that you will run into a lot of investors who will offer smaller amounts. These are helpful, but they should be found later. Initially, you must focus all your energy on finding the investor or investors who will take down 25 percent to 50 percent of your deal, and who in doing so will provide a magnet for the smaller investors.

- **Seek legal counsel.** Soliciting capital may bring several state and federal securities laws into play. You do not want to unwittingly run afoul of them, which may cause you to return capital you worked so hard to raise. Even though many deals are exempt from state and federal securities laws, there can still be a host of requirements on notification, documentation and the number of investors who can participate in the offering. Raising money is hard. Don't make it harder by unknowingly breaking the law.

- **Prepare a deal summary.** Technically, this should be your business plan's executive summary. As is mentioned in the chapter about business plans, the executive summary should be no longer than two pages and must function as a stand-alone document. This summary must describe the company, product or service, market, competition, key personnel, funding required, and use of proceeds and give a historical and projected financial snapshot. To stay within the one- to two-page length, you should write no more than one paragraph about each item.

- **Get referrals.** If an investor is interested in learning more about your business after the first telephone call or meeting, he or she might want to talk to someone else, such as a customer, licensee, franchisee, your accountant, attorney, or members of your advisory

Don't Forget
Investors are people, too. To strike a deal, you must be able to move beyond the language of attorneys and accountants and ignite imagination and curiosity.

Taking Action

One technique that is used by companies raising money is the publication of a regular newsletter. This keeps investors and potential investors up on the company as it makes progress.

board or board of directors. Plan for this question by figuring out who should talk. That way, when an investor asks to speak with someone, you can offer a name and a phone number rather than saying "I'll get back to you on that." Remember, you may never get the investor back on the telephone again. But if he or she has an action step and takes it, the mating dance is still on track.

- **Get introductions.** If your lead-generation process turns up investors you do not know, you must work ahead of time to get some kind of introductions. The best are when someone calls ahead of you and warns that you'll be calling. That way, you'll get an initial telephone call with the investor nearly 100 percent of the time.

  As a fallback, during the first conversation, if you can say in your first breath "Our mutual acquaintance Peggy Bennett suggested contacting you," chances of the call being successful—that is, the investor agreeing to look at something you send him or her—increase dramatically.

  Former employees, trade associations, accountants, lawyers or the person who supplied your lead in the first place all represent viable candidates to prepare the investor for your initial contact.

- **Choose a meeting venue.** If you have something in your factory or office worth seeing, such as a manufacturing process, you should always try to get the investor to come to your turf for the first meeting. However, if you work in a hovel or at home, it may not be a good idea to let the investor see your space. If this is the case, plan ahead of time a variety of meeting places where you know what's going on, such as the office of your accountant or attorney, or hotel lobbies you've visited that can accommodate an intimate conversation.

Lead Generation

If you ever trace your life's path in total, you may see that where you have ended is, to a great extent, the result of chance meetings and random events. The same theory applies to raising money. You never know whom you will meet who will put you in touch with the person who becomes your investor.

Here are some real-life examples of such serendipity:

A turkey restaurant owner looking to expand, got a referral, of all places, from the person who supplied him with ham (clearly not a major vendor) to a franchise development consultant. After that, it was almost biblical in the chain of names that led to the almighty investment capital. The franchise developer, named Bloomenthal, had a friend by the name of Levine, who had a friend by the name of Rosen, who had a friend by the name Erlich, who had a friend by the name of Freidman, who knew a merchant banker named Miller, who made the deal.

Or consider this story. The president of a homebased care-management company who had been raising money had the opportunity to make a presentation before an angel investor group. About 80 investors filled the room, making it a target-rich environment. His company was met by the investors with all of the enthusiasm normally reserved for a blood test. But a funny thing happened. Just before going "on stage," the entrepreneur was put in an anteroom with two other entrepreneurs scheduled to present that day. They started comparing notes and swapping the names of investors they had met. Our healthcare entrepreneur diligently followed up on these tips, and among them found his lead investor, who committed $200,000 to his company.

Raising money is a lot like finding a job. You must network, network, network. Ask for three names from every person you meet. One entrepreneur who had diligently saved the business cards of every

A Good Deal

Several electronic matching services, such as ACE-Net, provide quick and direct access to angel investors. These matching services may not lead you to capital right away, but they have the power to start you digging in the right vein.

person he had met over the years sent each one a letter asking for help in raising money or putting him in touch with investors. He found five investors, and a lot of encouragement for what he was doing.

If you are not such a pack rat, here are several paths you can take to start meeting investors. Many of these are described in greater detail in Chapter 12, about angel investors.

- Venture capital forums
- Fund-raising seminars
- Venture capital fairs
- Venture capital clubs
- Private capital networks (see Chapter 13)
- ACE-Net (see Chapter 13)
- Professional services, such as accountants and attorneys

Making Contact And Following Up

Now it's time to dial for dollars. Before picking up the telephone, you should have created a business plan and, where possible, gained some kind of entree to each of the investors you plan to approach. Now you must:

- **qualify the investor.** Your first task is ensure you and your would-be investor are a match. This must be done early in the process. After all, every investor has parameters and preferences, and if you don't fit within them, you should probably spend your time on other potential investors.

  One of the first things the investor will ask in your early conversations is who you are and what your company does, to which you should respond something like "We are the business that makes luxury travel affordable for 50 million middle-income Americans."

  Next, you might suggest some overall industry trends, but then you'll need to ask: "Do you typically invest in companies such as ours?" If the person you are talking to doesn't invest in companies like yours, it's time to gracefully bow out and move on. But remember to get three more names before you do.

- **answer questions.** If the investor has any interest, he or she will ask many questions. This is where writing a good business plan pays off. Because you've thought through every aspect of the business, you should be able to manage these questions.

It's important, however, to answer with confidence. The investor is evaluating you from the moment the conversation begins. Equity investors are not like lenders in this regard. They don't rely on cash flow to recoup their investment. They instead rely on you, the entrepreneur, to build value and sell the business to other investors until the point where it gets sold to the public or another corporation. The upshot is, if you can't convince this investor, he or she will most likely conclude you probably can't convince the next investor, and that, ultimately, his or her investment will remain trapped inside the company.

You want to show momentum because you want to leave investors with the feeling that things are happening quickly, that if they invested, their money would immediately be used productively and not sit around in limbo

One, Two, Three, Go!

The 20-minute pitch is standard operating procedure; you must be able to tell your story in this amount of time. The underpinning of the presentation is your business plan. Thus, in the allotted time, you must cover the major sections of the plan. You are trying to answer these questions in the investor's mind:

- What is the company?
- What are its strengths?
- How has it performed?
- Where is it going?
- How will it get there?
- What does it mean to me if it succeeds?

Whether you are meeting with one investor or a roomful, the best strategy is to walk them through a set of 10 to 15 slides that punctuate your remarks.

while you figure out the nuances of getting the business to the next stage of development.

- **get a meeting.** Your objective during the initial contact is to schedule a meeting with the investor. If your list of potential investors is well qualified, meetings will come easily. If not, getting an investor to agree to a meeting will be more challenging.

  Generally speaking, if the investor is interested in meeting, he or she will request more information, such as a business plan or business plan summary. Don't agree to send it out without getting something in return. Specifically, you want the investor to agree to meet on a certain date after he or she has reviewed the plan.

  Now it's up to you to make sure your business plan arrives on the investor's desk the next day. In addition, include some kind of sample or tangible evidence of your product or service. If you sell imported shelf-stable food

Because We Like You

Getting other people to like you is the subject of another self-help book. But here are the concepts outlined in Part Two of perhaps the greatest book ever written on the subject: *How to Win Friends and Influence People* (Simon & Schuster), by Dale Carnegie. Read them several times before you meet with a prospective investor.

- Become genuinely interested in other people.
- Smile.
- Remember that a person's name to that person is the sweetest, most important sound in any language.
- Be a good listener. Encourage others to talk about themselves.
- Talk in terms of the other person's interests.
- Make the other person feel important—and be sincere.

products, this is easy. If you manufacture waterbeds, this is more difficult. Even in difficult situations, it's worth considering creative solutions. Pictures, customer testimonials and videotapes can sometimes help bring a product or service to life. Anyone can send a bunch of papers in the mail that pile up on someone's desk. But product and service samples are picked up, toyed with—and considered.

Taking Action

Following are five steps to suggest the investor take after the close of the initial meeting. Have the investor:

1. read your business plan (assuming he or she has only read a summary to date).

2. try your product or service.

3. speak with one of your references.

4. have his or her attorney or accountant call you.

5. call someone he or she has worked with who understands your industry.

- **manage objections.** Typically, seeking the first meeting presents the first wall of objections: "The product is not developed enough," "The distribution channel is too crowded," "Your management team is too thin" or "It doesn't appear that you have established technical feasibility."

    If the investor is qualified to participate in your offering, you must be tenacious. Generally, when investors decline an opportunity, it's because they don't understand a certain aspect of the product, market, technology or your vision for the company. As a result, when investors say they don't want to meet, ask them why not, and then show them where their thinking is off.

- **prepare a formal presentation.** You cannot meet with an investor without having prepared a formal presentation. Remember, the investor is evaluating your ability to sell the company because it's how he or she will eventually get a return. If you show incompetence in this arena, even if the company shows promise, it spells trouble for your capital-formation efforts.

- **conduct the initial meeting.** There are straightforward objectives for the first meeting: Number one, make the investor like you. Second, commit the investor to some kind of action step.

You must get the investor to like you for a simple reason. If he or she doesn't, there's little chance the deal you are proposing will happen. Unlike a lender, who bases his or her decision on credit quality exclusively, an equity investor looks for personal chemistry, at least for earliy-stage offerings. Without some baseline affinity for the entrepreneur and what he or she is doing, there is no basis for an investment. Also remember that an equity investor can be romanced by business ideas and people, but it's unlikely that a lender would change the lending criteria simply because he or she liked the entrepreneur.

But you must do more than simply hit if off with the investor. The meeting must close with some sort of action on the part of the investor.

Finally, keep in mind that just like with the initial telephone conversation, you want to avoid ceding control of the process to the investor. Therefore, try to make the action steps conditional upon a second and, hopefully, closing meeting. For instance, you might say: "So you agree to try our product for two weeks and then meet with me to discuss your thoughts."

Closing The Deal

If things have gone according to plan, the date for the second meeting should have been set during the first. If not, getting this second meeting might take some effort and a bit of follow-up.

Regardless, the second meeting is deal time. And even if it's not, it's certainly the time to eliminate the investors who are not worth your time pursuing further.

You must pop the question in a way that involves the investor in the decision-making process. Also, you must do it in such a way that you force the investor to declare his or her interest or lack thereof. Here is a sample dialogue:

Entrepreneur: We have met twice. I appreciate the time you have taken to understand my company. Now that you know a little more, and since you clearly have some experience in these matters, I want to ask you an important question. How much capital do you think we should be raising?

Investor: Well, to tell you the truth, I'm glad you asked that. Because I have studied your plan, and I think you'll need much more than the $500,000 you initially sought. I think you need $750,000. Not right away but shortly after you commence marketing, which, according to this plan, could happen at the end of this year.

Entrepreneur: Comments like that let me know I've chosen the right course of action by seeking hands-on investors, who can provide not just capital but input. OK, of that $750,000, how much can you commit to?

Gotcha! At this point the investor has few courses of action. He or she can suggest a material amount, a small amount or no amount. If the answer is none, you can say goodbye to that investor and move on. If it's a small amount, you can solidify this investor's interest by telling him or her you are looking for a lead investor and asking if he or she will commit the dollars just suggested when a lead investor is found. Most will say yes. If the answer is a large amount, you have accomplished your objective: You've found a lead investor.

Getting from a yes to depositing money in the bank is beyond the scope of this book. However, if you have gone this far in the fund-raising process, you should have had at least some contact with an attorney who has significant experience in securities law. You will now need his or her counsel in drawing up the necessary subscription documentation, or understanding the securities laws exemptions you are taking advantage of.

Chapter 23

Writing A Business Plan

If you are raising capital, particularly equity capital, you need a business plan, period. Take note: A business plan is first and foremost a selling document. It is initially what sells outside investors on why they should take a risk with the company by offering capital.

Ironically, the "planning" value of a business plan is actually a byproduct. That is, it's only by committing to paper answers to all the questions an investor might ask that an entrepreneur will be prompted to seriously consider in detail how the business must run and what it needs.

For instance, how could the following typical questions from investors be answered without some hard thinking on the part of an entrepreneur: What will cause gross margins to improve as sales take off? Going forward, what percentage of your revenues will be recurring in nature? Or, there's always: Can you describe the skills, experience, salaries, and responsibilities of your new hires for marketing, finance and sales management?

Business Plan Structures

There is little agreement on precisely how a business plan should be structured. Much of this disagreement stems from the fact that companies at different stages in their life cycles require different business plans. That is, a company conducting research and development for a new product generally has less to talk about than a company with, say, 100 products, and several manufacturing operations.

This issue notwithstanding, following is a structure for a business plan, which is remarkably flexible and seems to cover all the bases from the perspective of an outside investor looking in.

- **Executive summary:** An abbreviated version of the plan that should be no more than two pages

Don't Forget

No one ever raised capital simply by writing a business plan. They raised money by writing it, then presenting and defending their plan before investors. Therefore, writing a business plan is not an end but the first step in the process of raising capital. It is, in effect, the blueprint for selling your deal to investors.

- **Description of the company and its business:** Provides detail on history, principal assets, products/services and properties

Taking Action

In business plans, bulk matters. If yours is light, add appendices. Also consider using Courier font. It is commonly accepted, large and will increase your page count.

- **Market analysis:** Describes the dimensions, changes and potential of the company's markets

- **Marketing operations:** Describes the specific tactics the company will deploy to capitalize on the opportunity identified in the market analysis

- **Key personnel:** Describes the background of the founders and operators of the business and validates their authority to make claims in the plan about the market, market opportunity and marketing strategy

- **Financial analysis:** Contains use of proceeds, summary historical and projected financial performance, detailed historical and projected performance, and assumptions to financial projections. In many cases, the financial analysis should include a comparable valuation analysis, which illustrates how the company stacks up financially against its competitors or similar public companies, as well as provides some measurement of what the company is worth. It's generally a mistake, however, to suggest a company's valuation if it's not profitable or is in its formative stages. In these instances, it's better to let the investor grow comfortable with the company and its prospects than to possibly short-circuit the entire sales process with a cold hard number.

- **Appendices:** Offers opportunity for show and tell

The one deviation to this business plan model occurs with manufacturing companies. Companies that manufacture can provide a detailed description of their operations in the section titled "The Company And Its Business," or can add a new section simply titled "Manufacturing Operations."

In addition, while in the model above, the section titled "Marketing Operations" provides the right context for showing how a service company will expand, it doesn't work so well for a manufacturer that will expand capacity for new markets. Accordingly, an additional section titled "Plan Of Expansion" is appropriate. Thus, in total, a manufacturer's business plan might have the following sections:

- Executive Summary
- Description of the Company And Its Business
- Manufacturing Operations
- Market Analysis
- Marketing Operations
- Plan of Expansion
- Key Personnel
- Financial Analysis
- Appendices

The following sections of this chapter will describe the purpose of each of the major sections of the business plan. They attempt to provide you, the capital seeker, with an insight into the capital provider's perspective. That is, they tell you what kinds of information the source of capital looks for and why. Rather than starting with the executive summary, however, which is generally the first part of the plan that investors read, we'll start with the company and its business and cover the executive summary last.

The Company And Its Business

When investors put money into a business, they need to feel two emotions: comfort and confidence. Specifically, comfort that the business opportunity and people running it are for real, and confidence that the business can succeed. This section of the business plan is where entrepreneurs make investors feel comfortable.

How? By describing everything about the business that is concrete and tangible. If the business is simply an idea, this is hard to do. But even if the business is a

Shop Talk
As noted, your business plan's executive summary must fit on two pages. In addition, when the plan is produced, make sure it is on facing pages rather than back to back, so that investors can take in the company in one glance.

Sample Tables Of Contents

Here are the tables of contents from three actual business plans:

A Chain of Pet-Supply And Animal-Theme Gift Shops

Table of Contents

Sample Tables Of Contents (cont'd.)

A Manufacturer Of X-ray Processing Equipment
Table of Contents

Sample Tables Of Contents

An Internet Promotions Company

Table of Contents

Don't Forget

Your business plan is not complete without a table of contents. In fact, a well-organized table of contents can draw an investor into the plan, whereas its absence could cause them to randomly browse and perhaps prematurely lose interest and put the plan down.

start-up engaged in product or service development but without revenues, there is a bigger story than you might think.

Look at the sample business plan outlines, starting on page 277. Note for instance the X-ray processing equipment manufacturer. Under the section of the business plan titled "The Company And Its Business," the company's products represent just one piece of the puzzle. The company's founder, who has used the plan to raise $1 million, says, "I never knew that there were so many dimensions to our company beyond its products until I started answering questions from investors."

In fact, you can write this section of the business plan simply by answering the following questions about your business. Of course, every situation is different, but the following questions should get you at least 90 percent of the way:

- When was this company started?
- Who else is an owner?
- What is the company's product or service?
- What are the advantages of the company's product or service over competitors?
- What has this company accomplished since its inception?
- Who are the company's strategic partners in the areas of distribution, technology, supply, product or service development?
- What outside professionals—i.e., accountants, lawyers or

Shop Talk

Due diligence is an investigation into the business and its products, markets, facilities, competitors and key employees. An investor's due diligence can be long and painful. And more than a few companies have gone out of business for lack of capital while investors dithered through due diligence. Therefore, a business plan should offer easily verifiable information that speeds up the process of due diligence and puts the investor in a state of readiness to proceed with the deal.

business consultants—have had a material impact on the company.

- Describe the company's facilities. Does it own or lease? What is the square footage?
- How many people does the company employ, and how are these employees organized? By product? By function? By department?
- What does the company own that is proprietary in terms of customer lists, technologies, licenses, patents or manufacturing techniques?
- How has the company been financed to date? Where did the capital come from?

As you answer these questions, remember the investor wants to be comforted. Accordingly, provide lots of facts, including cities, states, dates and telephone numbers, that investors can check if and when they start with their due diligence. For instance, if you outsource the assembly of your product, name the outfit that does it and provide its address, telephone number and any other contact information. Ditto for professionals. Got a patent? Great. Provide the U.S. patent number.

Market Analysis

Again, take the investors' perspective: What do they want to know next? Well, assuming you've done a good job describing how you have organized resources in the preceding section, the next question becomes, What are these resources organized to capitalize on? Specifically, what is the size of the market and what opportunities does it offer?

To write an effective market analysis, entrepreneurs must take off their business-owner hats and put on their captain-of-industry hats. Specifically, they must produce the analysis with a supreme understanding (or at least the appearance of a supreme understanding) of the events and trends creating opportunity and shaping the market.

Don't Forget
Prose is nice, but investors want to see upwardly trending graphs in the market-analysis section of the business plan.

A Good Deal

Unless your business plan contains sensitive information that can be used against you, do not include a confidentiality agreement. You stand a better chance of raising money if your plan's distribution is wide.

The overall objective of this analysis is to make a case for the market in which the company participates and thus, by association, make a case for the company's product or service itself. This is sometimes a tall order, even when the underlying market offers significant opportunity. Consider the manufacturer of X-ray processing equipment.

This company faced a problem in making a case for its products. Specifically, what angel investor, venture capitalist or investment banker would invest in conventional technology—the processing of X-ray film—when diagnostic imaging stands on the brink of a digital revolution?

The company astutely made its case in the market analysis by asserting that the market for conventional technology had more legs than was readily apparent. It backed this assertion up with the following points:

- Digital-imaging technology, though viable, would, in most instances, cost the majority of users more than $1 million to install and in addition would have introduced a new challenge in data management that many health-care institutions were unprepared to meet.

- Digital enhancements to conventional systems cost more than $100,000, still outside the range of many health-care practices.

- The filming and processing of X-ray film represent a revenue center for many small practices, and they would be unwilling to forgo this revenue when faced with capitated rates from health insurers.

- Chiropractic, veterinary, podiatry, D.O. and M.D. practices—the primary purchasers of conventional X-ray processing equipment—were actually increasing in number.

- Sales of X-ray film totaled some $7 billion annually, with the market dominated by global manufacturers such as Fuji, Kodak, AGFA and 3M, which were not simply going to let a multibillion-dollar market slip through their fingers.

- Most radiologists and physicians grew up on film-based diagnostic imaging and would resist a sudden shift to a new media.

- Finally, and most important, the United States, though a fertile market, represented a small portion of overall global demand. For many emerging industrial countries seeking to establish even a base level of health care, digital-imaging systems were not even a consideration. By contrast, however, conventional X-ray suites, with conventional X-ray film processors, are in hot demand in countries such as China, with its more than 55,000 hospitals.

It's important to note that a good market analysis doesn't simply make sweeping statements about trends in the market. Instead, it relies upon primary (i.e., original) research and published secondary research, government statistics, white papers or studies supplied by trade associations, and authoritative articles in the trade press.

According to angel investor Bill Simms in Sacramento, California, who invests for himself and and for a large corporation, "I continue to turn down business plans where the market analysis isn't wired tight and doesn't make a convincing case for the company's product or service."

Simms' stance makes great sense. After all, many investors are generalists with no specific industry knowledge or experience. Therefore, as a form of protection against being taken to the cleaners, many investors look for hard numbers backed by third parties to support the market analysis. Another reason for generating a market analysis backed by hard numbers concerns the investor's due diligence. That is, no one will invest in a company without taking some sort of independent look at the market. By offering an analysis with authoritative sources, you provide investors with a road map, which with any luck will get them to the closing table faster than if they floundered

Don't Forget

For many equity investors, marketing operations represent the nib of the plan. After all, it's what the company will do to capitalize on an opportunity that will increase earnings and hence the value of the equity investor's stake in the company.

alone, trying to see if the market offers a real opportunity.

Keeping the above points in mind, here are some of the questions your business plan's market analysis should answer:

- What is the market for your product or service in dollars?
- What is the market for your product in terms of units?
- What is the market's historical rate of growth?
- If the market is segmented many ways (e.g., the personal productivity segment of the software market), what were the rates of growth for the segments in which you are offering product or services?
- What is the projected rate?
- Why is there a deviation between historical and projected growth rates in the market for your product or service?
- What are the three primary determinants of demand?
- How is demand now satisfied in your industry; who are the major players?
- How has the market for the product changed in the past five years, and why?
- How do you anticipate it will change going forward?

Marketing Operations

The marketing operations section of a business plan makes the logical break between the opportunity defined by the analysis and the specific strategies and tactics the company will deploy to capitalize on the opportunity.

When writing your business plan's marketing operations section, keep in mind that it's not so much a great market opportunity that gets investors excited as it is a good solid marketing plan and a management team that inspires confidence it can execute the plan.

Describing marketing operations presents a different set of challenges for companies that are already selling their products and

Taking Action

Look at your historical financial performance and quantify the relationship between marketing activities and the net result. Thus armed, you are in a position to make your case for how financing more of the same will lead to increased profits.

raising capital for expansion vs. those that are raising capital to commence their initial marketing efforts.

Marketing Operations For Established Companies

Naturally, companies with a track record have it all over upstarts. Why? Because they have a historically proven algorithm for generating sales. For instance:

- Each manufacturer's representative will sell one unit a month.
- Every 1,000 catalogs mailed generates approximately $1,200 in new orders.
- The response rate on direct mail is 90 percent, and the pay-up rate on resulting subscriptions is 97 percent.
- The telemarketers are able to make appointments 27 percent of the time, and the direct sales force closes on about 9 percent of those appointments.
- The ratio of sales to media purchases for our infomercials is about 1.50 to 1.

Even if a business owner has never thought much about it, if there's a history, there is some reasonably reliable relationship between marketing activities and sales. The value of this relationship in raising money is incalculable. Specifically, it will lend an air of credibility to the company's projected financial performance, which for equity investors is perhaps the most important variable on which they base investment decisions.

Although companies that are already selling their product or service have an advantage over those that aren't, challenges still exist. Specifically, these companies must convince investors that their current way of selling products is:

- the optimal method of marketing.
- scalable; that is, it will work as well or better when enlarged by an order of magnitude.

The challenge is particularly difficult if the company is selling its product but not yet making any money. If the argument goes: "We simply need to run a higher unit volume over our fixed costs to reach profitability," that's fine. But be prepared to answer the following question: "Will throwing more money at marketing produce additional business at a reasonable cost, or will the additional expense offset the gains you are hoping for?"

Marketing Operations For Start-up Companies

Companies that haven't yet sold their product have a much tougher journey than their brethren that have some experience in the marketplace. And of these, companies with new or revolutionary products have the toughest sell of all. Why? Because the investor questions whether: 1) the customer will accept the product or service, and 2) whether the distribution channel will accept the product. Remember Internet cafes? Most failed because consumers proved unwilling to purchase online services in a retail environment.

Keeping these challenges in mind, most business owners go wrong in the marketing operations section of their business plan by making the following claim:

Upon financing, the company will engage in an integrated sales and marketing program consisting of advertising, public relations, trade-show exposition, direct selling through a company-paid sales force and the use of a manufacturer representative.

The problem with this approach as it relates to pitching an investor on your deal is that you are saying, in effect, you really don't know the best way to sell the product. When investors have the sense that you want to go to school on their money, they will probably say to themselves, "Not with my money you aren't!"

The whole business of raising capital for companies that have yet to sell a product or service is an imperfect Catch-22. However, the best way to overcome the process's inherent flaws is to reduce the marketing operations to one or two primary tactics.

For many companies, the old one-two punch delivers most of their sales anyway. Giant Dell Computer sells directly to consumers through catalogs and its own sales force. Amazon.com sells books over the Internet. Amway sells door to door. And the venerable Thighmaster became a household name by using infomercials.

For start-up companies, the beauty of reducing marketing operations to a one-two punch is that it then becomes feasible to conduct test marketing on a low-cost basis. With actual results in hand, no matter how rudimentary they may be, the business plan's credibility increases by a factor of 10.

Don't Forget
Any entrepreneur can make sweeping claims about what he or she will do once funded. But in the eyes of the investor, the entrepreneur who bases his or her claims on experience rather than supposition represents the best bet.

To see just how simple test marketing can be, consider the following low-cost techniques that almost any company can use:

Example 1: A janitorial company claims in its business plan that it will use advertising in local newspapers to promote free trial use of its service to commercial landlords in exchange for re-evalauting their existing maintenance contracts. **Low-cost test:** Run three advertisements in local newspapers, and record the response. When landlords call, use the occasion to poll them about needs, preferences and price sensitivities. Package these interviews as original market research to share with investors.

Example 2: A restaurant planning to franchise claims in its business plan that new sites will engage in so-called community-based marketing to draw customers from the surrounding 3-mile radius. **Low-cost test:** Saturate three neighborhoods near the existing restaurant with hand-delivered fliers that have a coupon offer. Distribute approximately 1,000 fliers per neighborhood and record the response rate of consumers who bring them into the restaurant to take advantage of the coupon offer. When customers visit the restaurant, offer a free dessert in exchange for completing a questionnaire. Compile these questionnaires, and use the results as original market research in the business plan.

Example 3: The manufacturer of a line of handheld garden tools claims in its business plan that it will sell its products through mass-market distribution channels. **Low-cost test:** Develop a list of 25 questions for buyers of garden tools at 25 mass-market retailers. Focus the questions on the requirements to gain shelf space, minimum order sizes, policies on payments and returns and the buyer's beliefs about the level of competitiveness in handheld garden tools. Survey the buyers by telephone. If a majority suggests a willingness to purchase products on a trial basis after a sales call from the company, compile their answers in the business plan, and write the marketing operation section of the plan so that direct selling is the primary marketing activity.

As a parting comment, whether or not your company is established, the marketing operations section of your business plan should answer these questions:

- What are the company's marketing objectives?
- What promotional tactics will the company use?
- What does each of these promotional tactics cost?
- What is the estimated or historical relationship between the company's proposed tactics and the resulting product or service sales?
- What are the primary channels of distribution for this product or service?

Key Personnel

Most investors say they don't even read business plans. But if you question them more closely, they will all tell you their own proprietary technique for skimming the plan to see whether the company merits a serious look. But many of these "proprietary" glances turn out to be remarkably the same. The investor reads the first paragraph of the executive summary, skims the balance and then turns to the plan's key personnel section.

It's simply human nature. Investors want to see who's running the show. They also want to know if there is any connection between themselves and the people involved in the company. And take note, some connection, no matter how small—as in "Their controller used to be a CPA at the accounting firm we used at my last company"—can make the difference between the investor deciding to take a closer look and the investor passing on the opportunity.

But that's just the first glance. Sooner or later, the serious investor

Don't Forget

When writing the key personnel section of your business plan, don't be modest; talk in terms of skills and experience instead of previous titles.

will settle down with the plan's key personnel section to take a critical look at the people behind the company. While the old saying in real estate is "location, location, location," the mantra for financing tiny companies is "management, management, management." And for better or worse, the first time a would-be investor meets the management team is in the biographical sketches written in the business plan.

Getting The Right Spin
On Biographies

So how must the biographical sketches be spun to do their work? Overall, the biographies of the founders and senior managers must be cast in terms of concrete skills and specific accomplishments, rather than titles and educational trophies.

A company with most, if not all, of its history ahead of it must offer the investor some assurances that the members of the management team can execute the plan. And the best way to do this is by showing a track record of execution.

Here is a biographical sketch cast two ways. Which is more inspiring?

James P. Morgan, Co-founder & Director of Marketing

Mr. Morgan has more than 15 years' experience in consumer-product marketing. Prior to co-founding the company, he was associated with Northstar Industries. He joined the company in 1985 as a marketing associate and during the next 15 years, rose to successively more responsible positions with Northstar. Prior to founding this company, Morgan was promoted to northeast regional marketing director of consumer products for Northstar Industries. He earned a bachelor's degree in business administration from Boston College. Currently, he is active in several business and civic organizations.

or . . .

James P. Morgan, Co-founder & Director of Marketing

Mr. Morgan has more than 15 years of experience in consumer-product marketing. During this time he has developed several critical skills related to the direct marketing of consumer products. Prior to co-founding the company, Mr. Morgan was associated with Northstar Industries. He joined the company in 1985 as a marketing associate, his primary responsibility being telemarkeing and qualifying prospects that responded to company advertisements. He enjoyed above-average response rates and, as a result, was promoted to manager of telemarketing sales training. In this capacity, Morgan created and published a direct-marketing manual that is still used by the company today. After three years in this capacity, he trained three individuals as his replacement and was promoted to a regional management position, fulfilling advertising and marketing functions. Specifically, Morgan hired, and was the point-of-contact for, regional advertising agencies to ensure their efforts were consistent with the company's national strategy and advertising campaign. In addition, Morgan oversaw the company's direct sales in the region by participating in sales calls, recruiting new personnel and directing quarterly sales promotions. He left Northstar last year to form the company. His responsibilities now include marketing planning, and recruiting and training the company's sales and marketing staff. Morgan earned a bachelor's degree in business administration from Boston College. Currently, he is a member of the Direct Marketing Association and the Chamber of Commerce Council on Marketing 2000 and is an advisor to the board of directors of the downtown enterprise zone business-incubation project.

Overcoming A Thin Management Team

Companies raising money are by definition needy. Financing the addition of new personnel is often the point of the business plan.

Still, it's difficult to overcome the challenges posed by an incomplete management team. After all, management is what the investors are investing in. And if there's no management in place, the question on the investor's mind becomes, What's the point here?

One way to overcome this problem is to include in the biography the individuals who will be hired once the company is funded. Investors know that it takes time to find employees, and they would prefer that entrepreneurs aren't looking on their nickel.

Therefore, if two companies are the same in every respect except that one has identified who it will hire and the other has simply suggested that it will hire once funded, the former company is a more attractive candidate in the eyes of the investor.

Granted, few emerging companies have this luxury. The fallback position would be to offer a menu of responsibilities and a biographical sketch of the person the company would hire. Here are biographical sketches from a company that contemplated the expansion of a retail chain of animal-theme gift shops. (The table of contents of this business plan was shown earlier in this chapter.) The only other biography alongside these was the founder's.

- **District managers:** Every five new stores opened will require a district manager. The duties of district managers are to maintain inventories at their locations, hire and manage personnel, staff locations when regular employee disruptions occur, manage cash and daily deposits, manage repair and maintenance of fixtures and equipment, create store displays, and coordinate with the company's merchandise buyer. Ideal candidates for district managers should have two years of experience in a retail environment.

- **Regional managers:** Every 20 stores require the addition of a regional manager. The duties of the regional managers are to oversee and manage the company's warehousing operations, direct purchasing and product distribution for stores in their territory, hire and manage district managers, inspect locations, develop and assist in execution of in-store promotions, and analyze territory for potential new sites. Ideal candidates for regional managers are district managers. Ideal candidates would have three to four years of

A Good Deal

Advisory boards can be a great deal for companies, especially when it comes to bulking up the key personnel section of the business plan. Not only do members of an advisory board add intellectual depth to the company, but they also increase the likelihood that outside investors seeing the plan for the first time will make a personal connection with the company.

experience in managing multilocation retail environments.

- **Chief financial officer, controller:** The company will hire a chief financial officer/controller in the first quarter after financing. The duties of the chief financial officer are to establish disbursement controls, design and oversee multiple commercial banking relationships, implement cash management, initiate and maintain corporate banking relationships, and develop and oversee accounting and financial management information systems. The ideal candidate has 10 to 15 years' experience with a publicly held retailer, specific knowledge about how to manage multilocation banking and cash-management activities, and undergraduate and graduate degrees in finance and/or accounting.

- **Marketing manager:** The company will hire a marketing manager during the first year following financing. The duties of the marketing manager are to establish and manage database marketing operations, oversee and assist with new-store-opening promotions, oversee and assist with new-store community-based marketing programs, and act as marketing consultant to regional managers. The ideal candidate will have 10 to 15 years of multistore marketing experience, good numerical and trend-analysis skills, experience working with printers and graphic designers, and a graduate degree in marketing.

- **Business development officers:** At the conclusion of the second year following financing, the company will hire two business development professionals. Their duties are to manage the building of 50 new stores per year. Specifically, to make final site selections, negotiate with landlords, hire and supervise contractors, and hire and promote district and regional managers. Ideal candidates have five to 10 years of experience in a retail chain, with a demonstrated track record of successfully opening new locations.

- **Buyer/purchasing manager:** During the second fiscal year following financing, the company will hire a full-time buyer. More than operational expertise, this buyer will provide creative leadership and help the company locate unique animal-theme products that its customer base will increasingly expect of our stores in clothing, pet products, gifts, cards and jewelry. To ensure the integration of this creative leadership at the store level, the buyer will also coordinate merchandising displays and holiday decorations. The ideal candidate has a college degree and at least five to seven years of experience purchasing for a multilocation retail chain.

Entrepreneurs gain mileage for including sketches of the people they will hire because it shows critical thinking and planning on the part of the entrepreneur. Simply saying you will hire additional people is merely a declarative statement.

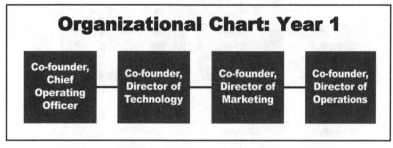

Organizational Chart: Year 3

Another device for overcoming an incomplete management team is to offer projected organizational charts. Here are some sample charts for a company at one, two and three years after financing.

Again, critical thinking about how an organization will grow once funded will win over investors more often than sweeping statements about organizational expansion.

Financial Analysis

The financial analysis section of the business plan incorporates many separate elements: summary historical financial performance, summary projected financial performance, use of proceeds, valuation analysis, detailed financial projections, assumptions to financial projections, and detailed historical financial statements.

Valuation Analysis

If you're raising equity capital, a valuation analysis is important. If you're raising debt capital, a valuation analysis is not as important. An equity investor wants to know the valuation because he or she is buying a hunk of the business. Its value determines the price the investor has to pay.

For instance, assume a business worth $10 million wants to raise $1 million. The investor who puts up the $1 million will get 10 percent of the company's equity. If the business is worth $2 million, the investor's $1 million jumps to 50 percent.

From the entrepreneur's perspective, a higher valuation preserves his or her equity position. And this is precisely why a valuation analysis is often more helpful than a one-line sentence that says, "The business is worth $3 million." An analysis provides some clue as to how the entrepreneur reaches his or her conclusions, as well as a basis for negotiation.

Unfortunately, developing a valuation analysis is beyond the scope of this work. However, many excellent guidebooks can guide you through the process (see Appendix A for a listing).

Use Of Proceeds

Many entrepreneurs handicap themselves by circulating a business plan that doesn't mention how the funds will be used. This is ridiculous. Would you put money into a business without knowing how it was going to be used? It's even more ridiculous considering just how easy it is to prepare a use of proceeds table. Here's one for a manufacturing company:

Purchase of mold dyes	$250,000
Raw materials	$125,000
Marketing	$300,000
Debt repayment	$125,000
Working capital	$150,000
Professional fees	$50,000
Total	**$1,000,000**

A service company might show proceeds with less emphasis on hard assets and more on working capital, marketing and personnel expenditures. For instance, one Internet-services firm anticipated the following use of proceeds:

Working Capital	$500,000
Marketing, development & administrative personnel	$570,000
Leasehold improvements	$100,000
Systems integration	$100,000
Professional fees	$80,000
Total	**$1,350,000**

The use of proceeds section can trip you up too. For instance, there must be some connection between it and the rest of the plan. If, as in the manufacturer's example, a company suggests $300,000 in marketing expenditures, the marketing operations section of the plan must be in sync. Sure, a company might be able to suggest a $600,000 or even a $1 million campaign by supplementing the proceeds with a percentage of the sales. But the plan can't show a $5 million or $10 million marketing campaign when the proceeds earmarked for these efforts are just $300,000 and total projected sales are just $3 million.

In addition, repayment of debt is a red flag for equity investors. They simply resist putting money into a company for the sole purpose of paying off someone else's debt. "There's no growth associated with it," is the common lament.

Shop Talk
The term "valuation" refers to a business's worth. When an investor asks "What is the valuation?" he or she is asking "What is this company worth?"

Summary Projected And Historical Financial Statements

Your business plan needs summary projected and historical income statements for three previous years and five future years. On the following page is a summary historical income statement. (The line items for the projected and historical statements should be the same.)

You must provide summary projected and historical financial statements because most investors like to look at the big picture first. Detailed financial statements, which are usually quite complex, don't offer a mechanism to do this. You just have to dig in. Therefore, if there's no big picture to look at, many investors will simply

Don't Forget

It's always good to reserve some of the proceeds for professional fees. It looks naive to suggest that a transaction of several hundred thousand to perhaps several million dollars can be completed without any fees being paid to lawyers, consultants and accountants.

put the plan aside until they have time to take a closer look. Of course, that may be the first step in a long, slippery road toward the investor never picking it up again. With all the challenges posed by raising money, why throw up another hurdle? Include the summary financial statements in the business plan.

Historical And Projected Financial Statements

Historical financial statements are mandatory. Unless you are doing pure research and development or are a start-up, there's little chance you will raise money without a set of historical financial statements. Giving an investor a business plan without financials is like giving a blind person a book to read without braille. There's no way he or she can make sense of it.

Summary Historical Income Statement

Sales	$1,000,000	$1,500,000	$2,000,000
Cost of sales	750,000	1,000,000	1,350,000
Gross profit	250,000	500,000	650,000
Selling general & administrative expenses	375,000	425,000	450,000
Operating income	($125,000)	$75,000	$200,000

Don't Forget
To inspire the maximum amount of comfort among potential investors, your plan should include financial statements prepared by a certified public accountant.

Even new businesses should have a full set of financial statements created after their first quarter in business. Why? Because founders of businesses often claim they are underpaid. If this is the case, their salary deficit must go on the books as a loan to the company and remain there year in and year out if there's any hope of the entrepreneur recovering this forgone compensation. Once the outside investors are part of the company, there will never be the opportunity for the entrepreneur to say in five years, "Now that the company is on its feet financially, I want the salary I passed up in the early years," unless of course, the loan has been known about from the beginning, and has remained on the company's books. Then there's a better-than-average chance of success. (To understand how investors look at these financial statements, refer to Chapter 21.)

The projected financial statements, on the other hand, consist of an income statement, balance sheet and cash flow statement. Each of these statements generally covers five years. Sometimes during the first two years it's wise to show the cash flow statements quarterly rather than annually. This helps the investor and the entrepreneur understand any seasonal fluctuations, which often have a significant impact on the business's cash flow.

Five years may seem like too far into the future to be making predictions. But keep in mind, investors have a specific reason for wanting to see the fifth-year forecast. They don't expect accuracy. But they'll have a good idea of the entrepreneur's thinking. That is, is he trying to build a $20 million empire? Or is he trying to build a $200 million empire? Keep this in mind as you develop years four and five of your projected financial statements.

Here are some more important ideas about developing financial projections. For the sake of brevity, these will be offered within the framework of the summary projected income statement, since the balance sheet and cash flow statement flow from it.

- **Sales:** First, refer to the marketing operations section of this business plan, which describes in detail some of the challenges associated with forecasting sales. As was mentioned, companies that have never sold their product or service must make some extraordinary efforts in guerrilla test marketing so they can make claims about future sales based on fact rather than guesswork. Anybody can guess, but anyone who does tends not to find financing.

Companies that do have sales must quantify the relationship between their sales and marketing efforts and the resulting sales. What sometimes challenges the credibility of the forecast is a company that has had fairly constant sales historically but is projecting geometric increases after funding. The big questions become "How and why?" If a company plans to use funding to do a higher volume of the same marketing program, it tends to deliver a proportional, not a geometric sales increase. If you already sell a product and are projecting big gains, you must be able to explain to an investor what qualitative changes you'll make to your marketing program to deliver the goods on sales.

- **Cost of goods sold and gross margin:** For many service companies, there is no cost of goods. Take professional service or consulting firms: They simply don't have raw-materials costs. In such cases, a discussion of the gross margin is not necessary. But manufacturers must discuss their gross margin. Companies that are already manufacturing or assembling products know— or should know— what it costs to make them. In fact, a manufacturer contemplating bringing in outside investors should be organized enough that it has a bill of materials for each product it makes and a companion schedule of component costs. If there are no secrecy issues, a bill of materials should be included in the assumptions to the financial projections as a means of offering proof positive on the cost estimates.

  Companies that have not yet commenced manufacturing but will upon financing need good estimates. If several manufac-

Taking Action

If you are outsourcing manufacturing, get an estimate from the manufacturing company and make it one of the appendices to your business plan.

turers provide parts, you'll need several estimates. Once you have them, it's simply a matter of aggregating.

If you are doing your own manufacturing, estimates are tougher to calculate but are even more vital to include in the business plan. Remember, the investor is looking for just two things from the plan: Comfort that the plan and the opportunity are for real, and confidence that the management team can pull it off. You can hit on both cylinders with a good estimate and completely stall with half-baked, sloppily prepared estimates. And if that's not enough to convince you to provide good estimates, remember, no one will invest in a company that does not know what it will cost to manufacture its products. Would you?

In truth, the cost of goods sold is simply a means to the gross margin. Gross margin is defined as sales less cost of goods sold and is usually expressed as a percentage. During a first and second glance, investors probably pay more attention to the gross margin than the cost of goods sold figure that produced it.

Investors look closely at the gross margin. It must not be too far out of kilter with industry norms. For instance, the National Restaurant Association reports that the gross margins for so-called full-menu table-service establishments are about 36 percent. Therefore, if you are opening a restaurant and your projected gross margin is 25 percent, that is a problem. The investor tends to ask, "Why should I invest in an embryonic company with below-average margins when I can invest in any number of public companies with average or superior gross margins?" Why indeed?

On the other hand, projected gross margins of 45 percent can provoke problems as well. The investor will question the credibility of the entrepreneur, wondering, "Doesn't he understand how this industry works?" Of course, breakthroughs in technol-

Don't Forget

Whatever your gross margins may be, for the purposes of making financial projections, it's best to pull them back a couple of percentage points. Why? Because a gross margin on a projected income statement is utopia. In real life there are strikes, stockouts, shrinkage, equipment outages and absenteeism.

ogy, or in marketing, management styles or products, are precisely what can change the economics of an industry and create an investment opportunity. So if your margins are truly above average, that's great. Have a credible explanation for what you are doing that allows you to beat the number that represents the collective knowledge and experience of your industry.

- **Selling, general and administrative expenses:** The easy part of SG&A are the general and administrative costs. This is the one place in your projected income statement where you might actually be able to let the spreadsheet software increase the expenses by a factor of 5 percent each year. Centralized administrative costs are not hard to calculate and should remain fairly constant even if there are significant revenue increases.

  But where companies go wrong in their projected income statement is with the "S," or selling, expenses. Estimating selling costs can be one of the most challenging aspects of developing financial projection because to do it right, entrepreneurs must be certain that their sales model works.

  Again, for products or services that have been sold before, these selling costs are known. The only exception occurs when an established company tries selling in a new venue, such as when giant book retailer Barnes & Noble began selling over the Internet.

  But for companies that are launching a new product or service, these costs are subject to guesswork. Unfortunately, nothing makes investors more jittery than guesswork. One way that selling expenses can tip off the investor that the entrepreneur isn't sure how to sell his or her product is when several different line items are listed under "selling expenses." For instance, if there are costs for advertising, direct mail, telemarketing, sales salaries, public relations and trade shows—it's too much, at least for a smaller company starting out. Remember, the most effective marketing operations rely on the old one-two punch, and in some instances, just the single punch. Keep this idea in mind when developing projected selling costs.

- **Operating income:** With respect to financial projections,

Don't Forget

Organize your assumptions to financial projections by the line items in the summary projected financial statements. That is, first list the sales assumptions, followed by your assumptions on selling and general and administrative expenses.

operating income is the bottom line. In a full-blown in-come statement, the only things happening below operating income are extraordinary gains and losses, which defy projection, and taxes, which despite the best efforts of tax reformers in government, also defy projection. Simply put, in most instances, it just doesn't add to the understanding of the business opportunity to project the future tax liability. And so, operating income is the bottom line.

Many of the concepts for building credible projected gross margins apply at the operating level as well. Specifically, build in conservatism rather than extremism so that it's possible to exceed the projections rather than fall short of them. And where operating margins exceed industry averages, have a tenable explanation. Just as technology, management styles and manufacturing techniques can cause a breakthrough on the gross margins, they can also have a positive effect on the operating margins.

For example, a Midwestern equipment-leasing company had a nearly vertical rise in revenues during start-up operations, and saw an opportunity to generate above-average operating margins. Why? According to a company executive, investments in technology would allow them to interface seamlessly with third-party sales organizations and deliver significant operating leverage. "After a certain point," he says, "we could handle large increases in lease volume with no increases in personnel costs on our end." Apparently, the strength of this reasoning delivered the goods and allowed the company to consummate an $11.25 million public offering in the fall of 1996. Even after the offering, the growth continued, and the company was bought out by a larger leasing company less than two years later, making millions for founders and shareholders.

Assumptions To
The Financial Projections

The last elements of the financial analysis section of the business plan are the assumptions to the financial projections. These are not mathematical equations, but they are not prose, either. Something of a hybrid mutation, assumptions are nonetheless the linchpin of the business plan. That is, they make the financial forecasts mesh with everything that comes before them.

Specifically, if the assumptions declare that marketing expenditures will be 9 percent of sales, and sales in year one are $2 million, the marketing budget must be $180,000, and the marketing strategies and tactics described in the plan had better be achievable for $180,000. If not, there's something wrong with the business plan.

The chart below shows the actual assumptions to financial projections for a manufacturer of photo-processing equipment. This company was successful in raising more than $1 million.

Financial Projection Assumptions

Pricing Assumptions

- The selling price of the MicroProcessor to dealers remains constant throughout the planning period at $2,850.
- The selling price of the MegaProcessor to dealers remains constant throughout the planning period at $6,900.

Direct Cost Assumptions

- MicroProcessor and MegaProcessor unit sales during the five years following financing are:

	Year 1	Year 2	Year 3	Year 4	Year 5
Micro	1,335	2,510	2,646	2,778	3,062
Mega	96	210	220	231	256

- Direct materials costs for MegaProcessor and MicroProcessor processors are:

	Year 1	Year 2	Year 3	Year 4	Year 5
Micro	$1,550	$1,375	$1,300	$1,300	$1,300
Mega	$2,000	$2,000	$2,000	$2,000	$2,000

Financial Projection Assumptions (cont'd.)

- In the first year following financing, the direct labor payroll—exclusive of benefits and payroll taxes—starts at an annual cost of $354,000 and rises to $510,000, for an average payroll cost of $432,000. With benefits and payroll taxes, the average direct labor payroll is $519,000.

- In the second year following financing, the beginning direct labor payroll is $510,000, and the ending direct labor payroll is $667,000, for an average payroll of $588,500. With benefits and payroll taxes, the average direct labor payroll is $695,500.

- In the third year following financing, the beginning direct labor payroll is $667,000, and the ending direct labor payroll is $770,000, for an average direct labor payroll of $718,500. With benefits and payroll taxes, the average direct labor payroll is $862,500.

- Payroll expenses remain flat for the fourth and fifth year following financing.

	Year 1	Year 2	Year 3	Year 4	Year 5
Average direct labor payroll	$432,000	588,500	718,500	718,500	718,500
Payroll taxes & benefits	$87,000	118,000	144,000	144,000	144,000
Total direct labor payroll	$519,000	706,500	862,500	862,500	862,500

- Rent and utilities are $3,000 per month at the beginning of the first year following financing, and $4,700 per month at the end of the first year, for an average rent and utility expense of $3,900. During the second year following financing, rent and utilities start at $4,700 per month and rise to $7,000 per month, for an average rent and utility expense of $6,000. During the third year following financing, rent and utility expenses stabilize at $7,000 per month.

Financial Projection Assumptions

Selling Cost Assumptions

- The company will pay the chief executive officer and executive sales manager a salary of $150,000, with an expense account equivalent to 100 percent of salary and benefits equivalent to 25 percent of salary.

- The company pays the sales manager a salary of $55,000, with an expense account of $15,000 and benefits equivalent to 25 percent of salary.

- The company adds salespeople in the following years at the following costs:

	Year 1	Year 2	Year 3	Year 4	Year 5
Number of salespeople	1	4	4	4	4
Salaries	$45,000	180,000	180,000	180,000	180,000
Expense account (90% of salary)	$41,000	162,000	162,000	162,000	162,000
Benefits/payroll expenses (20% of salary)	$9,000	36,000	36,000	36,000	36,000
Total	$95,000	378,000	378,000	378,000	378,000
Commission (percent of gross sales)	3.5%	3.5%	3.5%	3.5%	3.5%

- In the first year following financing (Year 1), the company hires one full-time salesperson, with an annual salary of $45,000.

- The salesperson hired in Year 1 has travel and entertainment expenses equal to 90 percent of salary.

- The salesperson hired in Year 1 has benefits and payroll expenses equivalent to 25 percent of salary.

Financial Projection Assumptions (cont'd.)

Administrative & Engineering Cost Assumptions

- The company's administrative staff consists of a receptionist, purchasing/materials administrator and bookkeeper at an average annual cost of $100,000. In the second year following financing, expenses for administrative staff will increase to $140,000. In the third year following financing, administrative costs are $190,000.

	Year 1	Year 2	Year 3	Year 4	Year 5
Administrative staff salaries	$100,000	140,000	190,000	190,000	190,000
Benefits/payroll expenses (25% of salary)	$20,000	$35,000	47,500	47,500	47,500

- The company's engineering personnel expenses remain constant, at 3 percent of sales, plus payroll taxes and benefits equivalent to 25 percent of salary.

Appendices

No business plan is complete without appendices. After all the ifs, ands and buts of the rest of the business plan, the appendices provide the investor a refreshing dose of reality. Specifically, the plan's appendices are where you show investors everything about the company that will give them additional dollops of comfort and confidence. Here are items typically found in the appendices of a good business plan:

- Product literature
- Patent certificates
- Company-sponsored research
- Sample sales contracts and agreements
- Publicity
- Trade articles
- Advertising literature or ad concepts under development

- Supporting financial schedules
- Licenses and permits
- Trade references
- Customer testimonials
- Site or personnel photos

There are no rules about what can go into the appendices of a business plan. While each company has its own story to tell, the general theory is to include items that increase the company's credibility with the investor.

When assembling appendices, it's important to make clear separations between different appendices. The many parts that can be included are graphically and visually disparate and, when presented without the guidance of cover sheets or separations, the effect is more confusing than enlightening.

Executive Summary

Even though it's presented first, the executive summary is written last because, if the rest of the plan is well written, the executive summary is simply a question of lifting sentences and stringing them together.

As was noted, the executive summary must be no longer than two pages. It must be written and structured in such a way that it can function as a stand-alone marketing document for the deal. To accomplish this, it must contain a paragraph or two about each of the major sections of the business plan. Specifically:

- The company and its business
- Market analysis
- Marketing operations
- Key personnel
- Financial analysis

The only deviation from the rest of the plan is the first paragraph of the executive summary,

Taking Action

Start drafting your business plan. For most of the financing sources outlined in this book, the first request they will make of you is to "send me your business plan." And as was mentioned earlier, when someone asks for a plan, it should be there the next day. So if you're serious about raising money, do the right thing. Start writing.

which should be a separate section called a summary statement, introduction or preface.

This statement is like the introduction to a book. It tells readers why they must read the plan. But unlike a book's introduction, which can run several pages, the introduction to a business plan, the executive summary, must get its work done in just a few paragraphs. Here is a sample summary statement:

Pope X-Ray Products Inc. manufactures X-ray processing equipment and has more than 30 years of experience inventing and manufacturing image-related equipment. Its products have a large, worldwide installed base and are recognized for quality, functionality and economy. The company has established a dealer network and has stimulated significant demand. Meeting this demand has been constrained by capital considerations.

Meanwhile, diagnostic imaging is undergoing evolutionary change, as traditional film is gradually being replaced by digital technology. Pope X-Ray seeks to exploit both markets. Specifically, the company has capitalized on the entrenched position, Third World potential and longevity of film radiography by continuing to build and distribute high-quality film processors. In addition, the company will enter the digital diagnostic market via the acquisition of technology to exploit the eventual replacement of film in developed countries.

To take advantage of these opportunities, the company seeks an equity capital infusion of $1 million to finance the expansion of its film processor manufacturing and sales activities. Based on this capital infusion, the company believes it can achieve sales of $9.5 million and operating earnings of $3 million within three years of financing. The company seeks another $3 million to acquire digital-imaging technology or assets that will enable it to enter the emerging market for digital imaging. Based on technology it has identified, developed by DMZ Systems, Ltd., Tel Aviv, Israel, Pope believes that it can achieve sales and operating incomes of $33 million and $11 million, respectively, within five years of financing.

Glossary

Accounts payable: a company liability that represents amounts due for goods or services purchased on credit

Accounts receivable: a company asset that represents amounts owed for goods and services sold on credit

Angel investor: a private individual who invests money in a business

Asset: that which is owned by a company and is expected to be used to generate future income

Audited financial statements: financial statements that offer the highest level of assurance by outside independent accountants that they constitute a fair representation of the company's financial position and operating results

Balance sheet: a "snapshot" of the assets, liabilities and owners' equity of a corporation for a given period

Capacity: volume

Cash flow: the net amount of cash generated by a company in an accounting period

Cash flow statement: the financial statement that reflects all inflows and outflows of cash resulting from operating, investing, and financing activities during a specific time period

Collateral: anything of value that can be pledged against a loan, including stocks and bonds, equipment, home equity, inventory and receivables; if you cannot repay the loan, the lender will look to your collateral as a backup source of repayment

Common stock: shares of stock that make up the total ownership of a company

"Coordinated Review" process: the collective review of a SCOR filing by a number of states to increase overall approval time

Cost of goods sold: the cost that a business incurs to produce a product for sale to its customers

Current assets: assets that are expected to be converted to cash within one year through a company's normal operations

Current liabilities: liabilities that are due for payment within one year

Debt financing: capital in the form of a loan, which must be paid back

Depreciate: the ability to write off each year the cost of equipment, vehicles or other fixed assets

Depreciation: allocation of the cost resulting from the purchase of a fixed asset over the entire period of its use

Dividend: the portion of a corporation's earnings that is paid to its stockholders

Due diligence: an investor's investigation of a proposed deal and of the principals offering it before the transaction is finalized; generally performed by the investor's attorney and accountant

Equity: the ownership interest in a company; also referred to as capital, net worth and owners' equity

Equity financing: capital received in exchange for part ownership of a company

Extraordinary gains: earnings from irregular occurrences such as insurance settlements or sale of assets like a company truck

Extraordinary losses: losses from irregular occurrences such as insurance settlements or sale of assets like a company truck; often a one-time occurrence

Factoring: the selling of a business's accounts receivables to a factor, who immediately pays the amount of the receivables, less a discount, and receives the payments when they arrive from customers

Filing date: the date on which a registration statement is received by the Securities and Exchange Commission

Fiscal year: a 12-month period ending on the last day of a month other than December

First-round financing: the money needed to actually get a company into business (i.e., to start sales); follows seed funding, which is used to get a company organized and up to the verge of entering the market

General and administrative expenses: periodic expenses incurred in running a business as opposed to those that can be directly allocated to the cost of producing a product or providing a service

Gross margin: gross profit divided by sales

Gross profit margin: the percentage of gross profit realized on goods sold after subtracting cost of goods sold from sales

Income: money received for goods or services produced or as a return on investment

Income statement: a financial statement that charts revenues and expenses over a period of time

Initial public offering: the first sale of securities (almost always stock) in a corporation under the regulations governing a public company

Inventory: the assets produced by a manufacturing business or the assets bought and sold for profit by a wholesaling or retailing business

Leverage: ratio of debt to equity; highly leveraged refers to a company with a high ratio of debt to equity; borrowed funds are generally used to increase a business's buying power

Leveraged buyout: acquisition of a company with a high portion of borrowed funds

Liabilities: the obligations for which a company has to pay money to others as shown on its balance sheet

Line of credit: an agreement between a bank and a customer whereby the bank agrees to lend the customer funds up to an agreed maximum amount; generally used for seasonal needs to finance inventory and/or accounts receivable

Liquidity: a company's ability to convert noncash assets, such as inventory and accounts receivable, into cash; essentially, a company's ability to pay its bills.

Loan agreement: written contracts specifying terms of a loan

Mezzanine financing: generally refers to the final round of nonpublic financing; allows a company to expand its operations sufficiently to qualify for an initial public offering

Nasdaq National Market System: the upper tier of the over-the-counter stock market where large companies trade

Nasdaq SmallCap Market: the second tier of the Nasdaq for those companies that don't meet the requirements of the Nasdaq National Market System

Net discretionary income: income available to pay cash dividends, repurchase common stock, retire debt, etc. after funding all investment projects

Net margin: the ratio of net income to net sales

Noncash expense: a cost, such as a depreciation, depletion or amortization, that does not involve cash flow but is shown on the income statement

Notes payable: short-term notes of less than one year, either under lines of credit or with a stated repayment date

Offering memorandum: a description of a securities offering, which is required to disclose all the factors a prospective investor would need to make a rational decision

Operating expenses: the selling and general and administrative expenses incurred by a business

Operating income: gross profit minus general and administrative expenses

Operating margin: the ratio of operating margin to net sales

Owners' equity: excess of total assets minus total liabilities

Primary research: original research conducted by an individual or organization

Private placement: the private sale of securities to raise capital

Promissory note: details the principal and interest owed on a loan and when payments are due; it also outlines the events that would allow the bank to declare your loan in default

Public company: a corporation that is allowed to sell securities to large numbers of people without having to investigate or qualify its investors

Public shell: a publicly traded company that is dormant

Ratio analysis: the use of certain financial ratios to compare the performance of a business with years past and with industry peers

Regulation A filings: securities filings that exempt small public offerings (less than $5 million) from most registration requirements with the Securities and Exchange Commission

Regulation D: the basic federal law governing private offerings of securities

Revenue recognition policies: the point in time during the sales cycle that a company reports its revenues on its books

Sales: the gross amount of revenue generated by a business

SB-1: a form used by small businesses to register offerings of up to $10 million worth of securities provided the company has not registered more than $10 million in securities offerings during the preceding 12 months

SB-2: a form used by small businesses to register securities to be sold to the public

SCOR offering: Small Company Offering Registration permits a company to raise up to $1 million in a 12-month period without registering with the Securities and Exchange Commission

Secondary research: research that has been published and may be found in the public domain

Second-round financing: the money raised and used for the expansion of a company that has demonstrated a basic viability in the market

Securities: stocks, bonds, promissory notes, and other financial obligations of a company

Seed money: the earliest investment in a company, usually before it is even organized as a company; commonly used to investigate a market or develop product technology

Small Business Investment Companies (SBICs): privately owned venture capital firms, licensed by the SBA, that invest their own capital along with money they've borrowed at a favorable rate from the government; SBICs may offer management services in addition to money

Specialized Small Business Investment Companies (SSBICs): privately owned venture capital firms that serve socially and economically disadvantaged entrepreneurs by investing in companies in economically depressed areas, and those owned by women and minorities

Subordinated: in reference to debt, a loan that is paid off after other debts have been repaid

Tax loss carryforward: losses that can be carried forward in time to offset taxable income in a given year

Underwriter: investment banker or broker who agrees to purchase and resell securities to the public

Venture capitalists: generally refers to institutional venture capital firms that invest other people's money and manage it for them; venture capitalists typically seek a high degree of involvement and expect a high rate of return in a short time

Warrant: the right to purchase securities at a specified price, usually within a specified time period

White Papers: an official statement or report published by the federal government that provides information on a particular issue and presents the government's own policy

Working capital: current assets minus current liabilities, or what would be left of current assets if they were used to pay current liabilities

Financial Resources

They say you can never be rich enough or young enough. While these could be argued, we believe "You can never have enough resources." Therefore, we present for your consideration a wealth of sources for you to check into, check out, and harness for your own personal information blitz.

These sources are tidbits, ideas to get you started on your research. They are by no means the only sources out there and they should not be taken as the Ultimate Answer. We have done our research, but business do tend to move, change, fold and expand. As we have repeatedly stressed, do your homework. Get out and start investigating.

As an additional tidbit to get you going, we strongly suggest the following: If you haven't yet joined the Internet Age, do it! Surfing the Net is like waltzing through a vast library, with a breathtaking array of resources literally at your fingertips.

Accounting And Taxes

Associations

American Accounting Association, 5717 Bessie Dr., Sarasota, FL 24233, (941) 921-7747

American Institute of Certified Public Accountants, 1211 Ave. of the Americas, 6th Fl., New York, NY 10036, (212) 596-6200, fax: (212) 596-6213, www.aicpa.org

Financial Executives Institute, 10 Madison Ave., P.O. Box 1938, Morristown, NJ 07926-1938, (973) 898-4600, fax: (973) 898-4649, www.fei.org

Independent Accountants International, 9200 S. Dadeland Blvd. #510, Miami, FL 33156, (305) 670-0580, fax: (305) 670-3818, www.accountants.org

Institute of Management Accountants, 10 Paragon Dr., Montvale, NJ 07645, (201) 573-9000, fax: (201) 573-9000, www.imanet.org

International Credit Association, P.O. Box 419057, St. Louis, MO 63141-1757, (314) 991-3030, www.ica-credit.org

Books

Accounting and Recordkeeping Made Easy for the Self-Employed, Jack Fox, John Wiley & Sons, www.wiley.com

Accounting for the New Business, Christopher R. Malberg, Adams Media, 260 Center St., Holbrook, MA 02343, (800) 872-5627, www.adamsmedia.com

Bottom Line Basics: Understand and Control Business Finances, Robert J. Low, The Oasis Press, 300 N. Valley Dr., Grants Pass, OR 97526, (541) 479-9464, www.psi-research.com

Day-to-Day Business Accounting, Arlen K. Mose, John Jackson and Gary Downs, Prentice Hall

The McGraw-Hill 36 Hour Accounting Course, Robert L. Dixon and Harold E. Arnett, McGraw-Hill

Simplified Small Business Accounting, Daniel Sitarz, Nova Publishing, 1103 W. College St., Carbondale, IL 62901, (800) 462-6420, www.nbnbooks.com

The Vest Pocket CPA, Nicky A. Dauber, Joel G. Siegel and Jae K. Shim, Prentice Hall

Magazines And Publications

Accounting Office Management & Administration, 29 W. 35th St., 5th Fl., New York, NY 10001, (212) 244-0360

Accounting Periods and Methods, IRS Publication #538

Management Accounting, 10 Paragon Dr., Montvale, NJ 07645, (201) 573-9000, www.imanet.org

Starting a Business and Keeping Records, IRS Publication #583

Taxes—The Tax Magazine, CCH Inc., 4025 W. Peterson Ave., Chicago, IL 60646, (800) 344-3734, www.cch.com

The Tax Adviser, Harborside Financial Center, #201, Plaza 3, Jersey City, NJ 07311-3881, (800) 862-4272, (201) 938-3858, www.aicpa.org

Your Tax Questions Answered, Plymouth Press, 100 Merrick Rd., #200 E., Rockville Centre, NY 11570, (800) 350-1007, fax: (516) 536-8852, www.irahelp.com

Business Valuation Books

A Basic Guide for Valuing a Company, Wilbur M. Yegge, John Wiley & Sons

Handbook of Small Business Valuation Formulas and Rules of Thumb, Glenn Desmond, John A. Marcell, Valuation Press

How to Price a Profitable Company, Paul B. Baron, Amacom

The Small Business Valuation Book, Lawrence W. Tuller, Adams Publishers

Small Business Valuation Book: Easy-to-Use Techniques for Determining Fair Price, Resolving Disputes, and Minimizing Taxes, Lawrence W. Tuller, ASIN

Valuing Small Business and Professional Practices, Shannon P. Pratt, McGraw-Hill

Valuing Your Privately Held Business: The Art & Science of Establishing Your Company's Worth, Irving L. Blackman, Irwin Professional Publishing

Understanding Business Valuation: A Practical Guide to Valuing Small to Medium-Sized Businesses, Gary R. Trugman, American Institute of Certified Public Accounts

Investor Networks

ACE-Net* Nodes

Advanced Technology Development Center, Georgia Institute of Technology, 430 10th St. NW, N-116, Atlanta, GA 30318; (404) 894-3575

Bay Area Regional Technology Alliance, 39550 Liberty St., #201, Fremont, CA 94538, (510) 354-3902

Ben Franklin Partnership, 3624 Market St., Philadelphia, PA 19104, (215) 382-0380

The Capital Network Inc., 3925 W. Braker Ln., #406, Austin, TX 78759-5321, (512) 305-0826

KTEC-Kansas Technology Enterprise Corp., 214 SW Sixth, #100, Topeka, KS 66603; (913) 296-5272

MERRA, P.O. Box 130500m Ann Arbor, MI 48113, (734) 930-0033

NJIT Enterprise Development Center, 105 Lock St., Newark, NJ 07103, (973) 643-5740

Technology Capital Network at MIT, 101 Main St., 9th Fl., Cambridge, MA 02142, (617) 253-2337

UCSD-CONNECT, MS-0176, Extended Studies & Public Service, University of California, San Diego, La Jolla, CA 92093-0176, (619) 534-6114

Visit the ACE-Net Web site at www.sba.gov/advo.

Nationally Focused Investor Networks

The Capital Network (TCN), University of Texas at Austin, 3925 W. Braker Ln., #406, Austin, TX 78759-5321, (512) 305-0826

Environmental Capital Network, 416 Longshore Dr., Ann Arbor, MI 48105, (734) 996-8387, http://bizserve.com/ecn

Investors Circle, 3220 Sacramento St., #21, San Francisco, CA 94115-2007, (415) 929-4910,

Pacific Venture Capital Network (PACNET), 4199 Campus Dr., Irvine, CA 92715, (714) 509-2990, fax: (714) 509-2997

Private Capital Clearinghouse (PriCap), 45 Lyme Rd., Hanover, NH 03755, (603) 643-7770, www.pricap.com

Seed Capital Network, 8905 Kingston Pike, #12, Knoxville, TN 37923, (423) 573-4655

Technology Capital Network at MIT, 290 Main St., Bldg. E-39, Lower Level, Cambridge, MA 02142, (617) 253-7163

U.S. Investor Network, P.O. Box 20161, Raleigh, NC 27619-0161, (919) 783-0614, www.usinvestor.com

Regionally Focused Investor Networks

Alaska: Alaska Investnet, Juneau Economic Development Council, 400 Willoughby Ave., #211, Juneau, AK 99801-1724, (907) 463-3662

Colorado: Colorado Capital Alliance, P.O. Box 19169, Boulder, CO 80308-2169, (303) 499-9646

Kansas and Missouri: Capital Resource Network, 4747 Troost Ave., Kansas City, MO 64110, (816) 931-6688

Kentucky: Kentucky Investment Capital Network, 67

Wilkinson Blvd., Frankfort, KY 40601, (800) 626-2930, (502) 564-7140

Montana: Montana Private Capital Network, P.O. Box 437, Poulson, MT 59860, (406) 883-5470

North Carolina: North Carolina Investor Network, P.O. Box 20161, Raleigh, NC 27619-0161, (919) 783-0614

Pacific Northwest: Western Investment Network (WIN), 411 University St., #1200, Seattle, WA 98101, (206) 441-3123

South Carolina: Private Investor Network, O'Connell Center for Entrepreneurship and Technology, University of South Carolina, Aiken, 171 University Pkwy., Aiken, SC 29801; (803) 641-3518

Start-up Assistance

Associations

American Bankers Association, 1120 Connecticut Ave. NW, Washington, DC 20036, (202) 663-5000, www.aba.org

American League of Financial Institutions, 900 19th St. NW, #400, Washington, DC 20006, (202) 628-5624

America's Community Bankers, 900 19th St. NW, #400, Washington, DC 20006, (202) 857-3100, fax: (202) 857-5581, www.acbankers.org

Association of Small Business Development Centers, 3108 Columbia Pike, #300, Arlington, VA 22204, (703) 271-8700

Bancard Services Trust Co. (provides a financial services help line and a government loan program), (818) 999-3333

Commercial Finance Association, 225 W. 34th St., #1815, New York, NY 10122, (212) 594-3490, www.cfa.com

Independent Bankers Association of America, 1 Thomas Cir. NW, #400, Washington, DC 20001, (202) 659-8111, fax: (202) 659-3604, www.ibaa.org

National Association of Small Business Investment Companies, 666 11th St. NW, #750, Washington, DC 20005, (202) 628-5055, fax: (202) 628-5080, www.nasbic.org

National Business Incubation Association (provides incubator-location assistance), 20 E. Circle Dr., #190, Athens, OH 45701-3751, (740) 593-4331, fax: (740) 593-1996, www.nbia.org

National Venture Capital Association, 1655 N. Ft. Myers Dr., #850, Arlington, VA 22209, (703) 524-2549, fax: (703) 524-3940, www.nvca.org

Service Corps of Retired Executives (national office), 409 Third St. SW, 6th Fl., Washington, DC 20024, (202) 205-6762

United Association of Equipment Leasing, 520 Third St., #201, Oakland, CA 94607, (510) 444-9235

Books

Creating a Successful Business Plan: A Step-by-Step Guide to Building Your Plan, Entrepreneur Media Inc., (800) 421-2300, www.smallbizbooks.com

Easy Financials for Your Home-based Business: The Friendly Guide to Successful Management for Busy Home Entrepreneurs, Norm Ray, Rayve Productions, P.O. Box 726, Windsor, CA 95492, (800) 852-4890

The Fast Forward MBA in Finance, John A. Tracy, John Wiley & Sons, www.wiley.com

Financing Your Small Business: How to Raise the Money You Need, Entrepreneur Media Inc., (800) 421-2300, www.smallbizbooks. com

Guerrilla Financing: Alternative Techniques to Financing Any Small Business, Bruce Jon Blechman and Jay Conrad Levinson, Houghton Mifflin

Money-Smart Secrets for the Self-Employed, Linda Stern, Random House

Understanding Financial Statements, Lyn M. Fraser, Prentice Hall

Venture Capital: Where to Find It, National Association of Small Business Investment Companies Directory, P.O. Box 2039, Merrifield, VA 22116, (202) 628-5055

Magazines And Publications

Bankers Digest, 7515 Greenville Ave., #901, Dallas, TX 75231, (214) 373-4544, fax: (214) 373-4545

Business Credit, 8815 Centre Park Dr., #200, Columbia, MD 21045-2158, (410) 740-5560, fax: (410) 740-5574, www.nacm.org

Business Start-Ups, Entrepreneur Media Inc., 2329 Morse Ave., Irvine, CA 92614, (949) 261-2325, www.entrepreneurmag. com

Corporate Financing Week, 488 Madison Ave., 12th Fl., New York, NY 10022, (212) 303-3300

Credit, American Financial Services Associations, 919 18th St. NW, 3rd Fl., Washington, DC 20006, (202) 296-5544, www.americanfinsvcs.com

The Secured Lender, 225 W. 34th St., #1815, New York, NY 10122, (212) 594-3490, www.cfa.com

Appendix B

Government Listings

Government Agencies

- Copyright Clearance Center, 222 Rosewood Dr., Danvers, MA 01923, (978) 750-8400, fax: (978) 750-4470, www.copyright.com
- Copyright Office, Library of Congress, 101 Independence Ave. SE, Washington, DC 20559-6000, (202) 707-3000, fax: (202) 707-6859, www.loc.gov/copyright
- Department of Agriculture, 1400 and Independence Aves. SW, Washington, DC 20250, (202) 720-7420, www.fas.usda.gov
- Department of Commerce, 14th St. and Constitution Ave. NW, Washington, DC 20230, (202) 482-2000, fax: (202) 482-5270, www.doc.gov
- Department of Energy, 1000 Independence Ave. SW, Washington, DC 20585, (202) 586-5000, www.doe.gov
- Department of the Interior, 1849 C St. NW, Washington, DC 20240, (202) 208-3100, www.doi.gov
- Department of Labor, 200 Constitution Ave. NW, Rm. S-1004, Washington, DC 20210, (202) 219-6666, www.dol.gov
- Department of Treasury, Main Treasury Bldg, 1500 Pennsylvania Ave. NW, Washington, DC 20220, (202) 622-2000, www.ustreas.gov
- Export-Import Bank of the United States, 811 Vermont Ave. NW, Washington, DC 20571, (202) 565-3946, fax: (202) 565-3380, www.exim.gov
- Internal Revenue Service, 1111 Constitution Ave. NW, Washington, DC 20224, (202) 622-5000, www.irs.ustreas.gov
- Patent and Trademark Office, Washington, DC 20231, (800) 786-9199, www.uspto.gov
- Printing Office, Superintendent of Documents, Washington, DC 20402, (202) 512-1800, fax: (202) 512-2250, www.access.gpo.gov/su_docs
- Securities and Exchange Commission, 450 Fifth St. NW, Washington, DC 20549, (202) 942-8088, www.sec.gov

• Small Business Administration, 409 Third St. SW, Washington, DC 20416, (800) 827-5722, www.sba.gov

SBA District Offices

The Small Business Administration has several types of field offices. Of these, the district offices offer the fullest range of services. To access all district office Web sites, go to www.sba.gov and then click on "Local SBA Resources."

Alabama: 2121 Eighth Ave. N., #200, Birmingham, AL 35203-2398, (205) 731-1344, fax: (205) 731-1404

Alaska: 222 W. Eighth Ave., Rm. A36, Anchorage, AK 99513-7559, (907) 271-4022, fax: (907) 271-4545

Arizona: 2828 N. Central Ave., #800, Phoenix, AZ 85004-1093, (602) 640-2316, fax: (602) 640-2360

Arkansas: 2120 Riverfront Dr., #100, Little Rock, AR 72202, (501) 324-5871, fax: (501) 324-5491

California: 2719 Air Fresno Dr., #107, Fresno, CA 93727-1547, (209) 487-5189, fax: (209) 487-5803

• 330 N. Brand Blvd., #1200, Glendale, CA 91203-2304, (818) 552-3210, fax: (818) 552-3286

• 550 W. C St., #550, San Diego, CA 92101, (619) 557-7252, fax: (619) 557-5894

• 455 Market St., 6th Fl., San Francisco, CA 94105-1988, (415) 744-6801

• 660 J St., Rm. 215, Sacramento, CA 95814-2413, (916) 498-6410, fax: (916) 498-6422

• 200 W. Santa Ana Blvd., #700, Santa Ana, CA 92701-4134, (714) 550-7420, fax: (714) 550-0191

Colorado: 721 19th St., #426, Denver, CO 80202-2599, (303) 844-3984, fax: (303) 844-6490

Connecticut: 330 Main St., 2nd Fl., Hartford, CT 06106, (860) 240-4700, fax: (860) 240-4659

Delaware: 824 N. Market St., #610, Wilmington, DE 19801-3011, (302) 573-6294

District of Columbia: 1110 Vermont Ave. NW, #900, Washington, DC 20005, (202) 606-4000, fax: (202) 606-4225

Florida: 100 S. Biscayne Bl., 7th Fl., Miami, FL 3313-2011, (305) 536-5521, fax: (305) 536-5058

- 7825 Baymeadows Wy., #100-B, Jacksonville, FL 32256-7504, (904) 443-1900, fax: (904) 443-1980

Georgia: 1720 Peachtree Rd. NW, 6th Fl., Atlanta, GA 30309, (404) 529-9865, fax: (404) 347-0694

Hawaii: 300 Ala Moana Blvd., Rm. 2-235, Honolulu, HI 96850-4981, (808) 541-2990, fax: (808) 541-2976

Idaho: 1020 Main St., #290, Boise, ID 83702-5745, (208) 334-1696, fax: (208) 334-9353

Illinois: 500 W. Madison St., #1250, Chicago, IL 60661-2511, (312) 353-4528, fax: (312) 866-5688

- 511 W. Capitol Ave., #302, Springfield, IL 62704, (217) 492-4416

Indiana: 429 N. Pennsylvania, #100, Indianapolis, IN 46204-1873, (317) 226-7272, fax: (317) 226-7259

Iowa: Mail Code 0736, 215 Fourth Ave. SE, #200, The Lattner Bldg., Cedar Rapids, IA 52401-1806, (319) 362-6405, fax: (319) 362-7861

- 210 Walnut St., Rm. 749, Des Moines, IA 50309-2186, (515) 284-4422, fax: (515) 284-4572

Kansas: 100 E. English St., #510, Wichita, KS 67202, (316) 269-6616, fax: (316) 269-6499

Kentucky: 600 Dr. Martin Luther King Jr. Pl., Rm. 188, Louisville, KY 40202, (502) 582-5971, fax: (502) 582-5009

Louisiana: 365 Canal St., #2250, New Orleans, LA 70130, (504) 589-6685, fax: (504) 589-2339

Maine: 40 Western Ave., Rm. 512, Augusta, ME 04330, (207) 622-8378, fax: (207) 622-8277

Maryland: 10 S. Howard St., #6220, Baltimore, MD 21201-2525, (410) 962-4392, fax: (410) 962-1805

Massachusetts: 10 Causeway St., Rm. 265, Boston, MA 02222-1093, (617) 565-5590, fax: (617) 565-5597

Michigan: 477 Michigan Ave., Rm. 515, Detroit, MI 48226, (313) 226-6075, fax: (313) 226-4769

Minnesota: MC 0508, 610-C, Butler Square, 100 N. 6th St., Minneapolis, MN 55403-1563, (612) 370-2324, fax: (612) 370-2303

Mississippi: 101 W. Capitol St., #400, Jackson, MS 39201, (601) 965-4378, fax: (601) 965-4294

Missouri: 323 W. Eighth St., #501, Kansas City, MO 64105, (816) 374-6708, fax: (816) 374-6759

• 815 Olive St., Rm. 242, St. Louis, MO 63101, (314) 539-6600, fax: (314) 539-3785

Montana: 301 S. Park Ave., Rm. 334, Helena, MT 59626-0054, (406) 441-1081, fax: (406) 441-1090

Nebraska: 11145 Mill Valley Rd., Omaha, NE 68154, (402) 221-4691, fax: (402) 221-3680

Nevada: 300 S. Las Vegas Blvd., #1100, Las Vegas, NV 89101, (702) 388-6611, fax: (702) 933-6469

New Hampshire: 143 N. Main St., #202, Concord, NH 03302-1248, (603) 225-1400, fax: (603) 225-1409

New Jersey: 2 Gateway Center, 15th Fl., Newark, NJ 07102, (973) 645-2434, fax: (973) 645-6265

New Mexico: 625 Silver SW, #320, Albuquerque, NM 87102, (505) 346-7909, fax: (505) 346-6711

New York: 111 W. Huron St., Rm. 1311, Buffalo, NY 14202, (716) 551-4301, fax: (716) 551-4418

• 26 Federal Plaza, #31-00, New York, NY 10278, (212) 264-1319, fax: (212) 264-7751

• 401 S. Salina St., 5th Fl., Syracuse, NY 13202-2415, (315) 471-9272

North Carolina: 200 N. College St., Ste. A-2015, Charlotte, NC 28202-2137, (704) 344-6563

North Dakota: 657 Second Ave. N., Rm. 219, Fargo, ND 58102, (701) 239-5131, fax: (701) 239-5645

Ohio: Superior Ave., #630, Cleveland, OH 44114-2507, (216) 522-4180, fax: (216) 522-2038

• Nationwide Plaza, #1400, Columbus, OH 43215-2542, (614) 469-6860, fax: (614) 469-2391

Oklahoma: 210 Park Ave., #1300, Oklahoma City, OK 73102, (405) 231-5521, fax: (405) 231-4876

Oregon: 1515 SW Fifth Ave., #1050, Portland, OR 97201-6695, (503) 326-2682

Pennsylvania: 900 Market St., 5th Fl., Philadelphia, PA 19107, (215) 580-2722, fax: (215) 580-2762

• 1000 Liberty Ave., Rm. 1128, Pittsburgh, PA 15222-4004, (412)

395-6560, fax: (412) 395-6562

Puerto Rico: Citibank Tower, 252 Ponce de Leon Blvd., Rm. 201, Hato Rey, PR 00918, (787) 766-5572, fax: (787) 766-5309

Rhode Island: 380 Westminster Mall, 5th Fl., Providence, RI 02903, (401) 528-4561, fax: (401) 528-4539

South Carolina: 1835 Assembly St., Rm. 358, Columbia, SC 29201, (803) 765-5377, fax: (803) 765-5962

South Dakota: 110 S. Phillips Ave., #200, Sioux Falls, SD 57102-1109, (605) 330-4231, fax: (605) 330-4215

Tennessee: 50 Vantage Wy., #201, Nashville, TN 37228-1500, (615) 736-5881, fax: (615) 736-7232

Texas: 4300 Amon Carter Blvd., #114, Ft. Worth, TX 76155, (817) 885-6500, fax: (817) 885-6543

- 9301 Southwest Fwy., #550, Houston, TX 77074-1591, (713) 773-6500, fax: (713) 773-6550

- 222 E. Van Buren St., Rm. 500, Harlingen, TX 78550-6855, (956) 427-8533, fax: (956) 427-8537

- 1611 Texas Ave., #408, Lubbock, TX 79401-2693, (806) 472-7462, fax: (806) 472-7487

- 727 E. Durango Blvd., Rm. A-527, San Antonio, TX 78206-1204, (210) 472-5900, fax: (210) 472-5935

Utah: 125 S. State St., Rm. 2229, Salt Lake City, UT 84138-1195, (801) 524-5804

Vermont: 87 State St., Rm. 205, Montpelier, VT 05602, (802) 828-4422

Virginia: 1504 Santa Rosa Rd., #200, Richmond, VA 23229, (804) 771-2400, fax: (804) 771-8018

Washington: 1200 Sixth Ave., # 1700, Seattle, WA 98101-1128, (206) 553-7310, fax: (206) 553-7099

- W. 602 First Ave., 2nd Fl. West, Spokane, WA 99201-3826, (509) 353-2810, fax: (509) 353-2829

West Virginia: 168 W. Main St., 6th Fl., Clarksburg, WV 26301, (304) 623-5631, fax: (304) 623-0023

Wisconsin: 212 E. Washington Ave., Rm. 213, Madison, WI 53703, (608) 264-5261, fax: (608) 264-5500

Wyoming: 100 E. B St., Rm. 4001, P.O. Box 2839, Casper, WY 82602-2839, (307) 261-6500

Small Business Development Centers

The following state Small Business Development Centers (SBDCs) can direct you to the SBDC in your region. You can access all state SBDC Web sites at www.smallbiz.suny.edu/sbdcnet.htm.

Alabama: Alabama Small Business Development Center, University of Alabama, Box 870397, Tuscaloosa, AL 35487, (205) 348-7011, fax: (205) 348-9644, www.cba.ua.edu./sbdc.htm

Alaska: UAA Small Business Development Center, 430 W. Seventh Ave., #110, Anchorage, AK 99501, (907) 274-7232, fax: (907) 274-9524

Arizona: Arizona Small Business Development Center Network, 2411 W. 14th St., #132, Tempe, AZ 85281, (602) 731-8720, fax: (602) 731-8729, www.dist.maricopa.edu/sdbdc

Arkansas: Arkansas Small Business Development Center, 100 S. Main, #401, Little Rock, AR 72201, (501) 324-9043, fax: (501) 324-9049, www.ualr.edu/~sbdcdept

California: California Small Business Development Center, Office of Small Business, 801 K St., #1700, Sacramento, CA 95814, (916) 324-5068, fax: (916) 322-5084, www.ca.gov/commerce/license/preface.htm

Colorado: Colorado Business Assistance Center, 1625 Broadway, #805, Denver, CO 80202, (800) 333-7798, (303) 592-5720, fax: (303) 592-8107, www.state.co.us/gov_dir/obd/sbdc.htm

Connecticut: Connecticut Small Business Development Center, University of Connecticut, 2 Bourn Pl., U-94, Storrs, CT 06269-5094, (860) 486-4135

Delaware: Delaware Small Business Development Center, University of Delaware, 102 MBNA America Hall, Newark, DE 19716, (302) 831-2747, fax: (302) 831-1423, www.dleawaresbdc.org

District of Columbia: Small Business Development Center, Howard University, School of Business, Rm. 128, 2600 Sixth St. NW, Washington, DC 20059, (202) 806-1550, fax: (202) 806-1777, husbdc@cldc.howard.edu

Florida: Florida Small Business Development Center, 19 W. Garden St., #300, Pensacola, FL 32501, (850) 470-4980, (850) 595-6060, fax: (850) 595-6070, www.floridasbdc.com

Georgia: Business Outreach Services, Small Business Development Center, Chicopee Complex, University of Georgia, 1180 E. Broad St., Athens, GA 30602-5412, (706) 542-6762, fax: (706) 542-6776, www.sbdc.uga.edu

Guam: Pacific Islands Small Business Development Center Network, UOG Station, Mangilao, Guam 96923, (671) 735-2590, fax: (671) 734-2002, http://uog2.uog.edu/sbdc

Hawaii: University of Hawaii at Hilo, Small Business Development Center Network, 200 W. Kawili St., Hilo, HI 96720-4091, (808) 974-7515, fax: (808) 974-7683, www.hawaii-sbdc.org

Idaho: Idaho Small Business Development Center, Boise State University, 1910 University Dr., Boise, ID 83725-1655, (208) 426-1640, fax: (208) 426 3877, www.idbsu.edu/isbdc

Illinois: Illinois Greater North Pulaski Small Business Development Center, 4054 W. North Ave., Chicago, IL 60639, (773) 384-2262, (800) 252-2923 (in Illinois)

Indiana: Indiana Small Business Development Center, 1 N. Capitol, #1275, Indianapolis, IN 46204, (317) 264-6871, fax: (317) 264-2806, www.isbdcorp.org

Iowa: Iowa Small Business Development Center, 137 Lynn Ave., Ames, IA 50014, (515) 292-6351, fax: (515) 292-0020, www.iowasbdc.org

Kansas: Small Business Development Center, 1501 S. Joplin, Pittsburg, KS 66762, (316) 235-4920, fax: (316) 235-4919, www.pittstate.edu/bti/sbdc/htm

Kentucky: Kentucky Small Business Development Center, 225 Gatton College of Business and Economics, Lexington, KY 40506, (606) 257-7668, fax: (606) 323-1907 http://gatton.gws. uky.edu/kentuckybusiness/ksbdc/ksbdc.htm

Louisiana: Louisiana Small Business Development Center, College of Business Administration, Northeast Louisiana University, Monroe, LA 71209-6435, (318) 342-5506, fax: (318) 342-5510, www.lsbdc.net1.nlu.edu

Maine: University of Southern Maine, Maine Small Business Development Centers, 96 Falmouth St., P.O. Box 9300, Portland, ME 04104-9300, (207) 780-4420, fax: (207) 780-4810, www.usm.maine.edu/~sbdc

Maryland: Maryland Small Business Development Center, 7100 E. Baltimore Ave., #401, College Park, MD 20740-3627, (301) 403-8300

Massachusetts: Massachusetts Small Business Development Center, University of Massachusetts, P.O. Box 34935, Amherst, MA 01003, (413) 545-6301, fax: (413) 545-1273, www.ump.edu/msbdc

Michigan: Michigan Small Business Development Center, 2727 Second Ave., #107, Detroit, MI 48201, (313) 964-1798, fax: (313) 964-3648, http://bizserve.com/sbdc

Minnesota: Minnesota Small Business Development Center, Dept. of Trade and Economic Development, 500 Metro Square, 121 Seventh Pl. E., St. Paul, MN 55101-2146, (651) 297-5773, fax: (651) 296-1290, www.dted.state.mn.us

Mississippi: Mississippi Small Business Development Center, University of Mississippi, 216 Old Chemistry Bldg., University, MS 38677, (601) 232-5001, (800) 725-7232 (in Mississippi), fax: (601) 232-5650, www.olemiss.edu/depts/mssbdc

Missouri: Missouri Small Business Development Center, 1205 University Ave., #300, Columbia, MO 65211, (573) 882-0344, fax: (573) 884-4297, www.missouri:edu/~sbdwww

Montana: Small Business Development Center, Department of Commerce, 1424 Ninth Ave., Helena, MT 59620, (406) 444-4780, fax: (406) 444-1872

Nebraska: Nebraska Business Development Center, College of Business Administration, University of Nebraska at Omaha, Rm. 407, Omaha, NE 68182-0248, (402) 554-2521, fax: (402) 595-2385, www.unomaha.edu

Nevada: Nevada Small Business Development Center, University of Nevada at Reno, College of Business Administration, MS 32, Reno, NV 89557-0100, (702) 784-1717, fax: (702) 784-4337, www.scs.unr.edu/nsbdc

New Hampshire: New Hampshire Small Business Development Center, 1000 Elm St., 12th Fl., Manchester, NH 03101, (603) 624-2000, fax: (603) 647-4410, www.nhsbdc.org

New Jersey: New Jersey Small Business Development Center, 49 Bleeker St., Newark, NJ 07102-1913, (973) 353-1927, fax: (973) 353-1110, www.nj.com/smallbusiness

New Mexico: New Mexico Small Business Development Center, Santa Fe Community College, 6401 S. Richards Ave., Santa Fe, NM 87505, (800) 281-SBDC, (505) 428-1362, fax: (505) 428-1469, www.nmsbdc.org

New York: New York Small Business Development Center, SUNY Plaza, S-523, Albany, NY 12246, (518) 443-5398, fax: (518) 465-4992, www.nys-sbdc.suny.edu

North Carolina: North Carolina Small Business and Technology Development Center, 333 Fayetteville Street Mall, #1150, Raleigh, NC 27601, (919) 715-7272, (800) 258-0862 (in North Carolina), fax: (919) 715-7777, www.sbtdc.org

North Dakota: North Dakota Small Business Development Center, University of North Dakota, P.O. Box 7308, Grand Forks, ND 58202, (701) 777-3700, fax: (701) 777-3225, www.und.nodak.edu/dept/ndsbdc

Ohio: Ohio Small Business Development Center, P.O. Box 1001, Columbus, OH 43261-1001, (800) 848-1300, (614) 466-2480, fax: (614) 466-0829, www.odod.ohio.gov

Oklahoma: Oklahoma Small Business Development Center, Stn. A, P.O. Box 2584, Durant, OK 74701, (580) 924-0277, fax: (580) 920-7471, www.osbdc.org

Oregon: Oregon Small Business Development Center Network, 44 W. Broadway, #501, Eugene, OR 97401-3021, (541) 726-2250, fax: (541) 345-6006, www.efn.org/~osbdcn

Pennsylvania: Pennsylvania Small Business Development Center, University of Pennsylvania, Vance Hall, 3733 Spruce St., 4th Fl., Philadelphia, PA 19104, (215) 898-1219, fax: (215) 573-2135, www.pasbdc.org

Rhode Island: Rhode Island Small Business Development Center, Bryant College, 1150 Douglas Pike, Smithfield, RI 02917, (401) 232-6111, fax: (401) 232-6933, www.risbdc.org

South Carolina: South Carolina Small Business Development Center, The Darla Moore School of Business, University of South Carolina, Columbia, SC 29208, (803) 777-4907, fax: (803) 777-4403, http://sbdcweb.badm.sc.edu

South Dakota: South Dakota Small Business Development Center, University of South Dakota, School of Business, 414 E. Clark St., Vermillion, SD 57069-2390, (605) 677-5498, fax: (605) 677-5427, www.usd.edu/brbinfo/sbdc

Tennessee: Tennessee Small Business Development Center, University of Memphis, South Campus, Bldg. No. 1, Box 526324, Memphis, TN 38152, (901) 678-2500, fax: (901) 678-4072, www.tsbdc.memphis.edu

Texas: Texas Small Business Development Center, 1100 Louisiana, #500, Houston, TX 77002, (713) 752-8400, fax: (713) 756-1500, http://smbizsolutions.uh.edu

Utah: Utah Small Business Development Center, 125 S. State St., Salt Lake City, UT 84111, (801) 957-3840, fax: (801) 524-4160, www.sbaonline.sba.gov

Vermont: Vermont Small Business Development Center, 60 Main St., #103, Burlington, VT 05401, (802) 658-9228, fax: (802) 860-1899, www.vtsbdc.org

Virginia: Virginia Small Business Development Center, P.O. Box 446, Richmond, VA 23218-0446, (804) 371-8258, fax: (804) 225-3384, www.dba.state.va.us

Washington: Washington Small Business Development Center, Washington State University, P.O. Box 644851, Pullman, WA 99164-4851, (509) 335-1576, fax: (509) 335-0949, www.sbdc.wsu.edu

West Virginia: West Virginia Small Business Development Center, 950 Kanawha Blvd. E., #200, Charleston, WV 25301, (888) 982-7732, (304) 558-2960, fax: (304) 558-0127, www.wvsbdc.org

Wisconsin: University of Wisconsin at Whitewater, Small Business Development Center, Carlson 2000, Whitewater, WI 53190, (414) 472-3217, fax: (414) 472-5692

Wyoming: Wyoming Small Business Development Center, 111 W. Second St., #502, Casper, WY 82601, (307) 234-6683, fax: (307) 577-7014, www.sbdc@trib.com

State Commerce And Economic Development Departments

Alabama: Alabama Development Office, 401 Adams Ave., Montgomery, AL 36130, (334) 242-0400, fax: (334) 242-2414, www.ado.state.al.us

Alaska: Alaska State Dept. of Commerce and Economic Development, P.O. Box 110800, Juneau, AK 99811-0800, (907) 465-2500, fax: (907) 465-5442, www.commerce.state.ak.us

Arizona: Arizona State Dept. of Commerce Business Assistance Center, 3800 N. Central Ave., Phoenix, AZ 85012, (800) 542-5684, (602) 280-1480, fax: (602) 280-1339, www.commerce.

state.az.us/fr_abc.shtml

Arkansas: Arkansas Economic Development Commission, Advocacy and Business Services, 1 State Capitol Mall, Little Rock, AR 72201, (501) 682-1060, fax: (501) 324-9856, www. aedc.state.ar.us

California: California Trade and Commerce Agency, Office of Small Business, 801 K St., #1700, Sacramento, CA 95814, (916) 324-1295, fax: (916) 322-5084, www.smallbusiness.commerce. ca.gov

Colorado: Colorado Office of Business Development, 1625 Broadway, #1710, Denver, CO 80202, (303) 892-3840, fax: (303) 892-3848, http://governor.state.co.us/gov_dir/obd/obd.htm.

Connecticut: Connecticut Economic Resource Center, 805 Brook St., Bldg. 4, Rocky Hill, CT 06067, (860) 571-7136, fax: (860) 571-7150, www.cerc.com

Delaware: Delaware Economic Development Office, 99 Kings Hwy., Dover, DE 19901, (302) 739-4271, fax: (302) 739-5749, www.state.de.us

District of Columbia: Office of Economic Development, 441 Fourth St. NW, Ste. North-1140, Washington, DC 20001, (202) 727-6365, fax: (202) 727-6703

Florida: Enterprise Florida, 390 N. Orange, #1300, Orlando, FL 32801, (407) 316-4600, fax: (407) 316-4599, www.floridabusiness. com

Georgia: Georgia Dept. of Community Affairs, 60 Executive Park S. NE, Atlanta, GA 30329-2231, (404) 679-4940, fax: (404) 679-4940, www.dca.state.ga.us

Hawaii: Business Action Center, 1130 N. Nimitz Hwy., 2nd Level, Ste. A-254, Honolulu, HI 96817, (808) 586-2545, fax: (808) 586-2544, www.hawaii.gov/dbedt

Idaho: Idaho State Dept. of Commerce, P.O. Box 83720, Boise, ID 83720-0093, (208) 334-2470, fax: (208) 334-2631, www.idoc. state.id.us

Illinois: Illinois Dept. of Commerce and Community Affairs, 620 E. Adams St., Springfield, IL 62701, (217) 524-6293, www. commerce.state.il.us

Indiana: Indiana State Dept. of Commerce, 1 N. Capitol, #700, Indianapolis, IN 46204-2288, (317) 232-8782, fax: (317) 233-5123, www.indbiz.com

Iowa: Iowa Dept. of Economic Development, 200 E. Grand Ave, Des Moines, IA 50309, (800) 532-1216, (515) 242-4750, fax: (515) 242-4776, www.state.ia.us/sbro

Kansas: Kansas Dept. of Commerce and Housing, Business Development Division, 700 SW Harrison St., #1300, Topeka, KS 66603, (785) 296-5298, fax: (785) 296-3490, www.kansascommerce.com

Kentucky: Kentucky Cabinet for Economic Development, Business Information Clearinghouse, 22nd Fl., Capitol Plaza Tower, Frankfort, KY 40601, (800) 626-2250, fax: (502) 564-5932, www.state.ky.us/edc/bic.htm

Louisiana: Louisiana Dept. of Economic Development, P.O. Box 94185, Baton Rouge, LA 70804-9185, (225) 342-5372, fax: (225) 342-5349, www.lded.state.la.us

Maine: Business Answers, Dept. of Economic and Community Development, 33 Stone St., 59 Statehouse Station, Augusta, ME 04333-0059, (207) 287-2656, fax: (207) 287-2861, www.econdev.maine.com

Maryland: Maryland Dept. of Business and Economic Development, Division of Regional Development, 217 E. Redwood St., 10th Fl., Baltimore, MD 21202, (410) 767-0095, fax: (410) 338-1836, www.mdbusiness.state.md.us

Massachusetts: Massachusetts Office of Business Development, 1 Ashburton Pl., 21st Fl., Boston, MA 02108, (617) 727-3221, fax: (617) 727-8797, www.state.ma.us/mobd

Michigan: Michigan Jobs Commission, Customer Assistance, 201 N. Washington Square, Victor Office Center, 4th Fl., Lansing, MI 48913, (517) 373-9808, fax: (517) 335-0198, www.state.mi.us/mjc

Minnesota: Minnesota Small Business Assistance Office, 500 Metro Square, 121 Seventh Pl. E., St. Paul, MN 55101, (800) 657-3858, (612) 282-2103, fax: (612) 296-1290, www.dted.state.mn.us

Mississippi: Mississippi Dept. of Economic and Community Development, Division of Existing Industry and Business, New Business, P.O. Box 849, Jackson, MS 39205-0849, (601) 359-3593, fax: (601) 359-2116, www.decd.state.ms.us

Missouri: Missouri Dept. of Economic Development, P.O. Box 118, Jefferson City, MO 65102, (573) 751-4982, fax: (573) 751-7384, www.ecodev.state.mo.us/mbac

Montana: Dept. of Commerce, Economic Development Division, 1424 Ninth Ave., Helena, MT 59620, (406) 444-3814, fax: (406) 444-1872, http://commerce/mt.gov

Nebraska: Dept. of Economic Development, 301 Centennial Mall S., P.O. Box 94666, Lincoln, NE 68509-4666, (402) 471-3782, fax: www.ded.state.ne.us

Nevada: Nevada State Dept. of Business and Industry, Center for Business Advocacy, 2501 E. Sahara Ave., #100, Las Vegas, NV 89104, (702) 486-4335, fax: (702) 486-4340, www.state.nv.us/b&i

New Hampshire: New Hampshire Office of Business and Industrial Development, P.O. Box 1856, Concord, NH 03302-1856, (603) 271-2591, fax: (603) 271-6784, http://ded.state.nh.us/obid

New Jersey: Dept. of Commerce and Economic Development, 20 State St., CN 820, Trenton, NJ 08625, (609) 292-2444, fax: (609) 292-9145, www.nj.com/business

New Mexico: New Mexico Economic Development Dept., P.O. Box 20003-5003, Santa Fe, NM 87504, (505) 827-0300, fax: (505) 827-0300, www.edd.state.nm.us

New York: Division for Small Business, Empire State Development, 1 Commerce Plaza, Albany, NY 12245, (518) 473-0499, fax: (518) 474-1512, www.empire.state.ny.us

North Carolina: Small Business and Technology Development Center, 333 Fayetteville Street Mall, #1150, Raleigh, NC 27601-1742, (919) 715-7272, fax: (919) 715-7777, www.sbtdc.org

North Dakota: Center for Innovation, Rural Technology Incubator, P.O. Box 8372, Grand Forks, ND 58202, (701) 777-3132, fax: (701) 777-2339, www.innovators.net

Ohio: Ohio One-Stop Business Center, 77 S. High St., 28th Fl., P.O. Box 1001, Columbus, OH 43216-1001, (614) 644-8748, fax: (614) 466-0829

Oklahoma: Department of Commerce, P.O. Box 26980, Oklahoma City, OK 73126-0980, (405) 843-9770, fax: (405) 815-5142, www.odoc.state.ok.us

Oregon: Oregon Economic Development Dept., 775 Summer St. NE, Salem, OR 97310, (503) 986-0123, fax: (503) 581-5115, www.econ.state.or.us

Pennsylvania: Pennsylvania Small Business Resource Center, Rm. 374, Forum Bldg., Harrisburg, PA 17120, (717) 783-5700, fax: (717) 234-4560, www.dced.state.pa.us

Rhode Island: Rhode Island Economic Development Corporation, 1 W. Exchange St., Providence, RI 02903, (401) 222-2601, fax: (401) 222-2102, www.riedc.com

South Carolina: Enterprise Inc., P.O. Box 1149, Columbia, SC 29202, (803) 252-8806, fax: (803) 252-0455

South Dakota: Governor's Office of Economic Development, 711 E. Wells Ave., Pierre, SD 57501-3369, (605) 773-5032, fax: (605) 773-3256, www.state.sd.us

Tennessee: Small Business Service, Department of Economic and Community Development, 320 Sixth Ave. N., 7th Fl., Rachel Jackson Bldg., Nashville, TN 37243-0405, (615) 741-2626, fax: (615) 532-8715, www.state.tn.us/ecd

Texas: Texas Dept. of Economic Development, Office of Small Business Assistance, P.O. Box 12728, Austin, TX 78711-2728, (512) 936-0223, fax: (512) 936-0435, www.tded.state.tx.us

Utah: Utah Dept. of Community and Economic Development, 324 S. State St., #500, Salt Lake City, UT 84111, (801) 538-8775, fax: (801) 538-8888, www.dced.state.ut.us

Vermont: Vermont Agency of Commerce and Community Development, Department of Economic Development, National Life Bldg., Drawer 20, Montpelier, VT 05620-0501, (802) 828-3211, fax: (802) 828-3258, www.state.vt.us/dca/economic/develp.htm

Virginia: Dept. of Business Assistance, Small Business Development Center Network, 901 E. Byrd St., #1400, Richmond, VA 23219, (804) 371-8253, fax: (804) 225-3384, www.dba.state.va.us

Washington: Business Assistance Division, Community Trade and Economic Development, 906 Columbia St. SW, P.O. Box 48300, Olympia, WA 98504-8300, (360) 753-4900, fax: (360) 586-0873, www.wa.gov/cted/lda/access.htm

West Virginia: West Virginia Development Office, 950 Kanawha Blvd., Charleston, WV 25301, (304) 558-2960, fax: (304) 558-0127, www.wvsbdc.org

Wisconsin: Department of Commerce, 201 Washington Ave., Madison, WI 53703, (608) 266-9467, fax: (608) 267-2829, www.commerce.state.wi.us

Wyoming: Wyoming Business Council, 2301 Central Ave., Cheyenne, WY 82002, (307) 777-5874, fax: (307) 777-6005, www.wyomingbusiness.org

Appendix C
Small-business-friendly Banks

Small businesses are in the best shape they have ever been in when it comes to obtaining microloans ($100,000 or less), according to a recent study by the SBA Office of Advocacy.

In fact, according to Jere Glover, the Advocacy Office's chief counsel, the number of loans approved in this category jumped 26.8 percent over a one-year period.

One reason for the rise is the increased use of business credit cards, which banks consider to be a revolving line of credit; this helps establish a credit history with the bank. "The other reason is credit-scoring," says Glover. "If you have a good personal credit record, banks are [more] willing to make you a small-business loan." The use of credit-scoring reduces paperwork and speeds up the loan process, resulting in lower costs for banks—and a greater willingness to lend.

The increase in the number of microloans is occurring even in the face of an industry seemingly consumed by mergers. "As the bank industry consolidates into fewer and fewer hands, a few people could make decisions to cut back [on small-business lending], and the effect on the business sector could be dramatic," Glover says, noting that so far the impact has been minimal.

Glover acknowledges that one reason small-business credit hasn't been affected may be the increasing number of smaller banking institutions setting up shop.

Another trend to watch is the increasing availability of loans online. But this will only work in certain situations, warns Glover. "It works for small amounts, when you can get a credit loan," he says.

The SBA's annual bank study shows an improving landscape for small-business lending, but with all the new forces being brought to bear on the industry, vigilance continues to be the watchword.

The following ranking lists the SBA's top two microbusiness-friendly banks in each state (where there were two) by the percentage of microbusiness loans per total assets. The list also includes banks whose microloans-to-assets ratio was 40 percent or higher.

The four variables measured are:

1. microbusiness loans-to-assets ratio

2. microbusiness loans-to-total-business-loans ratio

3. dollar volume of microbusiness loans

4. total number of microbusiness loans

Alabama

Independent Bank of Oxford, P.O. Box 3363, Oxford, AL 36203, (205) 835-1776

West Alabama Bank & Trust, P.O. Box 310, Reform, AL 35481, (205) 375-6261

Alaska

First National Bank, P.O. Box 100720, Anchorage, AK 99510, (907) 276-6300

Arizona

Bank of Casa Grande Valley, 1300 E. Florence Blvd., Casa Grande, AZ 85222, (520) 836-4666

Frontier State Bank, P.O. Box 1030, Show Low, AZ 85901, (520) 537-2933

Arkansas

Caddo First National Bank, P.O. Box 47, Glenwood, AR 71943, (870) 356-3196

Fidelity National Bank, 330 W. Broadway, West Memphis, AR 72301, (870) 735-8700

California

Cupertino National Bank & Trust, 20230 Stevens Creek Blvd., Cupertino, CA 95014, (408) 996-1144

Kings River State Bank, P.O. Box 997, Reedley, CA 93654, (209) 638-8131

Colorado

Cheyenne Mountain Bank, 1580 E. Cheyenne Mountain Blvd., Colorado Springs, CO 80906, (719) 579-9150

Bank of Grand Junction, 2415 F Rd., Grand Junction, CO 81505, (970) 241-9000

Connecticut

Lafayette American Bank, 130 N. Main St., Southington, CT 06489, (860) 620-5000

The Equity Bank, 1160 Silas Deane Hwy., Wethersfield, CT 06109, (860) 571-7200

Delaware

PNC National Bank of Delaware, 300 Delaware Ave., Wilmington, DE 19899, (302) 429-2274

NationsBank of Delaware, P.O. Box 7028, Dover, DE 19901, (302) 741-1000

District of Columbia

Franklin National Bank, 1722 Eye St. NW, Washington, DC 20006, (202) 429-9888

Florida

Northside Bank of Tampa, 12233 N. Florida Ave., Tampa, FL 33612, (813) 933-2255

Fidelity Bank of Florida, P.O. Box 540160, Merritt Island, FL 32954-0160, (407) 452-0011

Georgia

The Coastal Bank, P.O. Box 529, Hinesville, GA 31310, (912) 368-2265

Community Trust Bank, P.O. Box 1700, Hiram, GA 30141, (770) 445-1014

Hawaii

City Bank, 201 Merchant St., Honolulu, HI 96813, (808) 535-2500

Idaho

Panhandle State Bank, P.O. Box 967, Sandpoint, ID 83864, (208) 263-0505

D.L. Evans Bank, 397 N. Overland Ave., Burley, ID 83318, (208) 678-9076

Illinois

First National Bank-Employee Owned, 485 Lake St., Antioch, IL 60002, (847) 838-2265

The State Bank of Geneva, 22 S. Fourth St., Geneva, IL 60134, (630) 232-3200

Indiana

Peoples Trust Co., P.O. Box 190, Linton, IN 47441, (812) 847-4457

Scott County State Bank, P.O. Box 158, Scottsburg, IN 47170, (812) 752-4501

Iowa

Hartford-Carlisle Savings Bank, 100 First St., Carlisle, IA 50047, (515) 989-3255

Peoples Bank & Trust, P.O. Box 158, Rock Valley, IA 51247, (712) 476-2746

Kansas

The First National Bank of Conway Springs, 214 W. Spring Ave., Conway Springs, KS 67031, (316) 456-2255

First National Bank, 402 Main St., Palco, KS 67657, (785) 737-2311

Peoples Bank & Trust, P.O. Box 1226, McPherson, KS 67460, (316) 241-8450

Kentucky

Bank of Mt. Vernon, P.O. Box 157, Mt. Vernon, KY 40456-0157, (606) 256-5141

South Central Bank, 208 S. Broadway, Glasgow, KY 42141, (502) 651-7466

Louisiana

Community Bank of La Fourche, 3160 Hwy. 1, Raceland, LA 70394, (504) 537-6402

Community Trust Bank, 3921 Elm St., Choudrant, LA 71227, (318) 768-2531

Maine

United Bank, 145 Exchange St., Bangor, ME 04401, (207) 942-5263

Katahdin Trust Co., P.O. Box I, Patten, ME 04765, (207) 528-2211

Maryland

Maryland Permanent Bank & Trust Co., 9612 Reisters Town Rd., Owings Mills, MD 21117, (410) 356-4411

Bank of the Eastern Shore, 301 Crusader Rd., Cambridge, MD 21613, (410) 228-5800

Massachusetts

Luzo Community Bank, 1724 Acushnet Ave., New Bedford, MA 02746, (508) 999-9980

Bank of Western Massachusetts, 29 State St., Springfield, MA 01103, (413) 781-2265

Michigan

1st Bank P.O., Box 335, West Branch, MI 48661, (517) 345-7900

MFC First National Bank, 1205 Ludington St., Escanaba, MI 49829, (906) 786-5010

Minnesota

Pioneer National Bank of Duluth, 331 N. Central Ave., Duluth, MN 55807, (218) 624-3676

State Bank of Delano, P.O. Box 530, Delano, MN 55328, (612) 972-2935

Mississippi

Pike County National Bank, P.O. Box 1666, McComb, MS 39649, (601) 684-7575

First Bank, P.O. Box 808, McComb, MS 39648, (601) 684-2231

Missouri

First Midwest Bank of Dexter, 20 W. Stoddard, Dexter, MO 63841, (573) 624-3571

First State Bank of Joplin, 802 Main, Joplin, MO 64801, (417) 623-8860

Montana

Mountain West Bank of Helena, 1225 Cedar St., Helena, MT 59601, (406) 449-2265

Bitterroot Valley Bank Lolo Shopping Center, P.O. Box 9, Lolo, MT 59847, (406) 273-2400

Mountain West Bank of Great Falls, 12 Third St. NW, Great Falls, MT 59404, (406) 727-2265

Nebraska

Sapp City Bank, 9003 S. 145th St., Omaha, NE 68138, (402) 891-0003

Dakota County State Bank, 2024 Dakota Ave., South Sioux City, NE 68776, (402) 494-4215

Nevada

First National Bank of Ely, 595 Aultman St., Ely, NV 89301, (702) 289-4441

BankWest of Nevada, 2700 W. Sahara Ave., Las Vegas, NV 89102, (702) 248-4200

New Hampshire

Community Bank & Trust Co., 15 Varney Rd., Wolfeboro, NH 03894, (603) 569-8400

Bank of New Hampshire, 300 Franklin St., Manchester, NH 03101, (603) 624-6600

New Jersey

Panasia Bank, 183 Main St., Ft. Lee, NJ 07024, (201) 947-6666

Minotola National Bank, 1748 S. Lincoln Ave., Vineland, NJ 08361, (609) 696-8100

New Mexico

Peoples Bank, 1356 Paseo del Pueblo Sur, Taos, NM 87571, (505) 758-4500

Norwest Bank of New Mexico, P.O. Box 1107, Tucumcari, NM 88401, (505) 461-3602

New York

Olympian Bank, 512 86th St., Brooklyn, NY 11209, (718) 748-3500

Champlain National Bank, Court St., Elizabethtown, NY 12932, (518) 873-6347

North Carolina

Wilkes National Bank, 1600 Curtsbridge Rd., Wilkesboro, NC 28697, (336) 903-0600

Yadkin Valley Bank & Trust Co., P.O. Box 888, Elkin, NC 28621, (910) 526-6371

North Dakota

Kirkwood Bank & Trust Co., P.O. Box 6089, Bismarck, ND 58506, (701) 258-6550

Citizens State Bank, P.O. Box 127, Mohall, ND 58761, (701) 756-6365

Ohio

First National Bank of Pandora, 102 E. Main St., Pandora, OH 45877, (419) 384-3221

Citizens Banking Co., 10 E. Main St., Salineville, OH 43945, (330) 679-2321

Oklahoma

Bank of Cushing, P.O. Box 951, Cushing, OK 74023-0951, (918) 225-2010

Bank of Kremlin, P.O. Box 197, Kremlin, OK 73753, (580) 874-2244

Oregon

Community First Bank, P.O. Box 447, Prineville, OR 97754, (541) 447-4105

Security Bank, P.O. Box 1350, Coos Bay, OR 97420, (541) 267-6611

Pennsylvania

Pennsylvania State Bank, 2148 Market St., Camp Hill, PA 17011, (717) 731-7272

Old Forge Bank, 216 S. Main St., Old Forge, PA 18518, (717) 457-8345

Rhode Island

Washington Trust Co., 23 Broad St., Westerly, RI 02891, (401) 351-6240

South Carolina

Bank of Walterboro, 1100 N. Jefferies Blvd., Walterboro, SC 29488, (803) 549-2265

First National South, 307 N. Main St., Marion, SC 29571, (803) 431-1000

South Dakota

F & M Bank, P.O. Box 877, Watertown, SD 57201, (605) 886-8401

First National Bank in Garretson, P.O. Box G, Garretson, SD 57030, (605) 594-3423

Tennessee

Volunteer Bank & Trust, 728 Broad St., Chattanooga, TN 37402, (423) 265-5001

First Bank of Rhea County, P.O. Box 99, Spring City, TN 37381, (423) 365-9551

Texas

Navigation Bank, P.O. Box 228, Houston, TX 77001, (713) 223-3400

First Commercial Bank, 1336 E. Court St., Seguin, TX 78155, (830) 379-8390

Midland American Bank, 401 W. Texas, #100, Midland, TX 79701, (915) 687-3013

Woodhaven National Bank, 6750 Bridge St., Fort Worth, TX 76112, (817) 496-6700

Utah

Advanta Financial, 11850 S. Election Rd., Draper, UT 84020, (801) 523-0858

First USA Payment Tech., P.O. Box 57510, Salt Lake City, UT 84157, (801) 281-5800

Vermont

Union Bank, P.O. Box 667, Morrisville, VT 05661, (802) 888-6600

Citizens Savings Bank & Trust Co., P.O. Box 219, Saint Johnsbury, VT 05819, (802) 748-3131

Virginia

Benchmark Community Bank, P.O. Box 569, Kenbridge, VA 23944, (804) 676-8444

Chesapeake Bank, P.O. Box 1419, Kilmarmock, VA 22482, (804) 435-1181

Washington

First Heritage Bank, P.O. Box 550, Snohomish, WA 98291-0550, (360) 568-0536

First National Bank of Port Orchard, P.O. Box 2629, Port Orchard, WA 98366, (360) 895-2265

West Virginia

West Bank of Paden City, P.O. Box 178, Paden City, WV 26159, (304) 337-2205

First National Bank in Marlington, P.O. Box 58, Marlington, WV 24954, (304) 799-4640

Wisconsin

Stephenson National Bank & Trust, P.O. Box 137, Marinette, WI 54143-0137, (715) 732-1650

First National Bank Fox Valley, P.O. Box 339, Menasha, WI 54952, (920) 729-6900

Wyoming

Western Bank of Cheyenne, P.O. Box 127, 1525 E. Pershing Blvd., Cheyenne, WY 82001, (307) 637-7333

First Interstate Bank of Commerce, 4 S. Main St., Sheridan, WY 82801, (307) 674-7411

Index

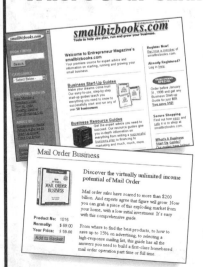

FREE ADVICE

When was the last time you got **free** advice that was worth something?

free issue!

Entrepreneur Magazine, the leading small business authority, is loaded with <u>free advice</u>—advice that could be worth millions to you. Every issue gives you detailed, practical knowledge on how <u>to start a business</u> and run it successfully. Entrepreneur is the perfect resource to keep small business owners up-to-date, on track, and growing their business.

Get your **free issue** of Entrepreneur today!

Call 800-274-6229 Dept. 5G9J9, or fill out and mail the back of this card.

Entrepreneur MAGAZINE

BREAK OUT

Business Start-Ups helps you **break** out of the 9–5 life!

free issue!

<u>Do you want</u> to get out of the 9–5 routine and take control of your life? <u>Business Start-Ups</u> shows you the franchise and business opportunities that will give you the future you dream of. Every issue answers your questions, <u>highlights hot trends</u>, spotlights new ideas, and provides the inspiration and real-life information you need to succeed.

Get your **free issue** of Business Start-Ups today!

Call 800-274-8333 Dept. 5HBK2, or fill out and mail the back of this card.

Entrepreneur's **Business Start·Ups**

MILLION DOLLAR SECRETS

free issue!

Exercise your right to make it big.

Get into the small business authority—
now at 80% off the newsstand price!

Yes! Start my one year subscription and bill me for just $9.99. I get a full year of Entrepreneur and save 80% off the newsstand rate. If I choose not to subscribe, the free issue is mine to keep.

Name ☐ Mr. ☐ Mrs. _____
(please print)

Address _____

City_____ State _____ Zip _____

☐ BILL ME   ☐ PAYMENT ENCLOSED

Guaranteed. Or your money back. Every subscription to Entrepreneur comes with a 100% satisfaction guarantee: your money back whenever you like, for whatever reason, on all unmailed issues! Offer good in U.S. and possessions only. Please allow 4–6 weeks for mailing of first issue. Canadian and foreign: $39.97. U.S. funds only.

5G9J9

Mail this coupon to **Entrepreneur** MAGAZINE P.O. Box 50368, Boulder, CO 80321-0368

OPPORTUNITY KNOCKS!!!

save 72%!

free issue!

Please enter my subscription to Business Start-Ups for one year. I will receive 12 issues for only $9.99. That's a savings of 72% off the newsstand price. The free issue is mine to keep, even if I choose not to subscribe.

Name ☐ Mr. ☐ Mrs. _____
(please print)

Address _____

City_____ State _____ Zip _____

☐ BILL ME

☐ PAYMENT ENCLOSED

Mail this coupon to

Entrepreneur's Business Start-Ups

P.O. Box 50347
Boulder, CO 80321-0347

Guaranteed. Or your money back. Every subscription to Business Start-Ups comes with a 100% satisfaction guarantee: your money back whenever you like, for whatever reason, on all unmailed issues! Offer good in U.S. and possessions only. Please allow 4–6 weeks for mailing of first issue. Canadian and foreign: $34.97. U.S. funds only.

5HBK2